SLAVERY AND MUSLIM SOCIETY IN AFRICA

Both authors, pere et fils, were born in New Zealand. Allan G. B. Fisher was Price Professor of International Economics at the Royal Institute of International Affairs, London. In 1946 he joined the International Monetary Fund in Washington, D.C. and retired in 1960 as chief editor.

His son, Humphrey J. Fisher, graduated from Harvard in 1955, took his doctorate from Oxford in 1959, and then worked for two years among Palestinian refugees in Jordan before joining the staff of the School of Oriental and African Studies, London University.

SLAVERY
AND MUSLIM SOCIETY
IN AFRICA

The Institution in Saharan and Sudanic
Africa and the Trans-Saharan Trade

by **Allan G. B. Fisher**
and **Humphrey J. Fisher**

DOUBLEDAY & COMPANY, INC.
Garden City, New York
1971

LIBRARY OF CONGRESS CATALOG CARD NUMBER 77–139019
COPYRIGHT © 1970 BY ALLAN G. B. FISHER AND
HUMPHREY J. FISHER
ALL RIGHTS RESERVED
PRINTED IN THE UNITED STATES OF AMERICA
FIRST EDITION IN THE UNITED STATES OF AMERICA

For
D.

Contents

Introduction   1

I   *The Size of the Slave Population*   11

II   *Slave Status and Religion*
PAGAN SLAVING   17
Jihad   21
ENSLAVEMENT OF MUSLIMS   28
SLAVE AND FREE STATUS   38
THE CONTRIBUTION OF SLAVES TO RELIGIOUS ACTIVITY   42
RELIGIOUS CONVERSION   45
EMANCIPATION   50
THE RETURN OF THE SLAVES   60

III   *Exports and Marketing*
SLAVE EXPORTS AND THEIR RELATION TO THE HOME
    MARKET   71
THE ARMS TRADE   80
SELECTION OF EXPORT MODELS   84
SLAVES ON THE MARCH   91

IV   *The Domestic Scene I: General Treatment*
GENERAL TREATMENT   99
SLAVE REVOLTS   107

V   The Domestic Scene II: Slaves in the Family

DOMESTIC DEMAND FOR SLAVES   115
CONCUBINES   115

VI   The Domestic Scene III: Slaves at Work

FREE AND SLAVE LABOUR   131
AGRICULTURAL WORKERS   132
ARTISANS   138
CARAVAN WORKERS   141
LUXURY SLAVES   148

VII   The Domestic Scene IV: Slaves and the
        State

COLONISTS   151
SOLDIERS   154
ROYAL SLAVES   163
EUNUCHS   171

VIII   The Domestic Scene V: Slaves as Currency

TRIBUTE   179
ALMS AND PRESENTS   185
SLAVES AS CURRENCY   188

IX   The Slave Market in Kuka   193

X   Conclusion: Anti-slavery Measures   201

Addenda   207
Bibliography   209
Index   211

ILLUSTRATIONS

1   Bagirmi slave-raid against the Pagan Kimre, 1872
2   The attack on Musfeia, 1823
3   An ivory porter
4   A slave caravan
5   Above, foot irons and, below, manacles for slaves, from the Fulani of Ngaundere in Adamawa
6   A Negress in Morocco
7   A slave in the block
8   A Ghadames bill of sale, including gold, male and female slaves, hides, pillow-cases, ivory, senna, perfume, camels, sacks and household slaves
9   Nachtigal's first grave, in Liberia

MAPS

North and West Africa   xii
Tropical Africa   xiv

MAPS

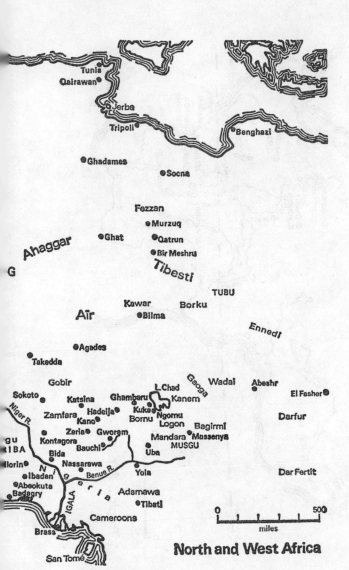

North and West Africa

Tunis
Qairawan
Jerba
Tripoli
Benghazi

Ghadames
Socna

Fezzan
Murzuq
Ahaggar
Ghat
Qatrun
Bir Meshru
G
Tibesti

TUBU
Kawar
Borku
Air
Bilma
Ennedi

Agades
Takedda

Gobir
Gaoga
Wadai
Abeshr
Sokoto
Katsina
Ghambaru
L. Chad
Kanem
El Fasher
Niger R.
Zamfara
Hadeija
Kano
Kuka
Bornu
Ngornu
Logon
Darfur
Zaria
Gworam
Bagirmi
gu
Kontagora
Bauchi
Mandara
Massenya
RIBA
Bida
Uba
MUSGU
Ilorin
Nassarawa
Benue R.
Yola
Dar Fertit
Ibadan
Abeokuta
Adamawa
Badagry
IGALA
Tibati
Brass
Cameroons
San Tomé

0   500
miles

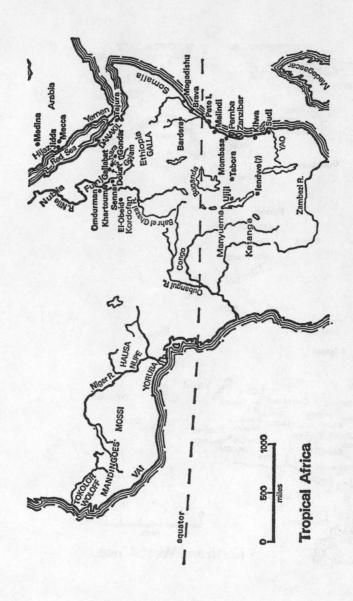

Tropical Africa

SLAVERY AND MUSLIM SOCIETY IN AFRICA

INTRODUCTION

The slave trade is one of the most arresting topics in African history. In the past three years at least seven major books[1] totalling some 2,500 pages have appeared on the African slave trade, to say nothing of numerous reprints of earlier works on the same subject. There is evidently interest in even the more restricted details; one of the seven books, *The fortunate slave*, concerns a single captive, Job ben Solomon, in the eighteenth century.

Yet, despite their voluminous detail, these studies are in some sense curiously restricted both in time and in location. Attention is drawn, almost irresistibly it would seem, to the trans-Atlantic slave trade, with some lesser commentary about the Indian Ocean and the east coast of Africa. And yet, slaves were already of critical importance in another sector of tropical Africa's export trade, the overland trade across the Sahara, centuries before the first slave crossed the Atlantic; and slave caravans, albeit increasingly small

[1] J. Pope-Hennessy, *Sins of the fathers*, London 1967; P. D. Curtin (ed.), *Africa remembered: narratives by west Africans from the era of the slave trade*, Wisconsin 1968; and *The Atlantic slave trade*, Wisconsin 1969; D. Grant, *The fortunate slave: an illustration of African slavery in the early eighteenth century*, London 1968; P. Verger, *Flux et reflux de la traite des Nègres entre le Golfe de Bénin et Bahia de Todos os Santos du XVIIe au XIXe siècle*, Paris 1968; W. E. F. Ward, *The Royal Navy and the slavers*, London 1969; L. Bethell, *The abolition of the Brazilian slave trade*, Cambridge 1970.

and furtive, were still slipping across the Sahara decades after the last slave sailed westwards. Of fluctuations in the Saharan trade we know little; it is likely that the Russian occupation of Georgia and the Caucasus, in progress in the late eighteenth and early nineteenth centuries, closing a well-established source of slaves for the Middle East from those areas, stimulated the demand for African slaves. In location, too, all eyes have been fixed on the coasts of tropical Africa to the neglect of the vast interior, where Muslim states and societies in particular provided a thriving domestic market to supplement trans-Saharan export opportunities.

The current trend in studies of African slave-trading and slavery is a little odd in another respect also. African history, at one time generally considered as little more than a series of footnotes to the chronicle of European penetration and colonialism, is now seen to have had an existence of its own, in many cases entirely independent of European presence or influence. The resources of archaeological evidence, oral tradition, Arabic archives, and many other records of the past, are now busily examined to further the discovery of this independent African history. The Atlantic slave trade, however, does not fit smoothly into this new perspective on African history; it is rather a part of the older view of African history as the history of Europeans in and about Africa. It is difficult to fathom why the Atlantic slave trade should maintain its popularity as a study among Africans, Europeans and Americans alike, while the independent African counterpart, in the interior of the continent, remains in the shadows; perhaps the unravelling of these reasons lies in the realms of psychology. This book attempts somewhat to redress the balance, by exploring a little the trans-Saharan trade, and rather more the domestic demand in the heart of Africa.

There are other reasons too for offering this survey. At a

time when economic studies in general, and development studies in particular, are increasingly in vogue amongst Africanists, there is some advantage in recalling, as we try to sketch in the historical background, that slavery and the slave trade were, among other things, economic factors. This book presents its examination, in part, in terms which may interest the economic historian.

Again, the book amounts almost to an essay in the sociology of African Islam, and may appeal to readers interested as much or more in the Islamic world as in the African.

And again, amidst the general development of African studies, often expressed in detailed investigations of specific and local topics, it is helpful to be reminded of the almost continental relevance of certain themes, such as the role of slavery in African Muslim society. Africa is a vast continent, where the student should expect to find a rich, and sometimes even bewildering, variety of social customs and institutions; yet students and other readers whose own main interests lie in a particular quarter may well profit from having their attention drawn to parallel circumstances elsewhere.

The reasons advanced in the preceding paragraphs may justify the appearance of this book, even though it is only a preliminary survey. That it is not more than this needs to be stressed. The nature of the sources make a complete study, at this stage, almost impossible. The number of books or other studies specifically devoted to slavery in Muslim Africa is very small; but the number of books which describe that society without any mention of slavery is probably smaller still. A complete analysis of all the relevant published references, to which unpublished archives would have to be added, would require many years, and result in a bulky, perhaps indigestible compilation. And even then,

oral tradition throughout the immense areas of Muslim tropical Africa would remain untapped. In this book we have
only begun to marshal the evidence.

The genesis of our book lies in the writings of Gustav
Nachtigal, a German physician, who travelled between
1869 and 1874 in various countries in the interior of Africa.
His travels were subsequently published, in German, in
three large volumes.[2] The original editions are now very
rare; they were reproduced in 1967 by an Austrian firm but
at rather a high price. Nachtigal's travels have not yet
found an English translator. We are now working on such
a translation, and in the course of this undertaking have
gathered together all Nachtigal's references to slavery, employing them as an important strand in this book. In the
absence of a complete translation, into any language, of
Nachtigal's book, his slavery material, incorporated here,
may in itself be a useful addition to the resources of those
students, particularly in Africa but also elsewhere, to whom
the original German, for linguistic or economic reasons, is
inaccessible.

To Nachtigal's information about slavery we have added
comparative details from other observers, including not only
outsiders such as other European travellers, and Muslim
visitors like Ibn Battuta in the fourteenth century and Leo
Africanus in the sixteenth, but also as far as possible the
views of African Muslims themselves, particularly concerning the Islamic theocracies which were set up during the
nineteenth century. We have also included some references
to the standard Muslim legal texts. The steady growth of
this comparative material means that Nachtigal is now,
though still a central figure, only one source among many.

[2] *Sahara und Sudan, Ergebnisse sechsjähriger Reisen in Afrika,*
vol. i, Berlin 1879; vol. ii, Berlin 1881; vol. iii, Leipzig 1889; complete reproduction, Graz 1967. All subsequent footnotes where no
title or author is indicated refer to *Sahara und Sudan.*

Nachtigal started from Tripoli; he crossed the Sahara, visiting Fezzan, Tibesti, Bornu, Kanem, Borku, Bagirmi, Wadai, Darfur and Kordofan, finally emerging in Egypt after more than five years. The area of our study centres on these lands which Nachtigal visited, with an important extension westwards to take in the Fulani empire of Sokoto, approximately the area of modern northern Nigeria. These states of the western and central Sudan are the main stage for our story; but we have ranged east and west, from Dakar to Zanzibar, throughout tropical Africa wherever Muslims are found, to add supplementary information, and have occasionally ventured into North Africa and the Middle East, and even as far as Brazil.

The nineteenth century is by far the best documented period, before European colonialism, for the history of the interior of Africa, and much of our discussion here necessarily relates to that time. We have, however, attempted to trace the outlines of earlier development right back to the beginnings of Muslim society in tropical Africa a millenium ago. It is on the other, modern, side that we have drawn our own dividing line, for the most part excluding the periods of European colonialism and subsequent independence. This dividing line by no means confines us to a very distant past. One of the last episodes which we record, in the pre-colonial period, concerns a eunuch sent from Wadai to serve the Holy Places in Mecca. Several years later, he sent word, by a returning pilgrim, to Sharif al-Din, an elderly eunuch occupying a very prominent position in the civil service of Wadai, inviting him also to come to Mecca, where life was easy and, thanks to the generosity of pilgrims, employment was lucrative, to spend his last days in prayer and study. The advice was not taken.[3] Nachtigal himself

3 H. Gaden, 'États musulmanes de l'Afrique centrale et leurs rapports avec la Mecque et Constantinople', Questions diplomatiques et coloniales, 1907, 439.

had known Sharif al-Din, and chronicled the first stages
of his career;[4] the invitation sent to Sharif al-Din, indeed
the original departure of the other eunuch from Wadai for
Mecca, fell within the lifetime of one of the present writers.

It is clear that slavery, as much in the local African Muslim
tradition as in the orthodox Muslim heritage, was a very
deeply entrenched institution, accepted alike by African
believers and learned lawyers as a matter of course. As far
as local practice is concerned, our whole book confirms the
importance of slavery in Muslim tropical Africa. Two examples, from Hausaland, may serve here as introductory
illustrations. One legend of the origin of the Hausa states
says that these derived from the six children of the first
founder, each of whom received special gifts: Kano and
Rano were dyers and weavers, Katsina and Daura were
traders, and Zaria and Bauchi were slave-dealers.[5] Again
in the traditional spirit, or *bori,* possession dances of the
Hausa—which are, however, not always well regarded by
stricter Muslims—there is represented one character called
Son Bawa, the desirer of a slave, who walks about weeping,
looking for a slave, and calling upon other spirits for help.[6]
   Turning to the orthodox Muslim heritage, there are two
legal texts which are of especial importance for us, since
both have been most highly esteemed in west and central
Muslim tropical Africa: the Risala of Ibn Abi Zayd from
the tenth, and the Mukhtasar of Khalil ibn Ishaq from the
fourteenth century. These are standard works of the Maliki
school of law, which predominates in North and West Africa, and in Upper Egypt. We have relied on them extensively for theoretical details. These details—those which follow immediately, and others noted at relevant points
throughout the book—are by no means rare curiosities of

   [4] iii, 164.
   [5] A. J. N. Tremearne, *Hausa superstitions and customs,* London
1913, 141; his collection of Hausa stories is full of incidental references to slaves.   [6] *ibid.,* 536.

the law: they are representative of some of the central portions of constantly used texts. But, while the details we cite are not rarities, neither, taken all together, do they make up a complete picture of Muslim Maliki law relating to slaves. For the most part, we cite only legal points having direct relevance to our African material.

To slaves as slaves, as a separate topic requiring specific attention, the two texts do not allocate much space. Ibn Abi Zayd is content with only a few lines: Be kind to those you possess [these might be animals as well as slaves]—and do not demand of them work beyond their ability.[7] But the incidental references to slaves are almost innumerable. In some cases, for example in the relationship of emancipation to inheritance and wills, slaves figure largely; in others, they may receive only passing mention. Yet at almost every point some special provision has to be made for them, since the law for slaves is so often slightly different from that for free men: the fifty oaths for homicide do not apply in the case of a slave;[8] may the trustee marry the female slaves in an orphan's estate?[9] if slaves are promised liberation on their master's death, is this set against the whole patrimony, or only against that third of it which is properly at the disposal of the testator?[10] The evidence of a slave is not admissible in court, but his confession, in cases not touching his master's property, may be;[11] the legal penalties inflicted on slaves differ somewhat from those of free men;[12] and so on.

[7] Ibn Abi Zayd al-Qayrawani, *La Risâla: ou épître sur les éléments du dogme et de la loi de l'Islam selon le rite mâlikite*, L. Bercher (ed. and tr.), Alger 1945, 323.

[8] Ibn Abi Zayd, 242.   [9] *ibid.*, 272.
[10] *ibid.*, 220-2.   [11] *ibid.*, 258, 262.
[12] *ibid.*, 252-4. Illustrations of this kind of thing may be found in African practice: for certain misdemeanours, free Tuareg are fined domestic animals, while slaves—on the orders of the senior chief, or Amenokal, for it is rare for a slave to be so punished by his own master—are flogged (J. Nicolaisen, *Ecology and Culture of the Pastoral Tuareg*, Copenhagen 1963, 440).

In some respects the position of the slave, acknowledged
at so many points, and with special provision made for him,
or her, yet of inferior status, resembles the position of the
tolerated non-Muslim. Calumnious imputation of fornication against a slave or a non-Muslim does not entail the
legal penalty of 80 strokes with the whip, which would
punish such a slander against a free Muslim.[13] A free
Muslim is not killed for murdering a slave or a non-Muslim,
though the opposite in either case means death; the *lex
talionis* does not apply between free and slave, or between
Muslim and infidel.[14] Neither a woman, a slave nor a non-
Muslim is able to give away a Muslim woman in marriage.[15]
And just as a slave does not inherit so a non-Muslim may
not inherit from a Muslim.[16]

In the tropical African setting, the Muslim law was not
always clearly applied, and it is difficult to draw a sharp
line between characteristics of African slavery which were
survivals from pre-Muslim practice, and those which were
imported later with Islam. Let us look again at the matter,
just mentioned, of inheritance. Slaves, according to the
clear teaching of the law, even if their state of servitude
is not absolute, do not inherit.[17] This disability is generally
true of slaves in Muslim tropical Africa; in Bornu it has
become proverbial that slaves do not inherit property.[18]
However, one observer, noting the same situation among
the Tuareg, has attributed it not to Muslim law but rather
to Tuareg traditional inheritance practice. Among the Tuareg, parents stand first in the line of inheritance from their

[13] Ibn Abi Zayd, 256.
[14] Ibn Abi Zayd, 249; whoever kills a slave owes his estimated
value to the slave's owner (250).   [15] *ibid.*, 180.
[16] Ibn Abi Zayd, 280. A non-Muslim slave suffers a double disability; he may not, for example, be freed as legal expiation for those
offences for which his owner may atone by freeing a Muslim slave
(228).   [17] *ibid.*, 280.
[18] P. A. Benton, *Primer of Kanuri grammar*, London 1917, 105-6.

children; slave owners are usually in the position of parents
to their slaves; and, as a slave always has a master, so the
property of any slave dying will pass to his master, *in loco
parentis*, not to the slave's own children.[19]

Such a situation in which the old custom and newer law
are mingled, has many precedents, even in Arabia at the
time of the Prophet. The newly revealed Muslim law then
was rooted in Arab custom, which custom however was
subject to considerable change: in the matter of slaves, the
new law, for example, attempted to raise their moral
status.[20]

The fact that the institution of slavery, in one form or
another, had deep roots in many parts of Africa long before Islam became a significant social influence there, and
that even in regions which were thoroughly islamized there
were many pre-Islamic survivals, demonstrates how misleading it would be to suggest a hard-and-fast distinction between Muslim and traditional slavery. Nevertheless, the
general pattern of slavery in the Muslim countries of tropical Africa, those through which Nachtigal travelled and
others, can fairly easily be recognized as different from that
in areas unaffected by Islam. Our study here is primarily
of Muslim masters and Pagan[21] or Muslim slaves. And,
since Muslim law is quite specific in defining slavery, however lax administration may sometimes have been, we are
spared the difficulties, which arise when such an institution
is found in an exclusively traditional society, of deciding

[19] Nicolaisen, 1963, 442.
[20] M. Khadduri, *War and peace in the law of Islam*, Baltimore
1955, 130.
[21] We use the word 'Pagan' for convenience, being shorter than
'traditional African religious' and more precise than 'non-Muslim'.
The term does not, of course, imply a unity among Pagan peoples
and beliefs corresponding to that among Muslims; nor do we in the
least intend any derogatory connotation.

whether it should be called slavery, or serfdom, or even the extended family, or whatever. How happily or unhappily slavery worked out in Muslim Africa, this volume attempts to give some indication.

CHAPTER I

THE SIZE OF
THE SLAVE POPULATION

In the nature of things statistical precision is not to be expected in any estimate of the number of slaves in Africa. Nachtigal made some valiant efforts to measure the total population of several of the countries which he visited, but he did not attempt to distinguish between free men and slaves, and indeed, as will be shown later (see pp. 38 ff.), it was often difficult to make a perfectly clearcut distinction. Clapperton did try to take account of this distinction for Kano in Hausaland, where he travelled nearly half a century before Nachtigal crossed the Sahara, but with variant results. In 1824 he judged that more than half the population of Kano, then totalling between 30,000 and 40,000, were slaves;[1] in 1827, however, he was told that there were 30 slaves in Kano to every free man.[2] According to Barth, slaves in Kano province in the 1850s were at least as numerous as free men,[3] and a modern writer has estimated the proportion of slaves to total population among the

[1] D. Denham and H. Clapperton, *Narrative of travels and discoveries in northern and central Africa in the years 1822, 1823 and 1824*, London 1826 (A. Major Denham's narrative, B. Captain Clapperton's narrative), B, 49.

[2] H. Clapperton, *Journal of a second expedition into the interior of Africa*, London 1829, with the Journal of Richard Lander from Kano to the seacoast, 171.

[3] H. Barth, *Travels and discoveries in north and central Africa*, 5 vols., London 1857–8, ii, 143–4.

Hausa at the end of the nineteenth century as ranging from 25 to 50 per cent.[4]

Stories of individuals owning huge numbers of slaves are frequent. There may well be a touch of fantasy in some of these large round numbers, which appear here and in other parts of our story: the natural inclination to inflate numbers may have been particularly difficult to resist in the absence of such countervailing elements as a property tax. It would be tedious to attach a sceptical qualifying phrase on each occasion; and in some cases, where the reporter is a careful eye-witness such as Nachtigal, even high numbers may be accepted.

Of Awdaghast, the eleventh-century Saharan town, it was said that a wealthy man might own as many as 1000 slaves.[5] Similar reports circulated of Timbuktu in the sixteenth century.[6] In the eighteenth century—though this is a non-Muslim example—some prazo, or crown estate, holders on the Zambesi boasted of slaves in tens of thousands: recent research suggests that in fact even 1000 was a large establishment for a prazo, and fewer than a hundred slaves was probably normal. Even so, a total slave population there of 30,000 in the eighteenth century is possible.[7] Clapperton, in Borgu in 1824, was troubled by the matrimonial ambitions of a friend, a portly Arab widow, the richest person in town and owner of 1000 slaves.[8]

[4] Irmgard Sellnow, 'Die Stellung der Sklaven in der Hausa-Gesellschaft', Mitt. des Instituts für Orientforschung, 1964, 88.

[5] Abou Obeid el-Bakri (eleventh century), Description de l'Afrique septentrionale, tr. MacGuckin de Slane, 1857, reprinted 1965, 317.

[6] Leo Africanus (sixteenth century), The history and description of Africa, tr. J. Pory, 1640, reprinted by Hakluyt Society, 3 vols., 1896 (hereafter Leo Africanus A), iii, 825; Description de l'Afrique, tr. A. Epaulard, 2 vols., Paris 1956 (hereafter Leo Africanus B), ii, 469.

[7] M. D. D. Newitt, 'The Portuguese on the Zambesi: an historical interpretation of the Prazo system', Journal of African History, 1969, 77.   [8] Clapperton, 1829, 81.

Nachtigal's observations supply further confirmation for large slave concentrations. The estate of Lamino, one of the most important men at the court of Kuka, the capital of Bornu, who died in February 1871, and for whom Nachtigal had a high regard, included several thousand slaves, who would on his death pass to other hands.[9] Many of them were occupied in tending Lamino's numerous horses and cattle[10] or in transporting supplies to his city residence from the country region which he controlled.[11] This was an exceptional case, but many other men of high rank had large slave establishments, whom Nachtigal saw gathered with their masters in the streets for the evening prayer.[12] Al-Hajj Ahmed Tangatanga was a Dongolan who had been persuaded by the king of Wadai to settle in Wadai, where he had become the most important merchant in the country,[13] and one of the four leading officials responsible for the maintenance of order in the capital, Abeshr.[14] Nachtigal travelled under his protection from Wadai to Darfur in 1874. On this occasion Tangatanga took with him 40 slaves, adding two more near the Darfur border, a Dinka deaf-mute and a young slave-girl for whom he traded one of his mares.[15]

However, the large numbers of petty slave-owners may have been as important as the exceptional cases of very wealthy men in filling out the total slave population. In the epidemic of 1870 in many houses in Kuka slaves 'by the dozen' lay stricken by fever.[16] Even among people of modest means the ownership of at least one or two slaves was normal in Bornu. The need for slaves was felt strongly in the small villages, where there were scarcely even the faint beginnings of any division of labour, and each household had to be almost entirely self-sufficient.[17] Even a penurious

[9] ii, 10–1.   [10] i, 602.   [11] i, 598.   [12] i, 625.
[13] iii, 69.   [14] iii, 62.   [15] iii, 317.   [16] i, 733.
[17] ii, 391.

scholar might hope to own a handful of slaves (see below, p. 43).

Slaves were naturally most in evidence wherever a significant fraction of the population enjoyed incomes which, judged by the local standards, might be regarded as comparatively comfortable. In poorer regions slaves were scarcer, but still not a negligible proportion in the population. Among the Budduma, the Kanuri nickname for the 'reed men' who lived on the islands in Lake Chad, while a poor man might be without any slaves, the average person owned two or three.[18] The Kanem desert was probably poorer still than Lake Chad, but Nachtigal's expectation that slave girls would be too few there to tempt Soliman, his unreliable Kanembu servant, to cultivate his taste for amorous adventure was certainly disappointed.[19] Even where the standard of living was desperately low for everybody, and slaves not easy to come by, their number was not negligible. Richardson, visiting the desert mountains midway between Tripoli and Ghadames in the 1840s, was told by a local shaykh that there were thirty slaves in his district, and wondered 'how the people could keep slaves when they can scarcely keep themselves'.[20] A similar situation confronted Nachtigal when he penetrated Tibesti, a rugged poor country in the central Sahara not visited again by a European until 1917.[21] His negotiations for the hire of camels once broke down because the young woman who owned them would accept in return nothing less than Sa'ad, another of Nachtigal's servants, who had already been an object of great interest among the women of the country.[22] According to a census of 1949, there were in Ahaggar, in equally rough country in the west-central Sa-

[18] Olive Macleod, *Chiefs and cities of central Africa*, London 1912, 227.   [19] ii, 31–2, 53.

[20] James Richardson, *Travels in the great desert of Sahara, in the years of 1845 and 1846*, London 1848, i, 63.

[21] i, 425.   [22] i, 355.

hara, 3960 fair-skinned pastoral Tuareg, and 1552 slaves, living in Tuareg camps.[23]

At one time, pioneer geographers of Africa, trying to visualize conditions in the interior, filled the Sahara with slaves. Cooley, for example, wrote:

> if the vast extent be considered of the region in which man has no riches but slaves, no enjoyment but slaves, no article of trade but slaves, and where the hearts of wandering thousands are closed against pity by the galling misery of life, it will be difficult to resist the conviction that the solid buttress on which slavery rests in Africa is—The Desert.[24]

Eye-witness reports from travellers in the Sahara soon corrected this impression, and it now appears that the significant fact is not that there were proportionately fewer slaves in the Sahara than in happier regions, but that the desert supported even as many as it did.

Even when full allowance is made for the difficulty of distinguishing between free and slave, the inadequate statistics, and simple boastfulness, it is clear that slavery was a highly important institution in each country through which Nachtigal passed, as in many other parts of Muslim Africa, and that slaves formed a substantial proportion of the population, in some areas perhaps even a majority. The complex and difficult problems which presented themselves when, after the slave trade had been eradicated, the colonizing European powers faced the task of getting rid of domestic slavery indicated clearly that the number of persons concerned was very large.[25] The importance of slaves, eco-

[23] Nicolaisen, 1963, 440.

[24] W. D. Cooley, *The Negroland of the Arabs*, London 1841, reprinted 1966, 139.

[25] According to one estimate published in 1908, a quarter of the population of the French West African territories which were under civil administration were not free. In Senegal there were 200,000

nomically and in other ways, is explored in subsequent
chapters.

'captifs', in Upper Senegal and Niger 600,000, in Dahomey 250,000,
in the Ivory Coast 500,000, and in Guinea 450,000 (G. Deherme,
L'Afrique occidentale française, Paris 1908, 383).

CHAPTER II

SLAVE STATUS AND RELIGION

Pagan slaving

There is next to nothing to be said about the number of slaves held by Pagan masters; and to the slave practices of Pagan people, Nachtigal made only a few incidental references. He noted, for example, among the Pagans in Bagirmi, the inclusion of slaves as part of the bride-price,[1] a procedure widespread also among Muslims elsewhere (see p. 186).

The slave in Pagan society sometimes ran the risk of serving purposes much more cruel. In Bagirmi again, the custom at one time obtained of burying alive two young slaves with the body of a dead chief.[2] This practice was quite common in non-Muslim Africa, and examples might be cited from both east and west.[3] In the Cape Mount area, in what is now modern Liberia, one or two slaves would accompany a nobleman to the grave, and hence it was usual for slaves to run away when their master was dying, returning only later.

'You will eat', they were mocked, 'of your Lords Cost,

[1] ii, 685. Among the Budduma, the gifts which a bride received from her parents included two women slaves; Macleod, 1912, 230.

[2] ii, 687.

[3] See R. Burton, *Lake regions of equatorial Africa*, London 1860, reprinted 1961, ii, 25–6, for the burial alive of female slaves at the funeral of a Wanyamwezi chief.

but not die with him; who excuse themselves, saying Life is sweet, and no man would willingly leave or have it taken away against his will.'[4]

The slave who fell into cannibal hands might come to an equally melancholy end. The reports about cannibalism, which appeared from time to time, often mention slaves as the victims. It should be added, however, that such reports are often secondhand. D'Ollone, in the hinterland of Liberia, contemplated reprisals against the local people, 'ces monstres qui nous offrent quelques captifs pour obtenir une paix qui leur permette de manger tranquillement les autres';[5] his report that 60,000 of Samori's followers, in the closing years of the nineteenth century, met this end seems merely hearsay. In Cameroon, German traders complained that their Hausa rivals sold slaves to cannibals, but there was no evidence for this, and the German administration thought on the contrary that the Hausa meat trade helped prevent cannibalism.[6]

Similar beliefs were indeed widely held among non-Europeans about Europeans themselves. Nachtigal's hopes of establishing useful contacts with some of the Pagans who thronged the war-camp of the fugitive king of Bagirmi were frustrated by their profound suspicion that white men were not only expert sorcerers, but also bought up black men as slaves, not in order to get them to work, but to satisfy their culinary tastes, or to provide blood for dyeing cloth red,[7] and in north Arabia Doughty was asked in 1876 about the land in the Christian seas where black men were bred up for eating.[8]

[4] J. Ogilby, *Africa: being an accurate description.* . . . London 1670, mainly derived from the Dutch of O. Dapper, 396.

[5] *Mission Hostains-d'Ollone, 1898–1900*, Paris 1901, 210.

[6] H. Rudin, *Germans in the Cameroons*, London 1938, 233–4, 299.   [7] ii, 621.

[8] C. M. Doughty, *Arabia Deserta*, London 1888, reprinted 1923, i, 149.

Other barbarities too were reported as being practised against slaves, such as sacrificial killing often in conjunction with a traditional secret society,[9] and simple cruelty. One traveller told of the first head of the Gizima clan of the Loma people in Liberia, who, among other things, kept a slave chained to a post, cutting pieces from him to feed to his dog, until the victim died and was replaced by another.[10] This, however, was said to have been at least 200 years before, and many such tales are similarly associated with a somewhat distant, and also perhaps somewhat legendary, past.

All these things are largely absent from Nachtigal's chronicle, and where they do appear, they are not specifically associated with slaves. He was told that ceremonial human sacrifice had continued at the court of Darfur up to the beginning of the nineteenth century, and that some traces of this practice still survived in his time among the distant hill tribes.[11] He was told too that cannibalism still obtained among several peoples in Wadai and Darfur, including even some nominal Muslims,[12] and that waterbags made of human skin were still sometimes brought into Darfur.[13]

The advance of Islam indeed effectively ended some of the harsher aspects of Pagan slaving; yet it was not the case that the slave in Pagan society had been entirely without rights. Circumstances of course varied greatly, but a survey of the position of slaves amongst various Liberian peoples reveals examples of the following benefits extended to slaves: the belief that upright slaves might hope for the same rewards in the next life as did other people;[14] the

[9] See for example G. W. Harley, *Notes on the Poro in Liberia*, Cambridge (Mass.) 1941, reprinted New York 1968, 14.
[10] G. Schwab, *Tribes of the Liberian hinterland*, Cambridge (Mass.) 1947, 22.
[11] iii, 440, 474.   [12] iii, 183, 195, 460.
[13] iii, 349.   [14] Schwab, 1947, 329.

opportunity for some independent farming; the possibility of some redress in cases of injustice; an arrangement by which a slave might himself change his master (see below pp. 58–9 for the parallel practice in Muslim society); the chance of freedom by purchase, gift, or on the master's death; the right of a slave in certain cases to inherit equally with his master's own sons; and permission granted in some societies to a slave to marry one of his deceased master's widows.[15] Indeed, one recent survey of Muslim Africa, taking account of such rights in the old societies, suggests that the liberalizing impact of Islam was probably of more importance in the case of captives and newly acquired slaves than for those who had already become established as domestic slaves or serfs.[16] Some non-Muslim peoples, such as the Kru on the West African coast, boast that they have never been slaves, nor dealt in slaves.[17]

The Pagan or near Pagan (for Islam was spreading amongst them) slavers of whom Nachtigal heard most during his travels were the Budduma. Nachtigal mentions their frequent raids upon the lakeshore Bornu villages, for whose inhabitants, both free men and slaves, the risk of being captured by the Budduma was a constant concern.[18] While travelling to Katsina, Barth once met a Bornu slave who had first been enslaved by the Budduma. Later captured by the Awlad Sulayman, the turbulent Arab tribe whose varying fortunes Nachtigal described at considerable length, he was finally taken from them by the Kelowi, a Tuareg tribe, but remained throughout a fervent admirer of the independent freebooters who had initiated his career as a slave.[19] Another of Barth's friends had been a counter-

[15] ibid., 441 ff.
[16] I. M. Lewis, ed., Islam in tropical Africa, London 1966, 51.
[17] Graham Greene, Journey without maps, London 1963, 44.
[18] ii, 371, 485.   [19] Barth, 1857–8, ii, 35.

raider against the Budduma, until they gave him a wife and he half-settled among them.[20]

A curious footnote to the contrast between Muslim and Pagan slave-owning arose in the British protectorate of Zanzibar and Pemba. There, in the early days, the British admitted the legality of slavery, as being sanctioned by Islamic law, to the support of which the British were then committed. But Sir John Kirk, the Consul-General, ruled that no slave could be the legal property of a Pagan, since slave-owning was recognized only by Islamic law, to which in turn only Muslims could appeal.[21] This is by no means the only context in which European colonialism, consciously or unconsciously, favoured Muslims over Pagans.

Jihad

The motives which impelled Muslim warriors in Africa to embark on slave raids against their Pagan neighbours were inevitably quite mixed. Strictly interpreted and between parties both of good standing, the *sharia*, or law of Islam, forbids any Muslim to enslave a co-religionist. On the other hand, *jihad*, holy war directed against non-Muslims, was approved by the *sharia*, and might, in some circumstances, be a positive duty. It was therefore natural that slave raiding, which in principle should be directed exclusively against non-Muslims, should acquire some of the characteristics of religious war between Muslim and Pagan.[22]

[20] *ibid.*, ii, 289–90.

[21] F. D. Lugard, *The rise of our east African empire*, Edinburgh 1893, i, 184–5.

[22] Pagans were the chief victims of Muslim slaving in Africa, but Christians might also on occasion be liable. In 1631 a revolt in Mombasa led to almost all the Portuguese there being killed, and among the African Christians in Mombasa many, refusing to recant, died as martyrs, while 400 were sent as slaves to the market in Mecca (G. S. P. Freeman-Grenville, 'The Coast, 1498–1840', in R. Oliver and G. Mathews (eds.), *History of East Africa*, Oxford 1963, i, 140).

The launching of a slave-raid was indeed only rarely marked by the procedures proper to a *jihad* (see the raid on Deba, p. 31 below), but the conclusion of the campaign, whether consecrated as *jihad* or not, might be much the same, and the subsequent fate of those who were captured on a slave raid had at least to some extent to be determined according to the principles of the Muslim law.

From the earliest days of Islam, enslavement had been one likely prospect for a prisoner of war. The law governing these prisoners of war was based on two Quranic injunctions, Surahs viii. 68 and xlvii. 4:

> It has not been for any prophet to have captives until he slaughters in the land.
>
> So, when ye meet *in battle* those who disbelieve, then *let there* be the striking off of heads until, when ye have slaughtered them, then make the bond strong. Then grant either favour afterwards, or ransom, till war lays down its burden.[23]

While the schools of law varied somewhat in details of the correct treatment to be accorded to prisoners of war, there were six principal alternatives: execution, usually

---

[23] These verses are cited in Khadduri, 1955, 127. A recent English translation, not yet complete, of the Quran offers the following modernist interpretation. It translates the first verse, 'It does not behoove a prophet to keep captives unless he has battled strenuously on earth', and continues with this commentary: '*i.e.*, as an aftermath of a war in a just cause. As almost always in the Quran, an injunction addressed to the Prophet is, by implication, binding on his followers as well. Consequently, the above verse lays down that no person may be taken, or for any time retained, in captivity, unless he was taken prisoner in a *jihad*—that is, a holy war in defence of the Faith or of freedom . . . and that, therefore, the acquisition of a slave by "peaceful" means, and the keeping of a slave thus acquired, is entirely prohibited: which, to all practical purposes, amounts to a prohibition of slavery as a "social institution". But even with regard to captives taken in war, the Quran ordains (in xlvii. 4) that they should be freed after the war is over.'

only in exceptional circumstances; ransom; exchange
against Muslim prisoners; taxation—the *jizya* and *kharaj*
taxes, nominally applicable only to People of the Book, that
is Christians and Jews; free release; and enslavement.[24] If
a *dhimmi*, or protected person (that is one who had agreed
to pay the *jizya*), broke his agreement and left Muslim territory to go to an enemy land, he became, unless he had been
driven to this resort by injustice suffered amongst the Muslims, liable to enslavement if he was ever again captured.[25]
There was general agreement that women and children
among the prisoners ought not to be killed, but rather enslaved and divided as spoil among the victors,[26] or, if their
circumstances merited it, included among those upon whom
the *jizya* was levied.[27] A captive woman, pregnant with
the child of a Muslim, might be kept enslaved; and, should
she have conceived before the father's conversion to Islam,
the child would be a slave like his mother.[28]

The distribution of booty was subject to certain regulations. A horseman, for example, got a double share, while a
slave, a woman or a minor, even if an active participant in
the campaign, received nothing.[29] Special restrictions applied to the distribution of enslaved prisoners: when they
were given out, husbands (if such had survived) and wives
should not be separated, nor parents and children.[30] In
tropical African practice the strict application of all these
rules often proved impracticable (see below pp. 161–2).

The combination of the legal position just outlined, the

---

[24] Khadduri, 1955, 127–8; Ibn Abi Zayd, 342; Khalil ibn Ishaq,
Abrégé de la loi musulmane selon le rite de l'Imâm Mâlek, i, 'Le
rituel', tr. G.-H. Bousquet, Publications de l'Institut d'Études Ori-
entales de la Faculté des Lettres d'Alger, 1956, 209.
[25] Khalil ibn Ishaq, i, 217.
[26] Khadduri, 1955, 129.
[27] Khalil ibn Ishaq, i, 209.
[28] *ibid.*
[29] Ibn Abi Zayd, 164; Khalil ibn Ishaq, i, 212–13.
[30] Khadduri, 1955, 130–1.

nature of the domestic demand to be described in Chapter
V, and the normal vicissitudes of warfare, may explain why
female slaves figure more prominently than male in Muslim
tropical Africa, and in the trans-Saharan trade, than in the
Atlantic trade. The possibility that this prominence, in turn,
is in part responsible for the readier absorption of Negro
slaves in North African and Middle Eastern society, than
in that of the United States, is interesting, but speculative.

The religious tension between Muslim and Pagan, coming to a climax in *jihad*, was sometimes reinforced in other
respects also. The biographer of Alooma, ruler of Bornu in
the latter part of the sixteenth century, mentioned more
than once and with evident approval his master's slave-
raiding during Ramadan.[31] In general, however, it might
be expected that the appropriate time for slave-raiding
would be determined by the seasonal changes of the solar
calendar rather than by the lunar calendar of the faith, and
in Nachtigal's experience there was, presumably for these
reasons, no Ramadan raiding. Further west, in the Senegal
area, during the flourishing period of the Tokolor theocracies in the later nineteenth century, there was often trouble between Muslims and the adherents of traditional secret
societies, such as the Komo. Once Tokolor horsemen broke
up a Komo festival, capturing two men in ceremonial cos-

[31] Ahmed ibn Fartua, *History of the first twelve years of the reign
of Mai Idris Alooma of Bornu* (1571–1583), H. R. Palmer (tr.),
1926, 40, 51. Muslim slaving during the Christian Lent is reported
from Ethiopia at the end of the fifteenth century, when Mahfuz,
ruler of Harar, began ravaging Ethiopia each year in Lent, killing
the men and enslaving the women and children, some for sale and
others for presentation to the Sharif of Mecca (W. Cornwallis Harris, *The highlands of Aethiopia*, 2nd ed., London 1844, ii, 53–4).
The purpose was to strike at the Christians when they were weakened by the severe fast of the eastern churches. As for Ramadan,
Muslims on *jihad* would legally be exempt from fasting. Richardson,
1848, i, 222, heard of some central Saharan raiders postponing
their activities until Ramadan was finished; he does not indicate how
important slaves were in the prospective loot.

tume. The Tokolor chief wondered at these strange creatures, and proposed burning them to discover their real identity, since evidently they could not be men. The unfortunate captives protested that they were in truth only men, and, stripped of their adornment, they were forthwith sold as slaves in the nearest market.[32]

Christian meddling with a quasi-religious exercise was not well received, whether it came from Europeans or from Africans, as, for example, in the banning of the slave trade by King Theodore of Ethiopia.[33] In April 1872 Nachtigal accompanied the forces of Abu Sekkin, the king of Bagirmi, who had been driven from his capital by an attack from Wadai, on a raid against the Pagan Kimre. Two of Nachtigal's servants played an active part in this expedition and, better equipped with firearms than the local forces, fired the first shots which made possible such success as the raiders eventually achieved. Fortunately, as Nachtigal observed, his men did not have much ammunition, and their skill was very limited. But they vigorously rejected Nachtigal's efforts to restrain them, maintaining that harrying Pagans who refused submission to a Muslim king and rejected the law of Islam was a purely religious matter in which a Christian had no right to interfere.[34] A variation on this theme comes from East Africa in 1804, where Dallons, a French slave-trader, said that the Zanzibaris put up the prices of slaves at will, and 'end by making us fear that we shall not obtain them at any price, because their religion, as they say, forbids

[32] L. Tauxier, La religion bambara, Paris 1927, 300.
[33] J. L. Krapf, Travels, researches and missionary labours during an eighteen years' residence in eastern Africa, London 1860, 84. Perhaps a similar annoyance is discernible amongst Pagans also. The following prayer was addressed to the Borfimor, the sacred object of the human leopard society in Sierra Leone. 'Make no trouble meet them. Make they get slaves. Make English no sabby they get slaves for get free. Make they gentry.' (T. J. Alldridge, The Sherbro and its hinterland, London 1901, p. 155.)
[34] ii, 630.

them to sell to white men'.[35] In 1855 Speke found Somalis greatly discomposed about rumoured British interference with the slave trade, which they regarded as their Quranic right.[36] Such resentment produced even livelier scenes during Ramadan in 1880, when Swahilis and Arabs from Mombasa, vowing to make soup of the livers of the Church Missionary Society missionaries, attacked the C.M.S. freed slave settlement at Freretown; the missionaries defended themselves with arms, and later admitted the possession of a white flag, bearing the word Freedom, to be unfurled as a signal for all the Mombasa slaves to rise against their masters.[37]

The concentration upon Pagans, and to a much lesser extent Christians, as the most eligible candidates for enslavement may have slowed down the spread of Islam. The exclusion from Islam in sixteenth-century Songhay of the masses, and especially the servile masses, has been explained as a consequence of the fact that a Muslim was *ipso facto* a free man.[38] It has been argued that later there was no consistent propagation of Islam by Arab traders in the East African interior because conversions would have restricted the supply of slaves,[39] or by the Turko-Egyptians and others advancing up the Nile, because the local people were

[35] G. S. P. Freeman-Grenville, *The East African coast: select documents from the first to the earlier nineteenth century*, Oxford 1962, hereafter Freeman-Grenville A, 1962, p. 199.

[36] J. H. Speke, *What led to the discovery of the source of the Nile*, Edinburgh 1864, 116–17.

[37] J. Gray, 'Zanzibar and the coast belt, 1840–84', in Oliver and Mathew, 1963, i, 245; R. Oliver, *The missionary factor in East Africa*, London 1965, 55–6.

[38] J. Rouch, *Contribution à l'histoire des Songhay*, Mémoires de l'Institut français d'Afrique noire, no. 29, 1953, 193.

[39] O. F. Raum, 'German East Africa', in V. Harlow and E. M. Chilver (eds.), *History of East Africa*, ii, Oxford 1965, 167; J.-C. Froelich, *Les Musulmans d'Afrique noire*, Paris 1962, 56; Oliver, 1965, 202.

more valuable as Pagan taxpayers or slave labour.[40] Nachtigal attributed a similar attitude to the Muslims of Bagirmi. Noting that they had made no effort to share the blessings of Islam with their Pagan neighbours, he explained this by the fact that for 300 years the Pagans had been regarded merely as a rich source of slaves.[41] One recent writer goes so far as to say that Muslim warriors were careful not to convert people who could be enslaved or heavily taxed; this, he maintains, was especially clear in Adamawa, the modern northern Cameroon.[42] In this respect, therefore, the suppression of slave-trading might be seen as removing one of the great obstacles to the spread of Islam;[43] with perhaps even the further corollary that, if Africa had ever become completely Muslim, slavery would inevitably have disappeared, in default of any Pagans who could legitimately be enslaved.[44]

These generalizations, in part correct, perhaps err in attributing too great a uniformity to the motives and practices of Muslims. Traders, and warriors on essentially secular campaigns, could scarcely be expected to display more than a tepid interest in evangelization. Where religious purposes were more to the fore, whether expressed militarily or peacefully, concern for the conversion of Pagans was widespread.

[40] R. C. Stevenson, 'Some aspects of the spread of Islam in the Nuba mountains', in Lewis, 1966, 211. He adds that massive slave-raiding, even if undertaken with little interest in extending the faith, and leading to the eventual return home of only a very few converted slaves, might nevertheless prepare the ground for Islam by breaking up traditional patterns of life.

[41] ii, 687.

[42] J.-C. Froelich, "Essai sur les causes et méthodes de l'Islamisation de l'Afrique de l'Ouest du XIe siècle au XXe siècle', in Lewis, 1966, 168-9.

[43] T. W. Arnold, The preaching of Islam, London 1913, 362.

[44] L. G. Binger, Esclavage, Islamisme, Christianisme, Paris 1891, 34-6.

Enslavement of Muslims

How significant in fact in African history has the concept been that a Muslim of good standing should in no circumstances be enslaved? Barth had some justification for the view which he expressed in 1857 that the Anti-Slavery Society in London was over-optimistic in believing a Muslim to be adequately protected against the risk of being enslaved.[45] Nevertheless, even if the protection enjoyed by a Muslim were limited and uncertain, several incidents show that conduct was sometimes influenced by scruples about enslaving fellow-Muslims.

It was noted as a sign of virtue in Askiya Muhammad I of Songhay in the early sixteenth century that he liberated from slavery those who could prove their right to freedom.[46] Alooma of Bornu released Muslim prisoners of free status after an expedition to Kanem in 1572-3 which he did not regard as *jihad*.[47] After an internal quarrel in Timbuktu in 1730 had ended in violence, the victorious general allowed free women to return to their families.[48] Bello, the son and successor of Uthman dan Fodio, creator of the Sokoto *jihad* of the late eighteenth and early nineteenth centuries, after defeating the rebel Abd al-Salam's supporters, released those who knew the Fatiha and the ritual of ablution, enslaving the rest.[49] When a combined Arab,

[45] Barth, 1857-8, ii, 189 n.; cf. J. Richardson, *Narrative of a mission to central Africa*, London 1853, ii, 223.

[46] Mahmud Kati ibn al-Haj jal-Mutawakkil Kati, *Tarikh el-Fettach*, O. Houdas and M. Delafosse (eds. and trs.), Paris 1913-14, reprinted 1964, 115.

[47] H. R. Palmer, *Sudanese memoirs, being mainly translations of a number of Arabic manuscripts relating to the central and western Sudan*, Lagos 1928, reprinted 1967, i, 36; Froelich, 1962, 50.

[48] *Tedzkiret en-Nisian*, O. Houdas (tr.), Paris 1901, 209.

[49] Haj Said, *Histoire de Sokoto* (attached to *Tedzkiret en-Nisian*), 313.

Bornu and Mandara slave-raid was proposed in 1823 the
sultan of Mandara havered, saying that the Pagan tribes
round about were all converting without force.[50] In the
same year Shaykh Umar's father, al-Kanemi, a pious Muslim who saved Bornu from Fulani attacks in the early nineteenth century, released prisoners taken on an expedition
against a rebel cleric, not wishing, as he said, to make slaves
of the wives and children of Muslims.[51] Nachtigal, who
thought that some of the near-Muslim tribes in Borku got a
raw deal from raiders who were no better Muslims than
they were, believed that the representations which he made
to the king of Wadai on their behalf were not without effect.[52] Nachtigal was himself with the Awlad Sulayman in
June 1871, when a raid into Ennedi was planned by them
to fill in the time while they were waiting for the date harvest. The raid was a failure, and among the prisoners whom
the Awlad Sulayman left behind when they withdrew was
a neighbour of Nachtigal's. After a few days, however, because of his religious status as a Murabid, he was allowed
to return on the mere promise of a ransom, the amount of
which was left undetermined, to be paid later.[53]

In almost every case, however, an alternative explanation
of the privileges of Muslim prisoners is possible. Askiya
Muhammad I, a usurper backed by the Muslim party, was
at least at the beginning of his reign anxious to curry clerical favour; the people of Kanem were kin to Alooma's
Bornu, and Alooma's principles did not protect the people
of Kano, Muslim but not kinsmen, against whom he also
warred; quarrels within Timbuktu were almost family
affairs; Abd al-Salam, an early and prominent supporter of
Uthman dan Fodio, clearly merited special handling despite his subsequent rebellion; Mandara and Bornu were

[50] Denham and Clapperton, 1826 A, 119.
[51] Denham and Clapperton, 1826 A, 167.
[52] ii, 145.   [53] ii, 95.

probably manipulating the 1823 raid as part of their struggle against the Fulani; al-Kanemi may have had some hesitation about crossing too harshly a cleric, even a rebellious cleric, whose supernatural powers were notorious; and any influence that Nachtigal may have had over the king of Wadai cannot be interpreted as purely Islamic.

In some instances scruples about enslaving members of a particular group appear to have had a tribal basis, which might or might not correspond with the general distinction between Muslim and Pagan. This might be true of Alooma's Kanem wars, just mentioned. A European slave-trader on the West African coast in the nineteenth century was told by a prince of Futa Jallon (now a part of modern Guinea) that Muslim courts there rescued Muslims from slavery, for the Fulani of that country detested the institution among themselves and among members of 'their caste', by which may be meant simply Islam; the same courts inflicted, for even the slightest offences, enslavement, as right and reputable, upon non-Muslims.[54] Of the Fulani on the Gambia in the eighteenth century it was said:

> As their Humanity extends to all, they are doubly kind to People of their own Race, insomuch that if they know of one of them being made a Slave, all the Pholeys [Fulani] will redeem him.[55]

The writer thought that all the Fulani were strict Muslims, but this seems unlikely as there are still Pagan Fulani on the Gambia today. The Budduma of Lake Chad observed the unwritten understanding that no Kotoko, Arab or Fulani might be enslaved, but the Kanuri, also Muslims, were not exempt from Budduma raids.[56]

[54] T. Canot, *Adventures of an African slaver: being a true account of the life of Captain Theodore Canot . . . his own story as told in the year 1854 to Brantz Mayer . . .*, London 1928, 95–6.
[55] Francis Moore, *Travels into the inland parts of Africa . . .*, London 1738, 32–3.   [56] Macleod, 1912, 227–8.

There are, moreover, equally numerous references to the enslavement of Muslims. In 1391–2 a letter came to Cairo from the ruler of Bornu, complaining that Arab tribes from the east were enslaving free Bornu Muslims, keeping some and selling others to Egypt, Syria and elsewhere.[57] Sonni Ali, ruler of Songhay in the later fifteenth century, though a Muslim of some sort himself, sometimes took free Muslims and gave them as slaves, adding insult to injury by pretending thus to bestow pious alms.[58] Between Askiya Muhammad I, usurping successor of Sonni Ali, and a Muslim cleric there was an agreement that the cleric's descendants should not be sold, but the chronicler Kati saw great numbers of them offered in the Timbuktu market despite their protestations.[59] Mansur, pasha of Timbuktu, before attacking Deba, a Pagan town, in the early eighteenth century observed the strict rules, first sending a messenger to offer the alternatives of conversion or taxation. The inhabitants agreed, submitting to the authority of God and the pasha; but a warlike officer of the pasha, unwilling to lose the opportunity for a raid, intercepted the messenger, and persuaded him to report a contrary answer. Deba was then attacked, the men killed, the children enslaved, and of the women some were killed and some enslaved. The town became a desert.[60] Despite the patent irregularity of these proceedings Kati felt no embarrassment in quoting, for an illustrative parallel, the Quranic verse (lxix. 7) describing the fate of some who ventured to deny God's prophets: 'and as for Ad, they were destroyed by a fierce roaring wind'. In the seventeenth and eighteenth centuries, raid and counter-raid between Timbuktu and the Tuaregs led to the enslavement of Muslim prisoners by both sides.[61]

[57] Ibn Fadl Allah al-'Umari, *Masalik al-absar fi mamalik al-amsar*, Gaudefroy-Demombynes (tr.), *L'Afrique moins l'Égypte*, Paris 1927, 40–2.

[58] Kati, 84.   [59] *ibid.*, 139–42; see also 15 n.

[60] *Tedzkiret*, 37–9.   [61] *ibid.*, 9–10, 11, 142.

In the early years of the nineteenth century, Abdullahi, brother of Uthman dan Fodio, charged some of his colleagues with selling free men in the market.[62] In the sole work known to survive from al-Hajj Jibril, Uthman dan Fodio's most respected teacher, the selling of free men ranks with adultery, wine drinking and manslaughter, among the things which 'our people' forbid.[63] The combined expedition of 1823 wound up in an attack on a Muslim Fulani town, Musfeia, in which the assailants were thrashed and Denham nearly lost his life.[64] (It was a slave of the Arab leader who restored to Denham his horse, and also rescued the flag of the pasha of Tripoli from the stricken field.[65]) Barth found that in the borderlands between the Fulani and Bornu it was difficult even to get guides, so risky had it become for anyone to venture outside his own town.[66] Bokari, the rebel governor of Hadeija, which was technically a part of the Sokoto empire, devastated the country to the gates of Kano, and thousands of slaves, Muslim and Pagan, passed to dealers through his hands.[67] Hausa traders in Adamawa handled, among other slaves, some Fulani sold to them by Pagan raiders.[68] After his accession, Zubayr, emir of Adamawa 1890–1901, failed in an attack on an outlying district to secure slaves which might be sent to Sokoto in exchange for his robe of office. When he came home he found the collector from Sokoto, to whom on such an occasion he might have to surrender all the fruits of his foray, waiting for the slaves; he then took the people of Fali,

[62] Abdullahi ibn Muhammad, *Tazyin al-waraqat*, M. Hiskett (ed. and tr.), Ibadan, 1963, 122.

[63] A. D. H. Bivar and M. Hiskett, 'The Arabic literature of Nigeria to 1804', *Bull. of the School of Oriental and African Studies*, 1962, 143.

[64] Denham and Clapperton, 1826 A, 131–8.

[65] Clapperton, 1829, 194.

[66] Barth, 1857–8, ii, 182, 187.   [67] *ibid.*, ii, 175–7.

[68] P.-F. Lacroix, 'Matériaux pour servir à l'histoire des Peul de l'Adamawa', *Études camerounaises*, 1952, 34.

near the capital of Adamawa, both free men and clerics, and gave them to the collector. A month later he followed the collector to Sokoto and received investiture and a flag.[69] At the end of the nineteenth century the emirs of Kontagora were enslaving Zaria Muslims.[70] The reign of Umaru, fourth emir of Bauchi, culminated in 1900 in a massacre in the town of Gworam, which had resisted a slave levy on its Muslim population.[71] As late as 1915 Ali Dinar, ruler of Darfur, accused the Muslim Kababish tribe of selling as slaves free Muslims, refugees from the French in Wadai.[72]

Baba of Karo, the Hausa woman who in 1949–50, at about the age of 60, told the story of her life to Mary Smith, recalled then the days when 'there was always fear; war, war, war—they caught a man and they made him a slave, or else they killed him'. She remembered that, before the British came and 'the world was settled', even Muslim clerics 'dared not travel freely, they would be kidnapped and sold in the market'. Baba gave not the slightest hint of any assured protection on which Muslims might rely against these risks.[73] Even today, similar memories live on here and there: recently, in Segu, a local family was still being derided because the father was enslaved while on pilgrimage; and in Ibadan the story is told of Malam Harun who set out for Mecca with some of his students, only to have the party broken up near Lake Chad, some of the

[69] R. M. East, *Stories of old Adamawa*, Lagos and London 1934, 91 ff. For a later instance of Zubayr again sending slaves to Sokoto, see below, p. 181.

[70] M. G. Smith, 'Historical and cultural conditions of political corruption among the Hausa', *Comparative studies in society and history*, 1964 (hereafter M. G. Smith, 1964 A), 177.

[71] S. J. Hogben and A. H. M. Kirk-Greene, *The emirates of northern Nigeria*, London 1966, 462.

[72] A. H. Theobald, *Ali Dinar, last sultan of Darfur, 1898–1916*, London 1965, 144–5.

[73] Mary Smith, *Baba of Karo*, London 1954, 47, 132.

students being killed and their teacher falling into slavery.[74]

Some of this maltreatment of Muslims arose from an aggressive disregard of the requirements of religious law. Such action, however, sometimes aroused serious qualms of conscience. A good deal of discussion has been reported of the implications of the curte of Ham, Gen. 9:20–7, which appeared to condemn to slavery the descendants of Ham, identified with the Negroes. Might not this, some were inclined to ask, be regarded as overruling the general prohibition of the enslavement of Muslims? This question was discussed at length early in the seventeenth century by Ahmad Baba, a scholar of Timbuktu who came from a Berber family, and to whom an enquiry had come from Tuat about the propriety of enslaving black Muslims, as was apparently happening frequently as a result of war between the Muslim rulers of the states in the Western Sudan. It was explained that there was sometimes difficulty in distinguishing between Muslim and Pagan prisoners of war, who differed from each other in no respect save in their religion. Ahmad Baba had no doubt that a Negro who had voluntarily embraced Islam should not in any circumstances be enslaved. 'The reason for enslavement,' he said, 'is unbelief. The position of unbelieving Negroes is the same as that of other unbelievers, Christians, Jews, Persians, Turks, etc.' For this reason he firmly rejected the view that the curse of Ham could be regarded as justifying the enslavement of Muslim Negroes. 'On the contrary, any unbeliever, if he persists in his original unbelief, may be made a slave, whether he is descended from Ham or not. In this respect there is no difference between the races.' The fact that these questions were raised at all and were then so seriously discussed indicates clearly enough that the prac-

[74] O. el–Nager, *West Africa and the Muslim pilgrimage,* Univ. of London thesis, 1969, 334 n.

tice of slave traders and of those who purchased slaves often diverged from the strict principles of the law.[75] Both Uthman dan Fodio and his son Muhammad Bello, in the Sokoto empire some 300 years later, cited Ahmad Baba as they examined the same problems.[76]

Even for those who were fully persuaded by such arguments as were adduced by Ahmad Baba, the definition of a Muslim 'in good standing' might present delicate problems to pious Muslims confronted by others who professed to be Muslims but who in the practice of their religion were found to be deplorably lax. Amongst the categories against whom *jihad*—leading, as we have seen, often to enslavement—might legally be waged some were quite clear, such as Jews and Christians, or polytheists, but others were more or less dependent upon definition, including apostates, deserters, highway robbers, and those who cause dissension.[77] To what extent did lapses from the true faith deprive a nominal Muslim of the immunity against slave-raiding which the *sharia* appeared to confer upon him, and make it legitimate, perhaps even obligatory, to launch a *jihad* against him? Heresy or apostasy might be regarded as an even more heinous offence than Pagan unbelief, for the example of a heretic might lead ignorant Muslims astray. Uthman dan Fodio considered the problem carefully, implicitly at least with special reference to the West African situation, and decided that in most cases the punishment meted out to erring Muslims must stop short of enslavement. Even he, however, admitted it under certain circum-

[75] G. Rotter, *Die Stellung des Negers in der islamisch-arabischen Gesellschaft bis zum XVI. Jahrhundert*, Bonn 1967, 49–52; Bivar and Hiskett, 1962, 111.

[76] J. O. Hunwick, 'A new source for the biography of Ahmad Baba al-Tinbukti (1556–1627)', *Bulletin of the School of Oriental and African Studies*, 1964, 588 n.

[77] Khadduri, 1955, 74 ff.

stances for apostates (*jama'at al-murtaddin*),[78] and if this doctrine were accepted there was an obvious temptation to impute apostasy to anyone whom, for quite other reasons, one might wish to attack. Denham thought that any people against whom war was intended was stigmatized, almost as a matter of routine, as being guilty of apostasy—kaffering, he called it.[79]

Whether enslaved originally by Pagans or by other Muslims—or, since conversion was not inevitably a passport to emancipation, enslaved as Pagans and subsequently converted—Muslim slaves frequently turned up in export markets. They were, for example, passing through lower Dahomey in the early eighteenth century.[80] Many domestic slaves in eighteenth-century St Louis and Goree were Muslim.[81] In Borgu, Hausa Muslim slaves were allowed freedom of worship.[82] In Yorubaland, near the Atlantic coast, Clapperton received an account of the local Paganism from a Bornu Muslim slave.[83] An eighteenth-century report mentioned that among the slaves in a slave-yard on the Sierra Leonean coast was 'a Mahometan [who] could read and write Arabick', who had been put in irons for the first time the day before; an American slave-captain also told of the loss of another Muslim slave who had died by 'the sulks', refusing food, despite beating and being offered the tastiest meals available, in despair at his enslavement.[84] In Bahia in Brazil there were large numbers of Muslim slaves, many of whom were able to read and write Arabic, and who en-

---

[78] A. D. H. Bivar, 'A manifesto of the Fulani jihad', *Journal of African History*, 1961, 241.

[79] Denham and Clapperton, 1826 A, 149.

[80] Paul Marty, *Études sur l'Islam au Dahomey*, Paris 1926, 11.

[81] J. D. Hargreaves, *Prelude to the partition of West Africa*, London 1963, 180–1.

[82] Clapperton, 1829, 74.   [83] *ibid.*, 51.

[84] C. P. Wadstrom, *An essay on colonization* . . . , London 1795, reprinted 1968, 83.

gaged in proselytizing activity among other slaves who had come to Bahia earlier.[85] Certain peoples, such as Mandingoes and Fulani, who were in Africa mainly Muslim, commanded higher prices from slave traders on the Liberian coast than the average slave; Mandingoes were much in demand in Cuba as the smartest type of domestic servant.[86] Some slaves rescued by the British and sent to Freetown were Muslims, including even Fulani who had fallen prey to their intended victims on slave-raids which did not go according to plan.[87]

There were also large numbers of Muslim slaves in the Mediterranean area, usually taken through direct action by Christians. Malta was a centre for preying on the shipping of Tunis and Tripoli, and there are estimated to have been 10,000 Muslim slaves on the island in 1720.[88] These, being allowed considerable freedom, were able to meet together for prayers. In 1749 an alleged slave plot in Malta led to trials, followed by tortures and executions.[89]

Nachtigal recorded several episodes which illustrated the uncertainty of the protection which their faith conferred upon Muslims, as well as the confusion which sometimes arose in distinguishing between slave and free man[90] or be-

[85] Verger, 1968, 361–8. Cf. V. Monteil, 'Analyse des 25 documents arabes des Malês de Bahia (1835)', and R. Reichert, 'L'insurrection d'esclaves de 1835 à la lumière des documents arabes des Archives publiques de l'Etat de Bahia (Brésil)', both in Bull. Institut fondamental d'Afrique noire, series B, Jan.-Apr. 1967, 88 ff. Also R. K. Kent, 'Palmares: an African state in Brazil', Journal of African History, 1965, 161–76.

[86] Sir Harry Johnston, Liberia, London 1906, i, 174.

[87] P. E. H. Hair, 'The enslavement of Koelle's informants', Journal of African History, 1965, 196–7; S. W. Koelle, Polyglotta Africana, London 1854, reprinted 1963, 18.

[88] J. Godechot, 'La course Maltaise', Revue africaine, 1952, 106.

[89] T. Zammit, History of Malta, Valletta 1929, 247–8.

[90] That such difficulties were not confined to the less settled frontiers of the Muslim world, such as tropical Africa, appears from the provision, in standard legal texts, of advice about what to do in the

tween the slave and the Muslim prisoner of war not yet exchanged or ransomed. In Tibesti, the fact that a man was a Muslim was not a decisive reason for not wanting to make a slave of him. The case of Sa'ad has already been mentioned (see above p. 14), and an effort was also made in Tibesti to kidnap another of Nachtigal's servants, indubitably a free man and a Muslim, on the ground that he was really a slave of the kidnapper's father.[91] The wilder marauding peoples of the desert were also not particularly precise in distinguishing between Muslim and non-Muslim when they were considering whom to plunder and take prisoner. Bu Aischa, the official leader of the caravan with which Nachtigal travelled from Murzuk, the capital of Fezzan, to Kuka, had once served the government of Fezzan before it became a Turkish province; the successful efforts which he made at that time to restore to the inhabitants of the Kawar oasis south of Fezzan their women and children illegally captured by the marauding Arabs were still remembered with gratitude by them.[92] In Wadai, there was no suggestion that Muslims were exempt from the condemnation to slavery whereby King Ali tried to protect foreign merchants against delinquent debtors,[93] a measure which may have been an extension of the principle which allowed a man to offer himself as a pledge for payment of a debt.

Slave and free status

Problems of status definition were clearly very real, as the following illustrations show. Prisoners of war were one of the main sources of supply in slave markets, but there was often also the possibility of ransom or exchange, and especially among the nomadic desert people, negotiations on

case, for example, when you have married a slave woman under the impression that she was free (Ibn Abi Zayd, 267).
[91] i, 289.   [92] i, 179, 519.   [93] iii, 63.

such matters might run on almost indefinitely. The Awlad Sulayman, with whom Nachtigal spent several months, were not themselves active slave-traders, but still held a number of unransomed prisoners. These were ranked above the despised real slave, but were treated in much the same way, the only practical difference, according to Nachtigal, between the two being that the prisoners could not be sold again.[94] Among the sedentary population of Borku too there were prisoners of war who had not been ransomed, but because of religious scruples had not been made slaves.[95]

King Ali of Wadai settled in his own country a great many of the prisoners, both free men and slaves, who had been taken when Massenya, the capital of Bagirmi, fell to his forces in 1870. He planned to use them to raise the local standards of housebuilding, handicrafts and agriculture, in all of which the people of Bagirmi far surpassed those of Wadai, who were described as the most barbarous of the Sudan peoples. The total number thus settled was commonly put at around 30,000; Nachtigal thought that half that number would be nearer the truth.[96] Most of the compulsory immigrants whom Nachtigal observed in Wadai were slaves, many of whom were distributed among the Wadai officials, or sold for export.[97] The status of some was uncertain, and despite his Muslim religious convictions, King Ali was not always able carefully to distinguish slave from free. At practically every audience which Nachtigal had with the king in 1873, disputes came before him about the status of captives from Bagirmi. The king had taken into his service a high Bagirmi official, whose duty it was to

[94] ii, 65.   [95] ii, 140.
[96] Oral tradition in the early twentieth century continued to use the figure 30,000, which was, however, said to be the number of Bagirmi killed or enslaved; Macleod, 1912, 143.
[97] ii, 727-8; iii, 83-5.

examine the genealogical trees of these individuals, and in their presence to make a report to the king. According to Nachtigal's information, the settlement experiment was highly successful; the forced removal of these people, slave or free, from Bagirmi benefited Wadai much more than all the treasures plundered in Massenya. The device adopted to settle disputes about slave status was, however, less effective. During Nachtigal's visit, some who claimed to be free were still being treated as slaves, though the market price for these 'hot' slaves, as the current jargon called them, was depressed by the element of risk below that offered for the 'cold' variety, about whose status there was no dispute. By means not clearly explained a good many 'hot' slaves accompanied the caravan with which Nachtigal eventually travelled from Abeshr to Darfur, and, as some difficulty was apparently feared in getting them out of the country, the caravan split into two sections, the one with the 'hot' slaves proceeding to the frontier by devious routes.[98]

Uncertainty about status was well exemplified by a 17-year-old boy, the son of a freedman, who had not realized that his status was that of a slave until he was suddenly transported from his home town to enter the service of Shaykh Umar, the ruler of Bornu,[99] with whom Nachtigal had established very friendly relations. This boy, with a younger colleague, was later lent to Nachtigal, whom he served faithfully for nearly three years (see p. 132).

Quarrels among Muslims increased the possibilities of dispute over such points. Shaykh Ahmad al-Bakkai, the distinguished Timbuktu scholar, remonstrating about 1861 with the invading champion al-Hajj Umar, cited, among other points, the complaint that al-Hajj Umar's troops had taken one of his own free wives, treating her as a slave while the slave of a *sharif* had likewise been taken by

[98] iii, 302–3.   [99] ii, 308.

them, but on the ground that she was actually a free woman.[100]

Nachtigal also referred to 'half-slaves' or 'half-free' men, men, for example, who were allowed to earn something on their own account in the great market of Kuka by selling firewood or straw for fence repairs,[101] men who tended the date-palm groves of their nomad masters in Borku between the date harvests,[102] or, at a much higher social level, among the officials who served the king of Darfur.[103] These men may well have been in one of the intermediary categories, specifically provided for by religious law (see pp. 54–5).

Such status problems may have been further complicated by the fact that in certain respects slaves and freemen were outwardly much alike. A slave often had, like a free man, the right to earn something for himself, and to own property, even to own other slaves. The master might ultimately be responsible for all his slave's possessions; the Maliki law provided, for example, that a man who had sworn an oath not to ride any beast of his own, and then rode his slave's, would be guilty of perjury.[104] The right of a slave to purchase his freedom would, however, have been purely nominal if he had been unable *de facto* to accumulate the means for this purpose. Clapperton said of the Sokoto empire that property-owning slaves were common, though on their death their property was inherited by their owners.[105] He qualified this by saying that masters inherited only if their slaves died childless; if this is correct it is a deviation from strict religious law, according to which, as we have already seen (see above p. 8), slaves, even if partially free, do not inherit. Clapperton's description of the combination of free

[100] MS. Arabe 5259, Bibliothèque nationale, Paris, ff. 67–8, 69; we are indebted to J. R. Willis for this reference.
[101] i, 672.   [102] ii, 139.   [103] iii, 429.
[104] Khalil ibn Ishaq, i, 192.   [105] Clapperton, 1829, 249.

enterprise and slave labour in agriculture is given below
(see pp. 133–4).

The contribution of slaves to religious activity

The possession of slaves facilitated religious study, and
other pious exercises, in various ways. Slaves might form
part of the alms which clerics received. Some earlier stories
of the largesse practised by pious rulers should perhaps be
regarded rather as moral anecdotes which might suggest an
example to their successors than as sober historical record,
but they no doubt indicate a widespread attitude to the uses
to which slaves might properly be put. A clerical chronicler
of the sixteenth century somewhat disingenuously praised
Askiya Muhammad I because, 'full of regard for the *ulama*,
he distributed slaves and riches generously to them to assure
the interests of the Muslims and to aid them in their submission to God and in the practice of the faith'.[106] On the
Prophet Muhammad's birthday the poets of Fez gathered
before the governor, and the best performer was proclaimed
the prince of poets; a little wistfully, recalling perhaps the
bounty which had once rewarded his own youthful verses
(see below p. 185), Leo Africanus looked back to the good
old days when every poet received 50 ducats, and the win-
ner 100 ducats, an excellent horse, a woman slave and the
king's own robe—130 years had passed '. . . since this cus-
tome, together with the maiestie of the Fessan kingdome,
decaied'.[107] Askiya Daud of Songhay, in the mid-sixteenth
century, had at his disposal a large property unexpectedly
inherited from one of his slaves. From this were given 100
cows to the muezzins of the capital, and to the sister of a
qadi 1000 sheep and goats. The numerous slaves which had
thus fallen into Daud's hands he divided into batches of

[106] Kati, 115.
[107] Leo Africanus, A, ii, 455; B, i, 214–15.

twenty-seven. One batch he sent to the chief cleric of the kingdom, one to the *imam*, and one to the main mosque, the women to make mats and carpets for the mosque, and the men to carry the clay and work the wood needed for its maintenance. Two batches were sent to the *qadi* of the capital, one for his own use, the other, or the proceeds from its sale, to be redistributed among those who had a legal right to alms; and one to a *sharif*, charged to share the bounty with all the other *sharifs* and their families. The members of this last batch, later freed, subsequently gave themselves out as also being genuine *sharifs*.[108] One high Songhay official, who murdered a rival in 1588, gave ten slaves and 100,000 cowries to students for a penitential recitation of the Quran on his behalf.[109]

Both teachers and pupils in Islamic schools might possess or be given slaves. Nachtigal observed that any impecunious scholar, attracted to Kuka from the neighbouring countries by the reputation of Shaykh Umar, the ruler of Bornu, for piety and generosity, and fortunate enough to gain his favourable attention, soon equipped himself with a few slaves.[110] Among the Fulani of nineteenth-century Masina, it was not rare for well-to-do families to give milch cows, or slaves, to the clerics who were teaching their children.[111] Another cleric, much impressed by the youthful learning of Shehu Ahmadu, the later founder of the Masina theocracy, gave him a slave, asking in return for his prayers; the slave subsequently rose to be a general of captives and freed captives in Masina.[112] In the Timbuktu area, when a pupil finished the memorization of the Quran, his teacher would receive five cattle, or a camel, or a slave, or the equivalent.[113] Even in poverty-stricken Mauritania,

[108] Kati, 196–9. [109] *ibid.*, 237. [110] i, 637.
[111] A. H. Ba and J. Daget, *L'empire peul du Macina*, i, The Hague 1962, 64.
[112] Ba and Daget, 52, 105; cf. 112–3.
[113] P. Marty, *L'Islam et les tribus du Soudan*, Paris 1920, ii, 83.

where students had to take turns to go out and care for the
animals, carrying their books or slates with them, a student
might occasionally have a slave to relieve him of this
work.[114] Even a teacher who had fallen into disfavour
might yet hope for something: Samori, the nineteenth-
century Mandingo leader in West Africa, after quarrelling
with his former master, defeated and captured him, and
then offered him, as one deeply versed in the Quran, wives
and slaves if he would freely remain with him.[115]

Beyond this direct involvement of slaves in education lay
the general contribution of slave labour, on the farms and
elsewhere, releasing slave-owners from such menial tasks
and leaving them free for study. In this respect, the abolition of slavery imposed by the European colonial authorities
had, quite unintentionally, the effect of checking Islam, as
both teachers and students found that they now had less
time for academic work.[116] The decline of Touba, founded
by the Jahanka in 1815 and one of the three main centres
of Islam in the area which is now the modern state of
Guinea, was attributed to the liberation of the slaves, which
obliged masters and disciples to farm for food.[117] On the
other hand, in the case of slaves of non-Muslim masters, the
abolition of slavery has sometimes led to the ex-slaves becoming Muslim; this is reported in parts of Mossi country.[118]

In some instances modern education reverses the old pat-

[114] Ahmad bin al-Amin al-Shinqiti, *Al-wasit fi tarajim udaba
Shinqit*, 1911, 493; partly translated by M. Teffahi, as Ahmed Lamine ech Chenguiti, *El Wasit*, Saint-Louis (Senegal) 1953, 115.

[115] A. Kouroubari, 'Histoire de l'Imam Samori', *Bulletin de l'Institut français d'Afrique noire*, series B, 1959, 547.

[116] V. Thompson and R. Adloff, *French West Africa*, London
1958, 149.

[117] M. Houis, *La Guinée française*, Paris 1953, 32.

[118] E. P. Skinner, 'Islam in Mossi society', in Lewis, 1966, 362;
almost all liberated slaves and serfs in Nobéré, a Mossi district, became Muslim.

tern, and the despised Negro, son or grandson of a slave, becomes a teacher. This has happened sometimes in Mauritania, where the Negroes have been much readier to take advantage of French western education than have the nomads. But racial antagonism in the country, rooted in past slavery, continues, and modern schools among the nomads are handicapped by being staffed often by Negroes, whom the nomads still regard as of slave status. One Negro teacher was stoned by his pupils for asking them to carry their own food sacks.[119]

Religious conversion

The tendency for slaves to adopt the religion of their masters has been widespread, in Africa and outside. The Portuguese crown, for example, towards the end of the seventeenth century, was concerned about heretical (that is to say, Protestant) foreigners in Brazil, who might own slaves and teach them heresy. It was suggested that heretics be forbidden to own slaves, or even that they be expelled from the country.[120]

Within tropical Africa, the adoption of Islam by the slaves of Muslim masters was, by and large, normal procedure. Many examples might be given of this, and often the procedure was deliberately fostered by the slave-owners. In 1606 a Portuguese Franciscan friar at Pate, on the east coast, heard of traders who came from Arabia to barter for African boys, who were then taken to Arabia, made Muslim, and kept as slaves.[121] Krapf, an early Anglican missionary, on a Persian ship in the Red Sea in 1838, witnessed some Galla slave boys being taught the Muslim prayer.[122] Later in the nineteenth century, Speke told how slaves

[119] Thompson and Adloff, 1958, 162, 532.
[120] Verger, 1968, 70.
[121] Freeman-Grenville, 1962 A, 162.   [122] Krapf, 1860, 20.

bought in Zanzibar were circumcised, and taught to distinguish between clean and unclean animals. They also
learnt some Arabic words and some even went on pilgrimage.[123] On his way from the West African coast to Futa
Jallon in 1873, Blyden visited a slave town called Fansiggah. Here the king had built a mosque among the Pagan
slaves; it was compulsory for children to learn the Quran,
and optional for their parents to attend prayers. Blyden thought this a widespread practice among Muslim
chiefs.[124]

Such attention by the master to the conversion of his
slaves had in part a practical purpose. Speke remarked that
until the slaves in Zanzibar had been circumcised, and had
learnt which meats were legally clean, they could not
slaughter and prepare food for their masters. Such practical
points applied throughout Muslim Africa. But they do not
provide a full explanation, for there was also, among some
masters at least, concern for the eternal salvation of their
slaves. Krapf commented that Muslim traders thought they
were behaving mercifully in selling as slaves Pagans, who
must in this way become Muslim,[125] a view reminiscent
of some earlier Christian argument about the trans-Atlantic
trade.[126] The feeling was sometimes ultimately recipro-
cated, as is suggested in the story of the enslaved Zanj king
(see pp. 62). Doughty found that the African slaves in
Arabia apparently bore no resentment over their condition,
and were even grateful for the opportunity of salvation.[127]

[123] J. H. Speke, *Journal of the discovery of the sources of the
Nile*, London 1863, xxv ff.
[124] H. R. Lynch, *Edward Wilmot Blyden: panafrican patriot*,
London 1967, 97.
[125] Krapf, 1860, 121.
[126] D. P. Mannix and M. Cowley, *Black cargoes, a history of the
Atlantic slave trade* (1518–1865), New York 1962, xii, 8, 26, 44,
58–60.
[127] Doughty, i, 554–5.

There is some evidence that the attempts of slaves to better their understanding of Islam did not always meet with a sympathetic reception. Among the Fulani of Adamawa, for example, such an effort was more likely to be received with irony than with approval by the master.[128] The dances of the free pastoral Fulani included prayers and the participation of the *imam*, while the dances of their slaves lacked such religious embellishment, though the slaves were Muslim and would on other occasions pray with their masters.[129]

It was not uncommon for slaves to join with their masters in joint fulfilment of standard religious obligations. Nachtigal, at almost the same time that Blyden was in Fansiggah, watching the Muslim instruction of slaves there, saw slaves and masters praying together in Bornu, in the streets at evening (see p. 13). In fact, to refuse to join in this way might have striking symbolic impact, as in 1926 in Sierra Leone, when slaves claiming freedom underlined their demand by praying separately from their masters in Ramadan.[130]

The religious obligations of a Muslim slave were somewhat laxer than those of his free colleague. The congregational prayer on Friday is required of all free Muslims, with certain exemptions as for disability. It was not required for a slave, though if he should happen to be present then he should join in.[131] It was recommended for a partially free slave, in the *mukātib* category (see p. 55) even without his master's permission: but for an ordinary slave, or even a

---

[128] P. F. Lacroix, 'L'Islam peul de l'Adamawa', in Lewis, 1966, 402.

[129] D. J. Stenning, 'Cattle values and Islamic values in a pastoral population', in Lewis, 1966, 394.

[130] Paper N. A. 13/1926, 5 May 1926, at Kabala District Office, Sierra Leone.

[131] Ibn Abi Zayd, 95.

mudabbar slave (see pp. 55–6) only with such permission.[132]

Al-Hajj Umar, arguing in favour of the superiority of the internal *jihad*, the struggle to control one's own evil inclinations, over the external, or military, *jihad*, said that the former was incumbent upon all, free and slave, male and female, while the latter was required only of free men, although participation was permitted to a slave who had his master's permission.[133]

Similarly a slave was not required to make the pilgrimage; indeed, should he do so, but without his master's permission, his pilgrimage was invalid.[134] With such permission, however, it was a valid act of worship, and indeed some schools of law allowed a slave to deputize as pilgrim for a free man.[135] Impressive legal complications may arise from these complex provisions: what is the position, for instance, of a slave whose master authorizes him to go on pilgrimage, but who is then bought by a new owner who is unaware of this authorization? or of a slave thus authorized who somehow vitiates, say by some ritual irregularity, his pilgrimage?[136]

These special exceptions and disabilities for slave Muslims did not mean that the slaves were necessarily any the less devout. Many authors, though some added that the Muslim education of slaves was often rudimentary, comment on the devotion, even fanaticism, of slaves.[137] The tale of the pious black slave, the 468th of the *Arabian Nights*, illustrates one popular Middle Eastern image of

[132] Khalil ibn Ishaq, i, 87.
[133] J. R. Willis, *The jihad of al-Hajj Umar al-Futiu: the doctrinal basis*, University of London thesis, 1970, 107 & note.
[134] Ibn Abi Zayd, 141.   [135] el-Nager, 1969, 13 n.
[136] Khalil ibn Ishaq, i, 175–6.
[137] See for example C. Snouck Hurgronje, *Mekka in the latter part of the 19th century*, Leyden and London 1931, 11; Richardson, 1848, i, 195.

such a slave: whose prayer was powerful enough to bring rain in time of drought, or to encompass the slave's own suicide, though his commercial value was low. The elder of the two slaves whose services were transferred to Nachtigal by Shaykh Umar was not merely a nominal but a deeply committed Muslim;[138] the younger one was a Muslim too, though less strict.

Slave status was not incompatible, in certain cases, with considerable religious learning—although in many of the available examples such learning may have been acquired before the individual's enslavement. Among Negro slaves in Bahia, Quran schools flourished; the police tried, during the disturbances and slave rebellion of 1835, to arrest the teachers of these schools, on the grounds that they were dangerous agitators.[139] It was possible for education so far to outweigh distinctions of slave and free status that a slave might teach freedmen in such a school.[140] Such literacy was not always a cause of concern to the authorities, even in the New World: a slave sold in Jamaica about 1805 was employed later as a storeman, keeping his accounts in Arabic since he could not read or write English.[141]

Though in the following instance the letters are mundane rather than religious, the story of Abd Masuma, a nineteenth-century slave poet in Mauritania, warrants retelling. Abd Masuma was deeply in love with his master's wife. His master, aware of this, tied him to a stake and left him to perish. There, another poet, who was himself in love and who had wandered for days seeking someone to complete a love poem for him, found him. Abd Masuma was unwilling to be released, and by that the wanderer knew that the captive was also in love. The wanderer recited some lines, and Abd Masuma did likewise, revealing that he was also a poet. The wanderer asked him to com-

---

[138] ii, 308.   [139] Verger, 1968, 341.
[140] ibid., 523.   [141] Curtin, 1968, 155.

plete the unfinished poem for him. Abd Masuma agreed, if
it should be a love poem. And so it was done.[142]

It has been said that slaves 'were readily accepted into
the clergy',[143] but it would seem that instances of this were
rare. According to the law, no slave might act as *imam* for
free men.[144] For freedmen, the opportunities for clerical
appointment were better. A curious episode, in Darfur in
the 1780s, illustrates this. The sultan of Darfur at that time,
Tirab, marched out with all his troops to confront a threatened attack from Kordofan; but, not wishing to leave his
capital empty, the sultan freed 100 of his slaves, making the
greatest of them *hākim*, or chief official, for the town. The
sultan also instructed each of his men to free one or more
slaves, and one slave of the *imam*, thus freed, was himself
appointed an *imam*.[145]

Emancipation

Slaves belonging to a real Muslim world, it has been said,
would be keen to give unmistakable witness of their new
faith, in order thus to win their freedom.[146] But while the
conversion of slaves to Islam was very general, converted
slaves could not count on emancipation. The ecstatic cry
of Blyden, nineteenth-century West Indian champion of
African Islam, that 'the slave who embraces Islam is
free'[147] may be true in an apocalyptic or spiritual, or perhaps a Pickwickian, sense; as a generalization about ordinary affairs it is unfounded. It is difficult to find anything

[142] H. T. Norris, *Shinqiti folk literature and song*, Oxford 1968,
57–8.
[143] Lewis, 1966, 51.
[144] Khalil ibn Ishaq, i, 77.
[145] Na'um Shuqair, *Tarikh al-sudan*, Cairo 1903, i, 118.
[146] C. Monteil, *Les Bambara du Ségou et du Kaarta*, 1924, 337.
[147] E. W. Blyden, *Christianity, Islam and the Negro race*, London 1887, reprinted 1967, 175–6.

in the historical record to justify Blyden's confident assertion that

> the introduction of Islam into Central and West Africa has been the most important, if not the sole, preservative against the desolation of the slave-trade. Mohammedanism furnished a protection to the tribes who embraced it by effectually binding them together in one strong religious fraternity, and enabling them by their united effort to baffle the attempt of the powerful Pagan slave-hunters.[148]

Blyden later commended the British occupation of Egypt, in 1882, as tending to supply a like preservative against the slave trade, but in this case against the Arab trade in Negroes.[149]

Freeing a slave was widely regarded as a meritorious act, but conversion and emancipation were only occasionally linked by deliberate policy. This appears to have been the case, for example, in the Masina theocracy of the early nineteenth century. There the slaves of the state, i.e. prisoners of war not voluntarily practising Islam, were settled in cultivable areas, under clerical overseers who both organized the farm work and without constraint initiated the captives in Islam. When such a slave could justify his faith, and pray without help, he was freed.[150] This may, however, have been more an ideal than what actually happened. The same account of Masina says, a little later, that a prisoner was kept for three days with the clerics, who tried to convert him; if he refused, he was executed on the third day, his body remaining unburied and his heirs having no rights of succession.[151] A somewhat comparable situation may have existed in Adamawa, where Uthman dan Fodio,

[148] ibid., 186.   [149] Lynch, 1967, 193.
[150] Ba and Daget, 1962, i, 66–7.
[151] ibid., 1962, i, 119 n.

in his initial instructions to the Emir Adama, said that slaves who had become true Muslims might be liberated;[152] but despite this Adamawa became the major slave reservoir of the Sokoto empire.

In the vast majority of cases, a slave had to look elsewhere for hopes of emancipation. Piety was one possibility. Both the Quran (Surah xxiv. 33) and the traditions of the Prophet urge the freeing of slaves, whether for heavenly or secular recompense. Maliki law cites the tradition: 'whosoever frees a slave who is a Muslim, God will redeem every member of his body, limb for limb, from hell-fire'.[153] However, such an act was only one of many virtuous observances open to the pious, and by no means the most prominent one. Bello, sultan of Sokoto, cited not only the tradition just quoted, but also the further commentary of the lawyers, to the effect that giving alms (sadaqa) was preferable to freeing a slave ('itq); freeing a slave was rewarded by freedom from damnation, but so was affirming the unity of God, while to repeat this ten times was equivalent to freeing four Arabs, or one hundred times, to freeing ten slaves.[154]

While such qualifications need to be mentioned, there are still many examples of slaves being freed as an act of individual piety. Mansa Musa, the celebrated fourteenth-century ruler of Mali, won added renown by emancipating a slave every day.[155] Of a certain cleric in Timbuktu it was recorded that he bought a large number of slaves, and freed them for the love of God and in view of the life hereafter.[156] Oral tradition recalls of Ngolo, later in the eight-

[152] M. Z. Njeuma, The rise and fall of Fulani rule in Adamawa: 1809–1901, University of London thesis, 1969, 176–7.

[153] F. H. Ruxton, Maliki law, London 1916, 351 n. 6.

[154] Muhammad Bello, Tanbih al-raqid, unpublished MS. cited in el-Nager, 1969, 367, 384–5.

[155] Kati, 55.

[156] Abd al-Rahman ibn Abdullah al-Sadi, Tarikh al-Sudan, tr. O. Houdas, Paris 1913–14, reprinted 1964, 84.

eenth century to become king of Segu and perhaps the strongest ruler of his day in the western Sudan, that he had been enslaved as a youth, but had been freed by his master, a cleric, on learning half the Quran.[157] Ngolo, however, was not a very reliable Muslim. Baba of Karo recalled that the reason why her grandfather had freed his slaves 'was because he wanted to be rewarded when he died—because of religion'.[158]

Pious emancipation might appropriately occur on the occasion of some religious festival, especially at the end of Ramadan. In Sokoto in 1824, several slaves were freed at this time, Clapperton's landlord himself liberating fifteen.[159] Or emancipation might follow the accomplishment, by the slave, of some special religious task, such as the pilgrimage (see p. 48). Emancipation might itself provide the occasion for a festival. The Hausa celebrated a slave's payment of his redemption money, and receiving his freedom, in much the same way as the naming of a baby on the eighth day after birth: a cleric shaved the head of the ex-slave, giving him a Muslim name and sacrificing a ram.[160]

The piety of the master might be stimulated by his own distress: in illness, for example, he might seek God's mercy through such devout acts. Uthman dan Fodio, condemning some Hausa, who were alleged to sacrifice a slave in the hope of recovery from a serious illness, added that to free a slave in such hope might be effective.[161] Similar emancipation was apparently quite well known on the east coast in more recent times.[162]

[157] C. Monteil, 1924, 47–8.   [158] Mary Smith, 1954, 40.
[159] Denham and Clapperton, 1826 B, 54, 127–8.
[160] J. S. Trimingham, The influence of Islam on Africa, London and Beirut 1968, 92–3.
[161] H. R. Palmer, 'An early Fulani conception of Islam', Journal of the African Society, 1914, 59.
[162] M. W. H. Beech, 'Slavery on the east coast of Africa', Journal of the African Society, 1916, 148.

In Muslim society, a master's death may sometimes confer freedom on his slaves. Clapperton said that this was
frequent among the Fulani,[163] but on the whole it seems
to have been rare in Africa. Jobson spoke of slaves and their
children remaining perpetual bondmen to their Mandingo
masters and their children.[164] In Adamawa, slaves were,
like other property, distributed among the heirs of a deceased master.[165] Speke contrasted the situation in Arabia,
where slaves would be freed in accord with Muslim law,
with the custom in Zanzibar of willing one's slaves to one's
heirs.[166] Sometimes African slaves sold outside Africa were
released when their master died. Speke's principal African
guide, Bombay, taken as a slave to India, had been freed
there on his master's death.[167] The man nominated by
Shaykh Umar as Nachtigal's guide on a six-month expedition to Bagirmi had been taken to Constantinople as a slave
in childhood, and there freed in consequence of the death
of his master.[168]

Speke is not altogether accurate in stating that Muslim
law requires the freeing of slaves on the master's death.
This is legally required only in the case of a slave who is
umm al-walad, mother of the child, that is to say a slave
who has born her master a child.[169] There is however a
special category of slave-to-be-freed, who is called mudabbar. A mudabbar slave has received his master's assurance
that, on the master's death, the slave will be freed: a situation much like that which obtained, for example, among
Christian masters in Brazil, who sometimes assuaged their

[163] Denham and Clapperton, 1826 B, 54.
[164] R. Jobson, The golden trade, or, A discovery of the River
Gambra, and the golden trade of the Aethiopians, London 1623,
reprinted 1932, 84-5.
[165] J.-C. Froelich, 'Le commandement et l'organisation sociale chez
les Foulbé de l'Adamawa', Études camerounaises, 1954, 19.
[166] Speke, 1863, xxvi.   [167] Speke, 1864, 211-12.
[168] ii, 303.   [169] Ibn Abi Zayd, 226.

consciences by making provision in their wills for freeing some of their slaves after their death.[170] In Muslim law, after such an assurance has been given, the *mudabbar* slave may not be sold, but he continues to work for his master, and his property is, at least in law, at his master's disposal. A master may still enjoy sexual relations with a female slave who is *mudabbar*. There are certain qualifications. A man may retract his last testament, if he wishes, including the provision to enfranchise a slave. A debtor whose patrimony does not cover his debts may not validly free a slave. Nor may a slave be made *mudabbar* unless he falls within that third of the estate over which the testator has powers of independent allocation. And again, if someone owns only part of a slave (i.e. the ownership is shared between two people) and he frees the slave, the slave does not become a free man until due compensation has been paid to the co-owner.[171] Some slaves might gain their freedom through their master's last will and testament when he had adopted this device to frustrate the expectations of avaricious heirs.

Another type of freed slave was the *mukātib*, a slave freed by *kitāba*, or contract. Under this arrangement, a contract was made between the owner and his slave, usually for the payment of a certain sum, and, after payment had been completed, the slave was released. Should he however fall behind in his instalments, he returned to his original state of unqualified servitude, and the master kept what had already been paid.[172] The *mukātib* slave was, in some respects, in a slightly stronger position than the *mudabbar*; we have earlier mentioned that it was recommended for the *mukātib*, but not for the *mudabbar*, to attend the Friday

[170] Verger, 1968, 491.
[171] Ibn Abi Zayd, 220 ff.; a vow to free someone else's slave is not binding (168).
[172] *ibid.*, 222–4.

prayer even without his master's authorization (see p. 47); similarly, if a *mukātib* slave makes a vow, his master should not prevent him from fulfilling it unless such fulfilment might interfere with the payments, while for another slave the master may forbid fulfilment of the vow, though the vow remains binding and the slave must resume it should he ever subsequently become free.[173]

We have already pointed out that the provision, in the legal texts, of the opportunity for the slave to earn the means to purchase his freedom, complements the traditional acknowledgment in many parts of Muslim Africa of the slave's right to own property (see pp. 20, 41). The income opportunities of slaves naturally varied greatly according to the type of employment to which they were assigned: slaves dwelling in town, and occupied in commerce or crafts, were more favourably placed than those on the farm or in the mines. This was the case also in Brazil,[174] where the *mukātib* arrangement had a close parallel, just as did the *mudabbar*. A slave in Brazil might oblige his master to free him, by offering his cost price; newborn slaves were being sold for the equivalent of £5 in 1816, and if this were offered at the baptism, the master had to free the slave. Some slaves asked important people to stand as godparents, hoping that they would not allow their godchildren to remain in slavery.[175]

Another variety of emancipation which figures prominently in the legal texts is emancipation granted as a form of *kaffāra*, or legal expiation for some wrongdoing. The necessary (i.e. *wājib*) expiation for non-intentional homicide was to free a slave. If this was beyond your resources, you should fast for two consecutive months. Even if your offence is pardoned, you were still encouraged to fulfil the expiation.[176] For breaking Ramadan intentionally, the ex-

[173] Khalil ibn Ishaq, i, 139.   [174] Verger, 1968, 488.
[175] ibid., 1968, 515.   [176] Ibn Abi Zayd, 250.

piation was also either to free a slave, or to fast two subsequent months, with a further alternative of giving a *mudd*, approximately a peck, of grain to each of sixty poor persons.[177] This last alternative was the one preferred by the law.[178] To atone for a broken oath, you might give ten poor free Muslims a *mudd* each, or more, or you might clothe them, or you might free a slave; or, if you were too poor to manage any of these alternatives, you might fast three days.[179] It was not permitted to combine the alternatives, for example freeing half a slave and feeding five poor people.[180] Whoever swore to renounce sexual relations with his wife—this was called *tazāhara*—might resume them only after the expiation of freeing a believing slave, without bodily defects, whom the master owns fully and whose servitude is total.[181] The definition of the slave suitable for emancipation in a case of *tazāhara* is the standard also in violations of Ramadan or in broken oaths.[182] (The contrary case, in which a wife or concubine intends a voluntary fast involving sexual abstinence, was not allowed without the master's permission.[183]

It is not easy to find many practical illustrations of these acts of compensatory emancipation in the African sources, but at least two categories—violations of Ramadan, and *tazāhara*—are mentioned as of actual importance in East Africa.[184]

So deeply ingrained was the idea that to free a slave was a fitting expiation for wrongdoing, that it may be found

[177] *ibid.*, 120–2.   [178] Khalil ibn Ishaq, i, 134.
[179] Ibn Abi Zayd, 166–8; Khalil ibn Ishaq, i, 188–9.
[180] Khalil ibn Ishaq, i, 188–9.
[181] Ibn Abi Zayd, 188; but p. 190 says that there is nothing wrong with freeing a one-eyed slave, or an illegitimate child but adds that among Muslims of the Maliki rite, it is better to pray and fast.
[182] Khalil ibn Ishaq, i, 134, 188–9.
[183] Khalil ibn Ishaq, i. 137.   [184] Beech, 1916, 148.

also in heretical Muslim sects. For example, among the eccentric teachings of the Baraghwata, in eleventh-century Morocco, was a ban on killing cocks, since these birds were believed to indicate the hours of prayer; and whoever killed one was liable to the penalty of liberating a slave.[185]

Another possibility of change for the slave, though not equivalent to emancipation, is found in a curious custom reported in variant forms from the western Sahara and Sudan. According to one account, if a discontented slave succeeds in cutting the ear of a free man, not his master, or of a child of such a free man, then the slave passes to the wounded man and can be redeemed only at enormous cost. An unusually amiable chief, the *Almami* of Dimar, was said little by little to have lost both ears in this way.[186] Another description says that the person seeking transfer must try to cut the ear of his prospective master, or to kill his horse.[187] Yet another, speaking of the Kel-Air Tuareg, says that the act sealing the transfer is to cut the ear of a child or a horse of a free man, or to kill his camel.[188] A more recent statement says that, among the Tuareg, if a slave cuts a piece from the ear of a riding-camel of another master, that other master must take him as compensation for the damage done, and the original owner has no claim or redress.

It is an extreme loss of prestige for a Tuareg to lose his slave in this way, just as it is a great mark of honour

[185] Ibn Abi Zar al-Gharnati, *Roudh el-Kartas*, A. Beaumier (tr.), Paris 1860, 181.

[186] W. W. Reade, *Savage Africa*, London 1864, 582.

[187] R. Caillié, *Journal d'un voyage à Tembouctou* . . . , Paris 1830, reprinted 1965, i, 155–6; he however speaks of a tributary, rather than a slave, and adds that the fugitive takes all his livestock and possessions with him; should he be recaptured before cutting the ear, or killing the horse, he is beaten and loses all his property.

[188] P. Marty, *L'Islam et les tribus dans la colonie du Niger*, Paris 1931, 245–6.

for the new master, who will receive his new slave with favour and give him clothes and a camel with a saddle.[189]

Emancipation in Africa was sometimes a regulated, formal business. In Sokoto, the letter of manumission had to be signed before a *qadi*, and attested by two witnesses.[190] Such a letter was called *'atāqa*. Richardson, in the desert between Socna and Murzuq in 1846, heard slaves on their way north singing of their lost homes in Bornu and Mandara, and adding, 'O God, give us our Atkah, let us go to our dear home.'[191] Richardson's own servant, Said, was anxious to receive his *'atāqa*, lest he be stolen and sold again.[192] Said's circumstances were somewhat unusual. He had been a slave of Sidi Mustafa, the Consular Agent of Britain in Jerbah, near Tunis. When it was discovered that Sidi Mustafa was keeping slaves, he was dismissed as Agent. Hoping to be reinstated, he prepared a document stating that he had freed all his slaves, and presented this to the British Consul-General. He was not, however, reinstated, and subsequently tried to resume power over his slaves, or ex-slaves. Said thus had to run away—which he did—in order to secure his freedom in practice, though he remained technically a free man because of the paper with the Consul-General.[193] Richardson reassured Said about his

[189] Nicolaisen, 1963, 441–2. These provisions, in a distant and curiously inverted form, perhaps echo the law of Moses on Sinai, that the master shall pierce the ear of a slave who does not wish to go free, as a sign of his perpetual bondage (Exodus xxi. 6).

[190] Denham and Clapperton, 1826 B, 54.

[191] Richardson, 1848, ii, 377. Whittier, the American poet, wrote a poem based on this song reported by Richardson, including these lines:

Hear us, save us, make us free;
Send our Atka down from thee!

[192] Richardson, 1848, i, 147.   [193] *ibid.*, i, 14.

legal position; but on at least one occasion a Saharan Tuareg chief did try to confiscate Said for himself.[194]

Denham, returning to Tripoli in 1825, applied through the Consul-General for the Pasha to set his seal to the freedom of a Mandara boy whom Denham had purchased, this being the only legal way for a Christian to free a slave in a Muslim country.[195] Other explorers, such as Richard Lander, who were able to free their slaves under Christian governments, in Lander's case in 1828 at Cape Coast in the modern Ghana, presumably followed a less complicated procedure.[196] For the two slaves lent to Nachtigal, he promised to have a letter of emancipation drawn up, which would be formally validated by Shaykh Umar before they left Kuka, so that there should be no question about their status on their return home.[197] Nachtigal, however, made no comment on the practical problems of legal documentation in a country where slavery was commonplace, paper rare, and clothing not normally designed as a receptacle for documents. Lugard in East Africa had feared complications arising from freedom papers, which might be lost, abandoned, or even sold—in fact, thought Lugard, a freed slave might even sell both his paper and then himself, a double profit.[198] Such problems are said to have seriously impaired the efficiency of anti-slavery decrees in Ethiopia at various times during this century.[199]

The return of the slaves

Enfranchised slaves often made no effort to return to their native country but continued to reside near their old mas-

[194] ibid., i, 432.
[195] Denham and Clapperton, 1826 A, 311.
[196] Lander, in Clapperton, 1829, 326–7.
[197] ii, 309.   [198] Lugard, 1893, i, 225–6.
[199] M. Pollaud-Dulian, Aujourd'hui l'esclavage, Paris 1967, 38.

ters, still acknowledging them as their superiors, and presenting them yearly with a portion of their earnings.[200] Nachtigal noted that in Tripoli a slave who had been given his *'atāqa* often developed with his master a relationship similar to that of a freedman in ancient Rome, with permission to establish an independent household if he wished to marry.[201] This sort of relationship is called *wilaa*, which may perhaps be rendered patronage.[202] Barth had met several freed slaves in Africa,[203] and Nachtigal frequently referred to them. Nachtigal's servant, Sa'ad, recruited in Tripoli, was a freedman of a respectable citizen of that town, to which he subsequently returned.[204] Another servant, Ali of Mandara, also recruited in Tripoli at the beginning of Nachtigal's expedition, was a man of uncertain legal status; though he proved incorrigibly untrustworthy, he was retained in Nachtigal's service for some time, lest, if abandoned far from his native country, he might relapse into slavery.[205] Among the Negroes in Murzuq were some freedmen who had found a new home in Fezzan,[206] and in Kuka itself many freed slaves were curious to visit Nachtigal.[207] In Ghadames, a considerable number of Negroes, the offspring of liberated slaves, were settled in the Arab suburb.[208] Such Negro groups were found outside Africa as well: in India, for example, colonies of Negroes survived long after they had ceased to be slaves, and the explorer Burton, having learnt their lan-

---

[200] Denham and Clapperton, 1826 B, 113. Cf. Beech, 1916, 145, for the same sort of pattern in East Africa.
[201] i, 17.
[202] Ibn Abi Zayd, 220 ff.; cf. F. D. Lugard, 'Slavery in all its forms', *Africa*, 1933, 9–10, commenting on the Hanafi code.
[203] Barth, 1857–8, i, 17, 86.
[204] i, 22.   [205] i, 489.   [206] i, 97.
[207] i, 641.   [208] Richardson, 1848, i, 229.

guage, was surprised to find on his arrival in East Africa that he already knew Swahili.[209]

Some among the freed slaves, however, moved about, and numbers of them eventually returned to their original homes. An early, picturesque and presumably partly legendary example of such return is provided by the well-known story of a king on the Zanj coast, probably southern Somalia or northern Kenya. In AD 922 a ship from Oman was driven by accident upon the coast. Ship and crew were kindly received, but repaid this hospitality by kidnapping the local king. He was sold in Oman, and taken to Basra, where he learnt to pray, to fast, and to read parts of the Quran. Sold again, he was taken to Bagdad, where he finished learning the Quran, and prayed in the congregation of the mosque. He then ran away with a party of pilgrims from Khorasan, and with them performed the pilgrimage to Mecca. He joined a returning pilgrimage caravan to Cairo, and thence begged his way up the Nile. Twice he was seized as a slave by other Negroes, but escaped, and finally returned home to resume his throne. Later, the same Oman ship was driven again on the same coast. The king again received his kidnappers well, forgiving them their offence since it had led to his own salvation. His only regret was that he had never reimbursed his owner in Bagdad for the losses suffered when he ran away. He would have liked to send him the purchase price, multiplied ten times as damages for the delay, but decided against entrusting this commission to his visitors, whom he released after guarding against a second kidnapping.[210]

[209] Lugard, 1893, i, 183 n.
[210] Freeman-Grenville, 1962 A, 9 ff. A better substantiated account of a slave of royal blood concerns Médicon, a nephew of a Bornu ruler, who was enslaved in the fighting which broke out in Bornu during one of his uncle's pilgrimages. Médicon, his rank un-

Less dramatic, but better documented, instances abound in later times. For much of the first five centuries of Islam, there was peace between Nubia and Egypt, and many slaves were sold north down the Nile. It has been estimated that in the eleventh century AD there were 50,000 slaves in Egypt. These provided a main prop of the Fatimid régime; many became Muslim, and some may have returned home when the Fatimids fell.[211] In the west, Denham and Clapperton, starting from Tripoli in 1822, had several freed slaves in their caravan. The pasha had freed twenty-four from the castle, sixteen of them women. An elderly notable, Muhammad D'Ghies, had freed three Bagirmi slave girls, all under twenty, sisters. Two had been his own property; when he learnt that three sisters had been brought to Tripoli, and the third had been sold to someone else, he searched for her, bought her, and freed her so that she might return with the other two.[212] On the way Denham mentions thirty freed slaves leaving the caravan at Lari, to take the road to their home in Kanem.[213] The caravan with which Barth travelled from Tripoli included sixteen freed

recognized, was sold to North Africa, but his uncle later sought him out and he was redeemed. A French doctor, himself a slave, met him in Tripoli in 1669. We are not told what, if any, were the religious consequences of Médicon's temporary enslavement. C. de la Roncière, 'Une histoire du Bornou au XVIIe siècle par un chirurgien français captif à Tripoli', *Revue de l'histoire des colonies françaises,* 1919, 86–8.

211 Y. F. Hasan, 'The penetration of Islam in the eastern Sudan', in Lewis, 1966, 151. An even earlier instance of the return of freed slaves, from the Yemen to the Niger bend, has been suggested (Houdas, in al-Sadi, 5 ff.) in the case of the first *za* of Koukiya, original cradle of the Songhay empire. There is no hint that this man was a Muslim; his return, if such it was, may indeed have antedated Islam. However, there is no direct evidence that he was Negro; this is surmised from the fact that the chronicles do not comment on his race, which they might have done had he been in any way locally unusual.

212 Denham and Clapperton, 1826, xxxi–xxxii.

213 *ibid.,* 1826 A, 49.

slaves.[214] Bowen, a Baptist missionary who was in West Africa, closer to the coast, at the same time that Barth was moving about in the interior, met a Yoruba woman who had returned home after having been, so she said, to Constantinople. Yoruba slaves were, he was told, to be found in Tripoli, Fezzan, and many other places.[215] Among the Negroes whom Nachtigal observed in Murzuq there were, in addition to those more or less permanently established there, also pilgrims and freedmen who were trying to get back to their own countries.[216] As late as 1906 there were many freed slaves in Tripoli, from Wadai, Kanem, Bornu and Bagirmi, anxious to join Hanns Vischer's caravan on his journey to Bornu.[217] One of these, a pilgrim, had been taken as a slave from Bornu to upper Egypt sixty years earlier, and had served as a corporal in the Sudanese army, being with Gordon at Khartoum.[218] A leader of the Sanusiya was said to have bought a caravan of slaves on its way from Wadai to the coast and, having freed and educated them, sent them back to Wadai as Sanusiya missionaries.[219] The emancipation enforced by European colonial authorities sometimes had the effect of allowing ex-slaves to return home bearing with them the seeds of Islam.[220]

The slave's return was not necessarily a once-and-for-all event. Koelle, the missionary and distinguished pioneer linguist, working in Freetown in the mid-nineteenth century,

---

[214] A. A. Boahen, *Britain, the Sahara, and the Western Sudan, 1788-1861*, Oxford 1964, 186; Richardson, 1853, i, 8, 163.

[215] T. J. Bowen, *Adventures and missionary labours in several countries in the interior of Africa from 1849 to 1856*, Charleston 1857, reprinted 1968, 218.

[216] i, 97.

[217] Hanns Vischer, *Across the Sahara*, London 1910, 18.

[218] *ibid.*, 21.

[219] H. Duveyrier, *La confrérie musulmane de Sidi Mohammed ben Ali es Senousi . . .* , Rome 1918, 16–7; cited by E. E. Evans-Pritchard, *The Sanusi of Cyrenaica*, Oxford 1949, 16.

[220] Marty, 1920, ii, 180.

met a native of Falaba, in the north-eastern interior of modern Sierra Leone. This man had been enslaved by the Fulani, and had later found his way to Freetown, whence he had visited Falaba several times.[221] Nor is the return always associated with emancipation. Another of Koelle's linguistic informants in Freetown had been one of the slaves sent in tribute to Bauchi; despite this uprooting, the slave had been able to keep up his own language, both because he found many of his countrymen in Bauchi, and also because he was able, while still a slave, to return occasionally to his own home.[222] Early British administrators in north-eastern Nigeria reported that a particular people there, the Wurubo, had been an unprofitable investment as slaves, for they quickly died in captivity; yet the Wurubo women had proved good concubines for their Fulani masters, 'if allowed to be in constant communication with their own people'.[223]

Nor was the return home always a happy one. Duncan, travelling in West Africa in 1845, met in Yoruba country a freedman who had been born in Bornu. This man had been taken in the wars and sold, passing eventually to Bahia, where he worked for 21 years, partly for a Liverpool firm. Finally freed, as the slave of a British subject, he returned to Whydah on the West African coast, and thence to his native town.

> But now the spell was broken, and all his happy dreams of more than twenty years had vanished. His native town had twice been burnt down by the enemy, and was chiefly inhabited by strangers from a far coun-

221 Koelle, *Polyglotta Africana*, 1854, 3.
222 Koelle, *Polyglotta Africana*, 19.
223 F. H. Ruxton, 'Notes on the tribes of the Muri Province', *Journal of the African Society*, April 1908, 383.

try. He was now an obscure stranger, and looked upon
with suspicion, and his long-cherished home was to
him a desolate waste.

He resolved to attempt a second return, this time to Bahia.[224]

There were also Muslim slaves returning across the Atlantic to the West African coast. In Dahomey, for example,
the returned slave or freedman was clearly a pioneer Muslim, for Islam was established there as much by slaves coming from Brazil as by Muslims descending from the interior.[225] Even Liberia was a little affected. In 1829 a freed
slave, Abd al-Rahman, originally from Timbo in Futa Jallon, returned from America, coming to Monrovia. He
claimed to be a brother to the *almami* of Futa Jallon, and
the Liberians hoped that his homeward journey via Monrovia might stimulate their own connections, particularly in
trade, with Futa Jallon. But Abd al-Rahman died in Monrovia during the first rains.[226]

The religious impact of Muslim slaves returning is difficult to assess precisely. In the incidents listed above, several
have an explicitly Muslim aspect. And, while our overall
knowledge about the returning Muslim slave is still frag-
mentary, the potential religious importance of this category
of person is abundantly clear in the Christian history of
West Africa. Here, the return of the freed slaves is the
main early theme, first in the creation of the colony of
Sierra Leone, and then in the planting of Christianity in
southern Nigeria, especially Abeokuta, as freedmen passed

[224] J. Duncan, *Travels in western Africa in 1845 and 1846*, London 1847, ii, 175–7.
[225] Marty, 1926, 32–3, 51–2, 108, 145.
[226] S. Wilkeson, *A concise history of the commencement, progress and present condition of the American colonies in Liberia*, Washington 1839, 40.

from Freetown back to their native country.[227] The idea for the Nigerian return was apparently inspired by the example of two Hausa, emancipated in Trinidad, who passed through Freetown in 1837 on their way to Badagry and inland homewards.[228]

The religious transference of which slaves and ex-slaves might be the agents was by no means all one way and in favour of the dissemination of Islam amongst societies where it was previously little known. Newly acquired slaves coming from non-Muslim backgrounds into Muslim society might bring with them traditional beliefs and strange powers. In Ghadames, while the slaves as a group celebrated such festivals as that at the end of Ramadan, or *lailat al-qadr*, the Night of Power, late in Ramadan, they maintained also their own observances, such as a special dance at the cemetery of the slaves.[229] Richardson thought that most of the slaves in Ghadames came from Bornu;[230] but the commonest Negro language in the town was Hausa,[231] and when he was himself dispirited and unwell, the Negroes said that he was possessed by the *bori*, the spirits of traditional Hausa belief (see p. 6).[232] On his second journey, Richardson again had opportunity to see *bori* possession among Negroes, this time the servants of his own expedition.[233] Among the ex-slaves joining Vischer's caravan in 1906 were several Bagirmi women, who had been

[227] Subsequent expansion from Abeokuta provides further parallels: for example, when the Church Missionary Society began work in 1895 in Ado, the largest town in the Ekiti area of southern Nigeria, the first preacher was an Ekiti who had been enslaved and taken to Abeokuta, where he became a Christian (J. D. Y. Peel, *Aladura: a religious movement among the Yoruba*, London 1968, 51–2).

[228] C. Fyfe, 'Four Sierra Leone recaptives', *Journal of African History*, 1961, 82.

[229] Richardson, 1848, i, 223–4, 249–50, 279–80.

[230] *ibid.*, i, 148.   [231] *ibid.*, i, 281.

[232] Richardson, 1848, i, 361.   [233] Richardson, 1853, ii, 286.

brought to North Africa when quite young. Outstanding among these was Hawa, nearly six feet tall, who became a dominant and very valuable person in Vischer's party—in considerable measure because of the prestige given her by the fits of spirit possession to which she was subject.[234]

In Mauritania, such developments once took a more serious turn. There, sorcery was believed to be very widespread among the slaves of townspeople, particularly because so many slaves came from the Bambara, a Sudanese people skilled in such things. In the town of Tidjikdja, for example, a slave-owner who beat a slave would fall ill after one or two days, and soon die. A sorcerer slave always looked at the chest of a person, catching his heart and hiding it in the ashes, so that it became a ram: a man thus bewitched would not die as long as that ram was not slaughtered. This, as the chronicler recording these tales comments, is no doubt nonsense; but, he continues, it is true that if the sorcerer slave, threatened with death by the family of the bewitched, lays his hand on the breast of the bewitched person, he is loosed from the spell, and the same is true if the sorcerer dies. The people of Tidjikdja, distressed by these perils, contemplated killing their slaves, but desisted since there would then be none to care for the palm trees. So they brought instead, for a handsome fee, an expert from the Sudan, who gave the slaves something to drink. The expert departed; but the sorcery continued, until the people began killing all slaves suspected of it, and it decreased appreciably.[235]

Nachtigal said little about the general significance of returned slaves. He apparently took a poor view of the usual effects of experience of the Mediterranean Muslim world upon slaves taken there, for his guide to Bagirmi,

[234] Vischer, 1910, 52–3, 190–2.
[235] al-Shinqiti, 1911, 509–10; 1953, 137–8.

who had done very well for himself on his return to Kuka, he described as 'one of the few Negroes who brought anything useful back to his home on returning from a long stay in Europe'.[236]

[236] ii, 303. Barth, 1857–8, ii, 156, recalls his astonishment at meeting in Kano a Negro who had lived some twenty years, from his boyhood, in Constantinople. '. . . He had not only learned the language perfectly, but also adopted the manners, and I might almost say the features, of the modern Greeks.' Though Barth does not explicitly say so of this man, being a slave was the most likely qualification for such an opportunity.

CHAPTER III

EXPORTS AND MARKETING

Slave exports and their relation to the home market

The export slave trade from the Sudan region is of great antiquity. Already in the late ninth century, slave merchants even from Asia were established in Fezzan, dealing with suppliers to the south.[1] Later in the eleventh century, al-Bakri mentioned slave exports from Fezzan.[2] Ibn Battuta in the mid-fourteenth century commented that Bornu was renowned for its exports of excellent slave girls, eunuchs (*fityān*), and saffron-dyed fabrics.[3] Leo Africanus gave an interesting description of trade in Bornu at the beginning of the sixteenth century, Barbary merchants bringing war horses for the king, and receiving slaves in exchange. Though the king was very wealthy—his spurs and bridles, tableware, even dog chains were said to be pure gold—he preferred to pay only in slaves. And, as he went slaving only once a year, using his horses for this purpose, mer-

1 J. S. Trimingham, *A history of Islam in West Africa*, Oxford 1962, 32; Ibn Fartua, 5, 67.
2 al-Bakri, 29.
3 Ibn Battuta, *Travels in Asia and Africa, 1325–1354*, selections by H. A. R. Gibb, London 1929 (hereafter Ibn Battuta A), 336; *Voyages d'Ibn Batoutah*, tr. D. Defrémery and B. R. Sanguinetti, Paris 1858 (hereafter Ibn Battuta C), iv, 441–2. (This passage does not appear in *The Travels of Ibn Battuta*, tr. Sir Hamilton Gibb, Hakluyt Society, vol. i, 1958, vol. ii, 1962, with 2 vols. still to appear, hereafter Ibn Battuta B.)

chants had to wait until he returned from the annual expedition. If by chance the expedition was not sufficiently successful, the unfortunate Barbary merchant had to wait another year for payment.[4] About the same time, the Bornu rulers, having been driven a century before from Kanem east of Lake Chad, regained supremacy over their rivals there but never found it convenient to settle in Kanem again. Among the reasons for staying west of Lake Chad may have been the proximity of slave supplies to the south, and the relatively good trade connections north to Fezzan.[5] Denham found Bornu chiefly a rendezvous for caravans, exchanging principally slaves for imports from Barbary.[6] Barth in 1851 witnessed the departure for Fezzan of a caravan of about 750 slaves, and remarked that slaves were still at that time the main export of Bornu.[7] This was the same caravan that carried northwards the effects of his dead companion Richardson.

Some slaves travelled very long distances before they were finally disposed of, and the record of a few from Bornu, or even from Bagirmi, among those liberated in Sierra Leone in the first half of the nineteenth century[8] shows that the trans-Atlantic trade had some repercussions in these countries. The interest in exports which Nachtigal observed was, however, directed exclusively towards sales on the Mediterranean coast. In the trans-Saharan trade, slave exports continued to be the most important item throughout the first half of the nineteenth century and up to the time of Nachtigal's penetration into the Sahara and the Sudan. The number exported annually along the four main routes to the Mediterranean coast, Timbuktu to Morocco, Kano to Air and Ghadames, Bornu to Fezzan, and Wadai to Benghazi,

---

[4] Leo Africanus. A, iii, 833–4; B, ii, 480–1.
[5] Ibn Fartua, 5.   [6] Denham and Clapperton, 1826 A, 330–1.
[7] Barth, 1857–8, ii, 339.
[8] P. D. Curtin and Jan Vansina, 'Sources of the nineteenth-century Atlantic slave trade', *Journal of African History*, 1964, 185–208.

Buxton had estimated in 1839 at 20,000.[9] Any figure of this kind is obviously subject to a wide margin of error; Mauny thought Buxton's estimate conservative,[10] and Nachtigal, who put the exports from Wadai alone at 15,000 (presumably per annum), seems to confirm this.[11] But Boahen has proposed cutting Buxton's figure by half to 10,000; still, it might be thought, too substantial to be called 'only a trickle' compared with 70,000 believed to be crossing the Atlantic at the beginning of the century.[12] Buxton put the annual East African export of slaves at about 30,000. In 1858 the British Consul-General at Tripoli estimated that the slave trade constituted 'more than two-thirds of all the caravan trade' across the Sahara.[13]

By Nachtigal's time, however, this trade was definitely declining. Efforts, diplomatic and otherwise, to induce the governments of Turkey and the North African countries to outlaw the slave trade, and eventually to abolish the institution of slavery, had been, and were being, pursued with varying degrees of resolution and success. In Tunis the institution was formally abolished in 1846,[14] and in 1857 the Turkish authorities issued a *firman* which declared the final abolition of the Negro slave trade throughout the Sultan's dominions, with the exception of the Hijaz.[15] For many years there was a good deal of evasion of such decrees, and a substantial volume of clandestine trade persisted, as Nachtigal himself witnessed. He believed that it would be a long time before humanitarian expectations that the slave

[9] T. F. Buxton, *The African slave trade*, London, 2nd ed., 1840, 69.

[10] R. Mauny, *Tableau géographique de l'ouest africain au moyen age*, Dakar 1961, 379.

[11] iii, 266.   [12] Boahen, 1964, 128.

[13] Boahen, 1964, 127.   [14] *ibid.*, 140.

[15] *ibid.*, 155. The slave trade was made formally illegal in Saudi Arabia in 1936, full emancipation being announced for 1962 at a cost to the government of £6.5 million as compensation.

trade would be suppressed could find complete satisfaction.[16] Nevertheless the eventual disappearance of the trans-Saharan traffic can now be seen to have been inevitable.

Several observers have hazarded very high estimates of the profits to be won from the export trade in slaves. Harris, speaking of the Danakil on the north Somali coast in 1843, judged that the trade there yielded 300 per cent 'with the least possible risk or trouble to the merchant',[17] and Burton thought that trade in slaves who had been bought for 2 to 10 doti or tobes per head, and could be sold in Zanzibar for 10 to 15 dollars, realized nearly 500 per cent.[18] Some of these estimates were perhaps expansive, and the considerations of risk and loss to which attention is directed below (see pp. 93–98) suggest that slave-trading was not always a certain guarantee of a high-income status. Nevertheless, Nachtigal said that the trade had been very lucrative; on arrival at the Mediterranean coast, traders might count on getting for their slaves three or four times what they had paid for them, and despite wastage on the way, the almost complete absence of transport costs and the cheapness of the provisions required for the slaves meant that a very substantial profit might be expected; some traders, he thought, were therefore prepared to run considerable risks and, even when the trade was coming under growing government disapproval, to incur considerable expense to preserve at least part of this profit.[19]

So long as the export trade continued to be profitable it provided a powerful incentive to slave-raiding. It may have made necessary the continuance of the often savage methods of slave recruitment applied in the Sudan; for the possibility of being exported, in any particular case, may have

[16] i, 700–1.   [17] Harris, 1844, i, 336.
[18] Burton, 1860, ii, 61–2.   [19] i, 701.

meant that people would be much less willing voluntarily
to place themselves in servitude. That such voluntary action, under different circumstances, was not entirely fanci-
ful appears from the slaves of the Portuguese crown land
estates on the Zambesi. Here, while slaves were also acquired by raid, purchase or gift, it is estimated that a majority of the slave population in the eighteenth century were
clients who had attached themselves to a protector.[20] Their
prime function was to serve in the private army of the estate
holder, and though it was unlikely in any case that he
would sell his own soldiers some volunteers first extracted
a guarantee that they would not be sold abroad.[21] Particularly in times of famine and war the slave retinues on the
estates grew rapidly.[22] The Zambesi in the nineteenth century was also a main slave-exporting region, but even when
the geat estate holders dominated this trade, they continued
to observe the unwritten ban on selling their own people.[23]

Famine, which, as we have just seen, swelled the ranks
of the volunteer slaves on the Zambesi estates, also encouraged an intermediary variety of slave, not himself a volunteer, yet surrendered voluntarily by his people: these are
children, sold into slavery by their families in times of need.
Krapf says that the Wanika Pagans, nominally at least dependent upon the Swahili of Mombasa, sometimes had to
sell their own children to their overlords, when food was
very scarce.[24] In 1904-5, in parts of northern Nigeria, there
was famine, and slave-trading increased as a result. From
Adamawa and the Benue region, long-standing centres of
slave supply, many slaves were sold to southern Nigeria; a
British official, attempting to check the traffic, intercepted
and freed 200 children in less than three months. They
had been sold for between 1s. 9d. (in corn) and 10s. (in

[20] Newitt, 1969, 77.   [21] ibid., 76, 79.
[22] ibid., 77.   [23] ibid., 79.   [24] Krapf, 1860, 120.

salt); they were in lamentable condition, and 30 to 40 died in British hands.[25]

This resort, to the sale of children, may have been widespread in cases of extreme dearth, and *jihad* and slave-raiding, by contributing to such conditions, may thus indirectly as well as directly have enlarged the supply of slaves for the export market.

However, the export trade in slaves from the Sudan countries had always possessed a sound foundation in a flourishing domestic market for slaves, and Nachtigal's observations showed this still to be true in the early 1870s. Some 20 years before, Barth had estimated that slave-raiding in the Sudan as a whole was stimulated much more by domestic than by export demands.[26] In 1851 he guessed that slaves exported from Kano to Bornu and Nupe as well as northwards did not exceed 5,000 a year, while a considerable number were sold into domestic slavery in Kano or elsewhere.[27] Adamawa, described by him as a country 'based entirely on slavery' where many individuals had more than a thousand slaves each,[28] was also the main source of supply for the whole Fulani empire of Sokoto. Buganda provides a more recent, non-Muslim, example, though the export agents there were Muslim Arabs; in 1889 Mackay, an Anglican missionary, reported that the domestic demand there was very great, and that it was only the surplus, perhaps 2,000 a year, which the Arabs were able to export.[29] The various categories of domestic demand, involving the widespread use of slaves also for purposes of tribute, alms, marriage gifts, etc., will be examined later.

The decay of any traditional staple export market always

[25] Lugard, 'Northern Nigeria', *Journal of the African Society*, July 1906, 389, 401–2.
[26] Barth, 1857–8, i, xvii.   [27] *ibid.*, ii, 131–2.
[28] *ibid.*, ii, 478.
[29] J. W. H[arrison], *A. M. Mackay, pioneer missionary of the Church Missionary Society to Uganda*, London 1890, 434–5.

creates difficult problems of economic adjustment. Slaves were very important for the trade of Wadai and Bornu. Still more in Bagirmi, where slaves were the only significant export item, Nachtigal thought that, unless some kind of alternative profitable production could be developed by way of the Benue, the eastern tributary of the Niger, the condition of the country was likely to deteriorate as the slave trade contracted.[30] A visitor in 1911 was told that even during the first years of French influence Bagirmi had continued exporting some 5,000 slaves a year; she remarked,

> the action of the French in checking the slave trade, together with other raids and exactions, has fallen hardly on the ruling classes. It has put an end to the only means of livelihood they have ever known.[31]

In 1905 it was estimated that of the 750 slaves liberated by the British in Bornu Province since that area had been occupied by them in 1902, well over 600 were in transit from Bagirmi.[32]

In assessing the importance of alternative trading possibilities, it is worth noting that the establishment of the slave trade in a locality seemed sometimes to choke off other trade and commercial activity. Slave-raiding was destructive. Slave recruitment through kidnapping made people wary of venturing into public places, such as markets, to trade: the British in northern Nigeria, at the very beginning of their administration, acted on complaints of this kind, and convicted kidnappers, hoping that this would encourage particularly the reticent Pagan peoples to bring their produce to market.[33] Markets were traditionally places of truce, but this theory was not always effective protection: we have, for example, eye-witness accounts of Tubu raids on markets in the Lake Chad area even in this cen-

[30] ii, 668, 688.   [31] Macleod, 1912, 147–8, 150.
[32] Lugard, 1906, 402.   [33] ibid., 402.

tury,[34] raids which in the old days would certainly have included kidnapping.

Slaving possibilities might also affect the preferences of merchants. Among the Vai, on the west coast, the slave trade developed after the establishment there of Spanish factories, or trade posts, early in the nineteenth century. Soon all occupations save war and kidnapping were abandoned, and slave forays and hunts extended far into the interior. Civil war followed, and the European traders, refraining from interference, bought prisoners from both sides.

> Many a vessel bore across the Atlantic two inveterate enemies shackled to the same bolt, while others met on the same deck a long-lost child or brother who had been captured in the civil war.[35]

The Vai coast became one of the major centres of the Atlantic slave trade.[36] In Tajura, on the coast of the horn of Africa, Harris in the 1840s found no one interested in agriculture, every man being a merchant and waxing prosperous on slave exports. Amongst the commodities of trade which he lists, salt and slaves are the two principals.[37] The Yao, east of Lake Nyasa, later to become the most notorious slavers of all the indigenous East African peoples, first be-

[34] Boyd Alexander, 'Lake Chad', *Journal of the African Society*, April 1908, 231–2.

[35] Canot, 1928, 302–3. Ward (1969, 176) confirms this analysis, citing the views of a captain in the British West African squadron then patrolling the coast, and of a judge in Freetown. S. W. Koelle, who was there in 1850–1, says that Vai country had not extended further inland than fifteen or twenty miles until about 20 years earlier, when the chiefs were instigated by the Spaniards to expand (*Outlines of a grammar of the Vei language* . . . , London 1854, iii).

[36] P. E. H. Hair, 'Notes on the discovery of the Vai script . . .', *Sierra Leone Language Review*, no. 2, 1963, 41.

[37] Harris, 1844, i, 61.

gan trading to the coast with tobacco, hoes and skins, buying calico, salt and beads. At that time, the Yao did not
know the value of ivory or slaves.[38] Then the coast people
offered them guns and powder, asking in return for ivory
and slaves; and before long, the Yao were refusing to accept
any other commodities from their contacts in the interior.[39]
The slave trade became so much a part of the Yao national
heritage that children played a game, much like snakes-and-
ladders, in which beans represented traders and slaves on
their way to the coast; the loser was said 'to have died on
the way'.[40] Arnot, pioneer missionary in Katanga, on his
way thither in the 1870s, found many traders preferring
slaves to ivory.[41] From the Oubangi area of the Congo, it
was reported a little later that, although there was much
ivory there, the local people would exchange it only for
slaves, refusing any other trade goods.[42]

There is still some difference of opinion about the exact
relationship between the slave and the ivory trades. Some
authors argue that, although slavery and the slave trade
had been common in East Africa before the ivory trade became prominent, the ivory trade gave further stimulus to it
by increasing the demands for slave porters.[43] It has been
pointed out on the other hand that most of the slaves
brought to the East African coast were children and
women, who, though women were indeed sometimes employed for this purpose (see p. 147), did not make good

[38] Yohanna B. Abdallah, *Chiikala cha Wayao*, G. Meredith San-
derson (tr.), Zomba (Nyasaland) 1919, 27–8.
[39] *ibid.*, 30–1.
[40] H. S. Stannus, 'The Wayao of Nyasaland', *Harvard African
Studies*, 1922, iii, 359–60.
[41] F. S. Arnot, *Garenganze, seven years' pioneer mission work
in Central Africa*, London 1889, 164.
[42] H. Ward, *Five years with the Congo cannibals*, London 1890,
121.
[43] P. Ceulemans, 'Introduction de l'influence de l'Islam au Congo',
in Lewis, 1966, 176–7.

porters, and that the great ivory caravans consisted largely of professionals, or of slaves hired out by their masters; handling ivory, especially large tusks, was a matter for specialists.[44]

At the same time, the fact that the goods given in payment for the ivory had to be headloaded into the interior also meant that people were less likely to be enslaved there simply for the purpose of carrying ivory down to the coast, where they would themselves be sold as a subsidiary line of merchandise, and it would not be necessary to assemble a new batch of porters for each successive ivory caravan. For our purpose, however, a general analysis of the role of slaves, the part played by slave porters hired out by their owners is still significant.

Slave-raiding might on occasion be a useful lubricant for acquiring ivory, since captives could then be bartered back to their own people for ivory.[45] The Khartum merchants, in the eastern Sudan, were particularly active in thus holding captured people, and cattle, for ransom against ivory.[46]

The arms trade

As slaves were one, and often the major export item from the Sudan countries, they are frequently mentioned in conjunction with the staple imports. Slaves for salt was a widespread equation. In Mauritania it was said that a slave from the Sudan used to be bought with a bar of salt the length of his foot, but by the nineteenth century a camel load of salt was necessary to buy a slave, male or female, and even

[44] R. W. Beachey, 'The East African ivory trade in the nineteenth century', *Journal of African History*, 1967, 275–6.

[45] Ward, 1890, 189; Oliver, 1965, 99–100.

[46] Richard Gray, *A History of the Southern Sudan, 1839–1889*, Oxford 1961, 148.

then something might be owing, to be paid in grain.[47] Salt exporters from Mauritania went to the Sudan, and returned with slaves, some of whom were used to pay debts contracted at the time of the traders' departure, some sold to neighbouring people, while a few were kept for domestic work.[48]

Similarly slaves figure largely in the arms trade, in early days especially for horses, later for guns. In fact, to give the worth, in ammunition, of a slave was sometimes much like giving his price. In Liberia, for instance, the value of a slave boy was 15 kegs of powder, while a girl would fetch 10 kegs, or 100 sticks of salt.[49]

In the mid-fifteenth century, when slaves first became common in Kano, the *galadima* of Kano raided southwards, regularly sending slaves back to his ruler, who in return regularly supplied him with horses.[50] A little later in the same century, the ruler of Nupe sent 12 eunuchs to Kano in exchange for 10 horses.[51] In the early sixteenth century, Askiya Muhammad I of Songhay sold the children of slaves for horses.[52] During the same period the Berber chieftains of the southern Sahara sold horses in the Sudan at prices ranging from 10 to 15 slaves, according to quality. One Portuguese agent took horses from another Portuguese, and from a Genoese in Portugal's service, at the rate of 7 slaves each, and resold them to African dealers for 14 or 15 slaves.[53] Of Bornu Leo Africanus said that the king used

[47] al-Shinqiti, 1911, 493; 1953, 115. He reports that everything from the Sudan—cloth, horses, grain, as well as slaves—is bought with salt, and adds that it is said that some of the Sudanese sold their children for salt.

[48] *ibid.*, 1911, 493–4; 1953, 116.

[49] Johnston, 1906, i, 398; the average bride-price was 6 brass kettles, 15 kegs of powder, and 5 pieces of cloth.

[50] *Kano Chronicle*, in Palmer, 1928, iii, 109–10.

[51] *ibid.*, iii, 110–11.

[52] Kati, 106, 109.

[53] B. Davidson, *Black mother*, London 1961, 55–6.

to give 15 or 20 slaves to the Barbary merchants for one horse;[54] he reported 6 ducats as the price of a young slave of 15 years in Gao, where horses costing 10 ducats in Europe might fetch 40 or even 50.[55] He also mentioned the usurping ruler of Gaoga (see below p. 110) exchanging slaves for horses from Egypt.[56] By Barth's time the terms of trade had shifted against horses, for in Sokoto in 1853 a slave and a horse were of roughly equal value.[57] In Kuka, in 1870, a good riding-horse cost considerably more than a male slave of standard quality (see below, p. 197), but the disparity was much less than that reported earlier.

The decline in the relative value of a horse may have been brought about, in part, by the increasing prominence of the gun as the most favoured weapon. Difficulties of supply also played an important part in determining prices. Farther south, towards the forest, the prices of horses rose. In Bagirmi the best horses were worth 8 to 12 slaves, though Nachtigal had to be satisfied with much less for the horse which he sold there on behalf of the Sharif el-Medeni, his most trusted counsellor and friend in Kuka.[58] In northern Liberia a horse in the old days is said to have commanded as many as 100 slaves;[59] the horse was first seen in the Ganta area in Liberia late in the nineteenth century, and a chief bought one for 12 slaves.[60] While horses rose, guns fell in price nearer the Atlantic coast. Nupe became an

[54] Leo Africanus, A, iii, 833–4; B, ii, 480.
[55] ibid., A, iii, 826–7; B, ii, 471.
[56] ibid., A, iii, 835; B, ii, 482.
[57] Barth, 1957–8, iv, 180; Lacroix, 1952, 34.
[58] ii, 655.
[59] Schwab, 1947, 181; the price when Schwab wrote was £5 to £10.
[60] An elderly Mano informant told Schwab (1947, 69 and n.) that the first horse had been seen when his father was about 14 years old, and that a chief bought one eight years later in what was to become French Guinea.

important centre for the supply of muskets, which were traded there in exchange for slaves, as early as the middle of the eighteenth century.[61] Among the purposes of the Hausa raid, the date of which may be put approximately in the 1870s, and which is described in Sir Abubakar Tafawa Balewa's novel, *Shaihu Umar*, was the collection of slaves who could be sent to Bida, the main town of Nupe, in order to procure muskets.[62] Actually on the coast, a single slave might be the price of several guns.[63]

Some of the nineteenth-century Muslim leaders, particularly in the second half of the century, continued to indulge in this traffic. Samori in the 1870s, for example, regularly traded slaves for horses, guns and gunpowder.[64] Hoping to obtain supplies of these commodities by trade through Kong, in the Ivory Coast, he once sent the Kong rulers 100 young men, 100 girls, and gold.[65] In Samori's time, a repeating gun cost from two to four slaves, while a horse ranged from four to twelve; horses may have been especially valued for tactical reasons, giving leaders mobility, and providing an efficient means for taking captives.[66] In 1874, a little before the conquest of Darfur by Ismail Pasha, when the southern part of the country was being harried by the forces of Zubayr, the celebrated slaving lord, the Jellaba made a profitable business by clandestinely offering manufactured goods, weapons and gunpowder to both sides in

[61] *Kano Chronicle*, in Palmer, 1928, iii, 124.
[62] M. Hiskett (tr.), London 1967, 22.
[63] The Gio in Liberia formerly bought their guns from the Bassa, paying one slave for two guns; Schwab, 1947, 231. D'Ollone (1901, 85) in the hinterland of Liberia found a male slave worth four guns plus some other things, and a female three guns together with other goods.
[64] Hargreaves, 1963, 245; Kouroubari, 1959, 549, 556; M. Legassick, 'Firearms, horses and Samorian army organization, 1870–1898', *Journal of African History*, 1966, 103, 105, 106.
[65] Kouroubari, 1959, 555.   [66] Legassick, 1966, 106 and n.

exchange for slaves, which were said to be extraordinarily cheap there at that time.[67]

The arms trade for slaves was sometimes done on a credit basis, the arms being advanced so that the slaves, with which the arms were to be paid for, might be captured. This was apparently the position with the horses supplied to the sixteenth-century ruler of Bornu for his annual slave-raid (see above, page 71). Among the Vai, after a campaign warriors had to surrender a certain proportion of their captives, perhaps half, one-third or fewer, to the chiefs. The captives thus handed over were called war-ball, or gun-ball, and represented remuneration for the ammunition which the chiefs had provided at the beginning of the campaign.[68] The remaining captives stayed with the troops as booty, on the general pattern described below (see p. 161).

The interactions between slavery and war were thus often more complicated than a simple cause and effect relationship in which the need for slaves provided a motive for slave-raids. There was also the arms trade, which we have just described; and other possible links existed, such as the chance that captives from a successful raid might be drafted into the army, becoming slave-raiders themselves.

Selection of export models

On the criteria which guided the selection of slaves for the export market Nachtigal offered no general comment. There is a continuing strand dating back to pre-Muslim days which links sale into slavery, and in particular into slavery in foreign parts, with punishment. It has been suggested that this arises from the customary belief in many

[67] iii, 469.
[68] Koelle, *Outlines* . . . , 1854, 187; on p. 238 Koelle estimates that less than one-quarter of the Vai were Muslim in his time.

areas in Africa that each community is responsible for the crimes of each of its members; thus an individual who repeatedly involved his community in trouble might be sold into slavery.[69]

Al-Bakri, in the eleventh century, said that in many Negro countries it was the custom for a robbed man to be given the choice of either selling or killing the robber.[70] In the History of Sudi, on the east coast, it was said that a thief and his brothers were to be made slaves of the robbed man.[71] On the Gambia in the seventeenth century an adulterous couple would 'without redemption be sold away', the same being the penalty for other great offences, no wrongdoer being put to death; the Portuguese purchased people such as these for the West Indies.[72] Slaves exported from the Sierra Leone area in the eighteenth century were, apart from prisoners of war, usually criminals. In the coastal areas at least, sale was rare without some preceding offence, adultery, theft, debt or witchcraft.[73] Burton reported that the Wanyamwezi, in East Africa, generally sold only criminals and prisoners, save in times of great need, when even relatives might be sold.[74] He added that the Arabs preferred to purchase men sold under suspicion of witchcraft, as being less likely to decamp for home.[75] An attempt by a Muslim Galla governor to punish two clan chiefs for tribute default by selling them and their families led to renewed Galla civil war.[76] In Borgu, early in the nineteenth century, a woman violating the ban on intercourse during lactation would be sold; slaves in this area dreaded the sea-

[69] Lugard, 1933, 13; he thought that the practice still continued, though in secret.

[70] al-Bakri, 326.   [71] Freeman-Grenville, 1962 A, 232.

[72] Jobson, 1623, 72.   [73] C. Fyfe, *A History of Sierra Leone*, Oxford 1962, 8–9.

[74] Burton, 1860, ii, 33.   [75] *ibid.*, 31.

[76] E. Cerulli, 'Folk literature of the Galla of southern Abyssinia', *Harvard African Studies*, 1922, 41.

coast, fearing that they would be eaten by the whites, and
those sold there were generally prisoners of war or refrac-
tory and intractable domestic slaves.[77] In the twentieth
century, in the same area, a man who found his bride not
a virgin still had the right to ask of her seducer what punishment was merited, and the seducer had formally to admit
that to be sold as a slave with all his family would be just.[78]
In the Senegambia region Reade contrasted the Woloff,
who would sell their own children, with the Mandingoes,
who thought it wicked to sell a slave without just cause of
complaint.[79] In Sierra Leone in the early twentieth century, heavy fines punished adultery, especially with a chief's
wife, or interference with girls in Bundu, the secret society;
in earlier days, failure to pay would have led to enslavement.[80]

Many of the examples cited above come from Pagan
areas; and on the whole, the introduction of Islam, with its
prescribed system of punishments for a variety of crimes,
seems to have reduced resort to sale into slavery as a penalty.
Fyfe, whose comment on the position in the Sierra Leone
area has just been quoted, goes on to say that in some Muslim districts, where adulterers were flogged and witchcraft
was less common, slaves were regularly obtained by kidnapping.[81]

Canot reports a number of interesting instances from
Futa Jallon in the nineteenth century. When the *almami*,
or ruler, there gave permission to form a caravan to trade
to the coast, all roads were temporarily blocked in order to
build up a party of imposing size. Debtors were arrested;
if his property were insufficient to pay his debts, a delinquent Pagan was sold as a slave, but a Muslim was let off

[77] Clapperton, 1829, 94–5.   [78] Marty, 1926, 220.
[79] Reade, 1864, 447–8.   [80] Alldridge, 1901, 123, 142.
[81] Fyfe, 1962, 8–9.

with a beating.[82] Muslims from Futa Jallon were sold into slavery only for exceptional wrongdoing. Once, a Futa Jallon caravan brought forty slaves to the coast, at the Rio Pongo, for sale; the factor there wished to refuse eight of them, as sub-standard, but the caravan leader insisted that one at least of the eight should be taken. This man had slain his own son, and judges in Futa Jallon, finding in the Quran no punishment for such a misdeed, had condemned him to be sold to the Christians, a penalty which was regarded in that country as worse than death.[83] Even a daughter of the *almami* himself might so suffer, being sold away to the coast 'for salt'. In this particular case, the woman, whose name Canot gives us as Beeljie, had so resisted an elderly relative after having been forcibly married to him that she was sent home with an insulting message. This was regarded as behaviour grievous enough on her part to warrant her sale, even though her husband was accused of cruelty to his *harim*, and of eating unclean food. By an elaborate stratagem, Canot rescued her at the coast.[84]

Closely related to the practice of enslavement as punishment is that of punishing people who are slaves already by selling them abroad. In both cases the advent of Islam may have had a restraining effect, for not only does Muslim law prescribe certain punishments other than enslavement for free offenders, but specific penalties are also spelt out for

[82] Canot, 1928, 93. Maliki law does not authorize such punishment for the insolvent Muslim debtor, to whom it is rather lenient; on the other hand, a debtor may be jailed while his financial position is ascertained; Ibn Abi Zayd, p. 270. Incidentally, a slave authorized to trade on someone else's behalf is not to be sold for debts which he may then contract.

[83] Canot, 1928, 95.

[84] *ibid.* 178. Such treatment of a Fulani noblewoman, for such an offence seems extreme. But while Canot's account of the reasons for Beeljie's enslavement is at second hand, and may be somewhat distorted, there is no reason to doubt his identification of her, and he was both eye-witness of her sale at the coast and deviser of her rescue.

slaves (see p. 8). Clapperton said of Sokoto that the children of slaves were never sold unless after repeated punishment they continued to be unmanageable; usually the slaves
for sale were prisoners of war, or newly purchased duds,
and in Kano he was told that it was customary to send the
perpetrators of grave crimes, such as murder, to the coast
to be sold to the slave-dealers.[85] In Ghadames, incorrigible
thieves among the slaves were despatched to Tripoli.[86]

A profit motive may have entered in in both cases. Profits
in prospect from the sale of slaves may have encouraged
the application of enslavement as a proper punishment.
Canot, visiting the Matacan river, in north-west Sierra
Leone, for slaves, describes such a result:

> My merchandize revived the memory of peccadilloes
> that had been long forgotten, and sentences that were
> forgiven. Jealous husbands, when they tasted my rum,
> suddenly remembered their wives' infidelities, and sold
> their better halves for liquor in which to forget them.
> I was exalted into a magician, unroofing the village
> and baring its crime and wickedness to the eye of jus-
> tice. Law became profitable, and virtue had never
> reached so high a price.[87]

In Senegambia, where the effects of the slave trade were not
so strongly felt as elsewhere in West Africa, enslavement
nevertheless replaced fines as the most common punishment, and this situation obtained until the end of the Atlantic trade.[88] A corresponding line of argument might be

[85] Clapperton, 1829, 171, 214.

[86] Richardson, 1848, i, 194–5, 248–9; he thought that the slaves
often stole simply in order to eat.

[87] Canot, 1928, 219.

[88] M. A. Klein, *Islam and imperialism in Senegal: Sine-Saloum,
1847–1914*, Edinburgh 1968, 29. He quotes a French Governor of
Cayor: 'When a man has cohabited with a girl and he has had a
child by her, he must pay three slaves, and if he lacks the means, he

applied to the punishment of slaves by sale. One observer, commenting on the practice of the people of Brass not to execute slaves guilty of serious offences but to sell them in distant places, clearly discerned the principle of economy, although Brass, in eastern Nigeria, was not a Muslim area. 'Two grand results', he said,

> it will thus be seen, accrue from the transaction to the two parties immediately concerned—to the master an indemnity against loss, and to the slave rescue from a cruel death.[89]

As suggested in this quotation, enslavement or sale abroad was not in every case a harsher penalty than traditional practice might, had the export opportunity not offered, have demanded. Canot reported the arrival, amongst a caravan of various slave women from Futa Jallon, destined for the Atlantic crossing, of two with ropes around their necks; these, he said, would ordinarily have been burnt as witches, had not the *almami* of Futa Jallon been at that moment particularly distressed for gunpowder, which their sale might bring.[90]

Many writers have been attracted by the hypothesis which seeks to explain a large part, perhaps the great majority, of the slaves to be found in Africa, and in particular of those who crossed the Atlantic, in terms of the principle widely accepted in Africa that slavery was an appropriate punishment for certain offences. Edward Blyden, for example, believed that 'as a rule, those who were exported belonged to the servile and criminal classes'.[91] A modern

is enslaved himself. Those responsible for fights, constant theft, false accusation are condemned to considerable fines, which they are never able to pay, and then they are imprisoned and sold to the captains of ships.'

[89] Adebiyi Tepowa, 'A short history of Brass and its peoples', *Journal of the African Society*, 1907, 68.   [90] Canot, 1928, 95.
[91] Blyden, 1887, 126.

scholar has described the Atlantic slave trade as providing
Africans 'with a means of getting rid of criminals and other
undesirables'.[92] A more recent popular writer believes that
'until the Europeans came upon the scene, slaves were regarded inside Africa as useful and helpful people, whose
ownership carried with it specific obligations—to feed, to
clothe, to shelter and protect'; while properly insisting that
the status of domestic slaves differed from area to area and
from tribe to tribe, and not ignoring the fact of warfare and
kidnapping, he has listed as the more important reasons
for enslavement the custom of pledging one's self when in
default on a debt, and adultery, theft and certain other
crimes.[93] There have even been reproaches for failing to
put forward the punishment explanation even when the
information available about some particular episode that is
being reported has nothing whatever to say about it. Referring to eye-witness accounts of slaving expeditions returning to the market place in Kano with as many as a
thousand newly captured slaves, one commentator complained of the witness, that

> it does not appear that it struck him to inquire for
> what reason this was done. In my humble opinion if
> he had done so I think he would have found it to be
> the punishment for some insurrectionary rising against
> the Sultan of Sokoto, or for resistance to the mandates
> of some emir.[94]

Both in Pagan and in Muslim Africa slave status was
indeed often the penalty imposed for the commission of

[92] A. E. Afigbo, 'A reassessment of the historiography of the colonial period', in J. F. Ade Ajayi and I. Espie (eds.), *A thousand
years of West African history*, Ibadan and London 1965, 442.
[93] Pope-Hennessy, 1967, 88, 176.
[94] A. E. M. Gibson, 'Slavery in western Africa', *Journal of the
African Society*, 1903, 18–19. The reporter here criticised was C. H.
Robinson, a pioneer Hausa linguist.

some grave social offence, but the views just quoted imply an importance for this practice which the facts recorded in at least many parts of the continent do not justify. Even with such economic stimulus as has been outlined above, the sale as punishment principle is inadequate to account for the large masses of slaves, male and female, young and old, exported west, north or east. In Nachtigal's account of the sources from which the Kuka market drew its supplies of slaves (see p. 193) there is no hint that anyone was ever enslaved in Kuka as a result of the application of the principle of punishment. The Pagans enslaved by the Bagirmi raiders whom Nachtigal observed were collected quite indiscriminately, and there were no recognizable grades of either moral or physical quality to distinguish those who were despatched to the Kuka market and those who remained behind in Bagirmi. The picture of unscrupulous exporters dumping shoddy goods in overseas markets covers only the smaller portion of the trade: the majority of slaves for export, it seems certain, were re-exports, captives taken in war or raids.

Slaves on the march

Slave-hunting is by its nature a violent and brutal exercise, as Nachtigal was able himself to observe when he accompanied a raid in Bagirmi in 1872 (see above pp. 25-6). The results on that occasion were rather disappointing, only about fifty slaves;[95] some later raids were more productive.[96] Death during the slave-raid itself was only the first danger the slave had to face. He had then to pass through the marshalling yards. Conditions in the camp of Abu Sekkin, ruler of Bagirmi, were pretty grim for everybody, and many of the newly captured slaves who were herded together

[95] ii, 633.   [96] ii, 646.

there were soon reduced to a lamentable condition. Many fell ill; all had inadequate food. As a precaution against attempts at escape to their home country which was still not very far away, and in the absence of enough chains, slaves were fastened together by strips of raw hide, even those so physically weak that movement was difficult for them.[97]

The lot of slaves who survived raid and marshalling yard, to be then moved to an organized marketing centre, was no happier. They did not enjoy even the theoretical protection of the law, for the full slave law did not come into effect until the slaves were brought into safe Muslim territory: while still on the road they were simply booty.[98] There were hundreds of slaves in the caravan with which Nachtigal returned from Bagirmi to Kuka, and his story of the journey is punctuated throughout with references to the hardships imposed upon them, and their attempts at escape. He did not record the number which eventually reached Kuka, but observed that, in estimating the weight of the burden placed by the slave trade on its Pagan victims, it had to be borne in mind that for every one who arrived in Kuka there were probably three or four who died or disappeared on the way.[99] Other writers have made similar estimates. One account of the Sudanese marauder, Rabih, says that 'for each of the slaves who reached their journey's end, one must add at least five other individuals who perished either in the slave raids of the foregoing campaigns, on the journey, or through sickness following on a change

[97] ii, 652–3.

[98] Hurgronje, 1931, 18. According to the law, should a Muslim actually engaged on *jihad* kill someone in a category legally exempt from death, repentance, but no compensation, is necessary; if, however, the killing occurs after the booty has been assembled, then the person responsible must reimburse, to the *imam* who will add it to the booty, the value of the dead man; Khalil ibn Ishaq, i, 207.

[99] ii, 752.

of climate'.[100] Another French observer thought that the sale of one captive might represent a total decline of population of ten, defenders killed in attacks on villages, women and children dying of famine, old people, children and the sick who were unable to keep up with those who had captured them, or were killed on the road because a more numerous enemy was threatening, or who died of misery.[101]

Of the four slaves who accompanied Nachtigal from Bagirmi, being the price paid for the horse which the Sharif el-Medeni had sent with him to be sold there, only one arrived in Kuka. Nachtigal's guide lost five of the six in whom he had invested, and would have lost the sixth too, a girl who collapsed in a state of complete exhaustion near the end of the journey, if Nachtigal had not rescued her.[102] Even on the first day of the journey, despite strenuous efforts to keep them going by the use of the hippopotamus hide whip, some slaves had to be left behind.[103] It was the usual fate of such laggards to be killed by their disappointed masters, anxious to discourage any thought of feigning incapacity as a means of escape,[104] just as in the Congo area it was usual to kill slaves who fell ill while carrying ivory.[105] Some of the sick slaves were left behind as the price of a few measures of corn;[106] their physical condition continued to deteriorate, and many died.[107] Some did, indeed, succeed in running away, sometimes with at least tacit assistance from the inhabitants of the districts through which the caravan was passing, happy thus to come into possession of slaves for whom they did not have to pay anything.[108] (Burton in 1858, at Ujiji on the east shore of

100 J. Lippert, 'Rabah', *Mitteilungen des Seminars für orientalische Sprachen in Berlin*, 1899, *Afrikanische Studien*, 249–50.
101 Hourst, *Mission hydrographique du Niger*, 1896, cit. Deherme, 1908, 381–2.
102 ii, 758.   103 ii, 730–1.   104 ii, 734.
105 Ruth Slade, *King Leopold's Congo*, London 1962, 87–8.
106 ii, 732.   107 ii, 741.   108 ii, 743.

Lake Tanganyika, complained that the local people had a
bad name for selling slaves cheap, and then recouping
themselves by aiding and abetting desertion.)[109] If a slave
disappeared in a village, a hut-to-hut search was made in
which the inhabitants were asked to swear on the Quran
that they were not sheltering the missing person and did
not know where he or she was hiding, a procedure usually
quite ineffective.[110]

In none of the regions with which Nachtigal became
familiar was travel indeed at any time or for anybody organized like a Cook's Tour, but slaves inevitably had to
carry the heavy end of the stick. The most extreme illustration in Nachtigal's experience was seen near a spring
which he passed both on his way into Tibesti and on the
return journey thence, its immediate surroundings covered
with camel skeletons and bleached human bones, apparently the remnants of a slave caravan which had collapsed
when the spring was found choked up.[111] Vischer, who
crossed the desert early in this century, remarked that it
was always near a well that the greatest number of bones
was seen. He attributed this to slave children falling by the
wayside, and later dragging themselves to the well to find
the caravan gone; and also to sick animals being abandoned
there.[112] These explanations seem rather less plausible
than that of the clogged well, which might take considerable time to clear. Denham crossing the Sahara described
how slaves, belonging to an old Shuwa Arab going on pilgrimage, ran, speechless with thirst, the final miles to a
well; little children, thirsty and fever-stricken, were kept
moving only by the threat of the whip.[113] Many of these
might have perished had the well been blocked.

The writings of other early travellers abound with paral-

[109] Burton, 1860, ii, 61.   [110] ii, 748–9.
[111] i, 228–9, 368.   [112] Vischer, 1910, 226.
[113] Denham and Clapperton, 1826, A, 294–5.

lel instances. In 1827 Richard Lander, after the death of
Clapperton, travelled from Sokoto with a huge caravan of
Fulani and Tuareg. The caravan included fifty slaves who
had been sent as tribute to Bello, the sultan of Sokoto, from
Bauchi, but were being returned to their original master
since he had suffered heavy losses from attacks from Bornu.
These slaves were reported missing, and horsemen sent
back in search of them found thirty-five dead on the road,
unable while carrying their heavy burdens to keep up with
the camels and horses. The other fifteen were presumed to
have met the same fate.[114] The slaves in a caravan originally 3000 strong were found by Thomson living on grass
and roots, as they waited on the west side of Lake Tanganyika to be ferried across; already on the trip from Manyuema two-thirds of them had died of famine, murder or
disease.[115]

A little later on the same march just mentioned, Lander
met a party of thirty slaves on their way to Zaria as tax,
all apparently ill with smallpox, and the men bound neck
to neck with twisted bullock hide.[116] An epidemic amongst
slaves in transit, whether by land or sea, was much to be
feared. Canot, himself an experienced slaver, who had seen
smallpox break out on a slave ship, called it 'the most
dreaded and unmanageable' of calamities that might befall
a slaver.[117] Smallpox in a land caravan might condemn it
to wander almost as a plague ship, shunned by all—as
Thomson, though his was not a slave caravan, learnt with
bitter cost in East Africa.[118] Nachtigal noted that while
slave caravans sometimes brought smallpox into Fezzan,

[114] Lander, in Clapperton, 1829, 292.
[115] J. Thomson, *To the central African lakes and back*, 1881, ii,
73–4.
[116] Lander, in Clapperton, 1829, 292.
[117] Canot, 1928, 245.
[118] J. Thomson, 'To Lake Bangweolo and the unexplored region
of British Central Africa', *Geographical Journal*, 1893, 110.

the desert nomads whose encounters with such caravans were less frequent were thus less likely to contract diseases from this source.[119]

Cold was another killer. Al-Hajj Bashir, *wazir* of Bornu in 1851, and a friend of Barth, going on pilgrimage with a number of slaves for sale to defray expenses, lost 40 dead in a single night between Fezzan and Benghazi, through cold in the mountains, and swore that he would never again travel with slaves for sale. But Barth found it hard to make him sensible of the equal horrors of slave-hunting.[120] Vischer, in mountains south of Bir Meshru, came upon a large heap of camel bones, remains of a caravan from Bilma killed by intense winter cold. One of his companions had earlier himself been halted in the same place by cold, the water freezing in the waterskins, and the camels refusing to rise, being unable to stand upon their stiff legs.[121] At the other extreme, some slaves died in the fires which occasionally engulfed villages, particularly in the dry season: in western Bornu, in 1853, Barth heard reports of eight female slaves, fettered together in a hut, burnt to death in such a conflagration.[122]

There was the danger, too, that a slave caravan might be attacked. In 1824 Clapperton heard at Sokoto of freedom fighters, among the Gobir Hausa, capturing a Fulani caravan, 300 slaves and six Fulani women falling to them among the spoil.[123] Barth reported of a returning slave-raiding expedition in Adamawa, that it was attacked by the irate relatives of its captives, and these were successfully freed.[124] Bu Aischa, who led the party with which Nachtigal first crossed the Sahara, was unfortunate on his return

[119] i, 146, 434-5.   [120] Barth, 1857-8, ii, 296-7.
[121] Vischer, 1910, 230.   [122] Barth, 1857-8, iv, 47.
[123] Denham and Clapperton, 1826, B, 108-9.
[124] Barth, 1857-8, ii, 529.

journey from Kuka to Tripoli; starting out burdened with much property and many slaves, he was plundered of his possessions before he got home, though the marauders were said to have spared the gifts which he was taking from Shaykh Umar to the Governor-General of Tripoli.[125]

There is nothing to suggest that slave-traders were careful cost accountants, and the constant possibility of losses through exhaustion and exposure, hunger and thirst, disease and desertion, and robbery, must have made the trade, if sometimes very lucrative, inevitably an exceeding risky economic enterprise. And if slave-owners, handling their own property on the march, were not always careful, slave-drivers, responsible for the slaves only in transit, and moving them from one place to another at a charge of so much per head, were likely to be even less so. Richardson met such a caravan between Ghat and Ghadames, of slaves being brought to their Ghadamsi owners by Tuareg caravaneers. Richardson thought he espied two old men labouring after the group, but discovered on closer examination that they were two small children crawling.[126]

On the other hand, the slaves whom Nachtigal met daily in small caravans between Murzuq and Tripoli in 1869, and who had survived the often harrowing Saharan crossing, appeared cheerful and contented, apparently glad to be near the end of their toilsome and painful wanderings, and now reasonably well clothed and fed.[127] The company of seventy women slaves, whom Denham met on his way to Murzuq in 1822, were, he said, 'much better looking and more healthy' than any he had seen near the Mediterranean coast.[128] Other travellers' reports of caravans, often wholly or largely of women slaves, coming into North Africa were, however, not so reassuring,[129] and Denham described

[125] iii, 13.   [126] Richardson, 1848, i, 399–400.
[127] i, 64.   [128] Denham and Clapperton, 1826, A, xvii.
[129] Barth, 1857–8, i, 93, 184, 258–9.

how only the most robust reached the Fezzan—he saw over 100 skeletons from one slave caravan which had left Bornu with inadequate food—and how these survivors were fattened before going on to the Tripoli market.[130]

[130] Denham and Clapperton, 1826, A, 9–10.

CHAPTER IV

THE DOMESTIC SCENE I: GENERAL TREATMENT

General treatment

The fate of a slave who survived a raid upon his (or her) home, and the rigours of the journeys which then had to be made, naturally varied very widely. Some peoples accepted enslavement more easily than others: the eastern Arabs said that slaves from Ulungu quickly became unmanageable, dull and morose, and many committed suicide, a measure rarely adopted by other peoples in that area;[1] again, slaves from Okrika in eastern Nigeria

> have always proved refractory and incorrigible, and have often died broken-hearted, offering little or no encouragement to buyers to recruit their ranks with substitutes from that place.[2]

Some areas were more dispiriting than others: slaves isolated on the island of San Tome sometimes ate earth for suicide.[3] Nachtigal heard of similar despair in Tibesti (see p. 103).

[1] Thomson, 1881, i, 319–20; he adds, 'And yet as slaves in Unyanyembe [modern Tabora], they are vastly better off both in food and clothing than if they were free, besides having next to no work. It must therefore arise simply from grief at being separated from their country and kindred, and from a certain sense of degradation attending slavery.'

[2] Tepowa, 1907, 67.

[3] D. Crawford, *Thinking black: 22 years without a break in the long grass of central Africa*, London 1914, 2nd ed., 75.

'Everywhere,' Nachtigal observed, 'Islam brings with it a mild administration of the institution of slavery.'[4] Especially in Fezzan, where the population was gentle and good-natured, slaves, treated as members of the family, seldom sought to return to their homes, and in Tripoli too a slave was usually treated with humanity.[5] Even the Awlad Sulayman, brutal and cruel as their general behaviour frequently was, commonly treated their slaves in humane fashion and accepted them into the family circle. Nachtigal quoted several cases of slaves who had no desire whatever to return home. His guide and protector on his journey into Awlad Sulayman country, a man for whom he expressed a high regard, owned one small boy of 13 who steadily refused to be ransomed by his father, a prosperous man who frequently attempted to negotiate his release.[6] Another man, not, strictly speaking, a slave, but an unransomed prisoner of war, highly skilled as a tracker, was given the greatest freedom to practise his expertise, and never showed any sign of wanting to escape.[7] A slave girl, who had an aged relative in the same family under her complete control, was apparently a contented member of the family group.[8]

A recent study of slaves among the Tuareg describes how, through the classificatory kinship system and in particular through avoidance and joking relations, slaves are incorporated into the same social pattern as their masters, and made an integral part not only of the society but also of the actual family. While it is rare for a slave to eat with his master, and slaves live with wind and sun screens rather than in tents, there is otherwise little difference, and clothing and ornaments of free and slave are much the same.[9] This sort of incorporation, of slaves into the slave-owning society, was quite common in Africa. In Hausaland, a slave,

4 i, 133.
5 i, 17.   6 ii, 66.   7 ii, 65–6.   8 ii, 46.
9 Nicolaisen, 1963, 442 ff.

if acquired young enough, might be given the tattoo marks of his master's people.[10] In North Africa, a bondman frequently took the name of the tribe of his master, and some North Africans, settled subsequently in the Middle East and claiming ancestry from the old North African colonist tribes of Arabs, may in fact derive partly from Sudanese slaves of those tribes.[11]

In some places, the incorporation of slaves within the slave-owning society was furthered by special organizations amongst the slaves themselves. In Mecca, each community of Negro slaves had its own shaykh, who settled disputes amongst the members of his community, issuing judicial sentences which were carried out by a supporting official, the *naqīb*.[12] In Ghadames, there was but a single shaykh of the slaves,[13] who thus described his own functions to Richardson:

> Be it known, oh Christian! I am the Shaykh of the slaves, my name is Ahmed. I am from Timbuctoo. The people of Bambara are the finest in the world. They are brave—they fear none. Now, hear me: I know all the names of the slaves in Ghadames: I watch over all their conduct, to punish them when they behave badly, to praise them when they do well. They all fear me. For my trouble I receive nothing. I am a slave myself. I rarely punish the slaves. We have always here more than two hundred. If you wait, plenty of slaves will soon come from Soudan![14]

[10] Tremearne, 1913, 102.

[11] Doughty (1923, i, 140) suspected this of the people of el-Ally, a town in northern Arabia founded by Berber pilgrims, although the people themselves denied such admixture.

[12] Hurgronje, 1931, 11.

[13] Here also called the *qā'id al-wasfān*, head of slaves; Richardson, 1848, i, 304.

[14] Richardson, 1848, i, 101–2; *cf.* 112, 141–2.

There was also a street of the slaves in Ghadames, where
the slaves used to gather and talk.[15]

Evidence of the sometimes comfortable circumstances of
slaves comes from various quarters. Here is an East African
description:

> No starved and ill-used slaves are to be seen, for on
> cases of inhumanity being reported to the Sultan [of
> Zanzibar], the sufferers are at once set free, and made
> safe from the brutality of their masters. Indeed, this
> class seem to have a remarkably easy time of it, and
> have ten times more real liberty than thousands of our
> [British] clerks and shop-girls. They are commonly al-
> lowed to engage themselves out to work; and no cara-
> van ever goes up the country without a number of
> slaves among the porters. A jolly-hearted crew they are,
> whose motto in life is, 'beer, women, and ease'.[16]

Parallel instances of the possibility of intervention, should
a slave be ill-treated, might be cited. Among the Tuareg a
runaway slave may be reclaimed by his owner, but the senior chief may intervene in cases where the slave has been
misused or inadequately clothed.[17] According to Muslim
law the judicial authority might decree the enfranchisement
of a slave whose master had intentionally done anything to
him which appreciably diminished his value, or would in
the eyes of the world be considered degrading or humiliat-

[15] ibid., i, 147.
[16] Thomson, 1881, i, 17. Doughty (1923, i, 553–4) says of slaves
in Arabia, that their condition was always tolerable and often happy
(though somewhat harder actually within the holy cities), slave-
owners often freeing slaves, marrying them out, and endowing them
somewhat with camels or palms. Freedmen growing prosperous might
marry into the free class, though only among members of the somewhat despised smiths' caste.
[17] Nicolaisen, 1963, 442.

ing, e.g. the amputation of a part of the body or cutting off the hair of a beautiful female.[18]

Slave conditions in general were, however, by no means idyllic, particularly in countries which imposed poverty-stricken limitations upon even the free. The life of a slave in Tibesti was inevitably comfortless and harsh. He was subjected there to 'continuous hunger treatment', and his position was particularly hopeless, since the physical conditions of the country made it practically impossible to run away; cases were known where slaves from Bornu had committed suicide.[19] Desert conditions which the Awlad Sulayman accepted as a matter of course placed a very severe strain upon slaves from more fertile countries in the south. Nachtigal was on one occasion astonished to find himself, while on the march, delivering an exhausted slave girl of her newborn infant; the father, presumably a fellow-slave, no one could identify.[20] A poem from Mauritania illustrates what may have been the general opinion about the comforts to which slaves were entitled, though it suggests that in practice these were sometimes enlarged. The poem begins: This world is topsy-turvy but the world to come is sure; and it includes the line:

The slave is owner of two flowing shifts, while the slave girl keeps her weight through drinking milk.[21]

Under harsh circumstances, an enterprising slave might try to run away. Slave dealers in Ghadames had iron manacles and leg fetters—made, ironically, in the Negro lands —to prevent slaves from escaping, though these were apparently not very much used.[22] Slave caravans coming to Ghadames did occasionally lose runaway slaves, although such fugitives in the desert almost certainly perished.[23] A

[18] Ruxton, 1916, 352; Ibn Abi Zayd, 227.   [19] i, 355–6.
[20] ii, 230–1.   [21] Norris, 1968, 30.
[22] Richardson, 1848, i, 266–8.   [23] Richardson, 1848, i, 369.

slave girl in Tibesti, who gave Nachtigal much useful information about her home country, Ennedi, had been eager to escape, even after bearing her master a child. She had, accordingly, for some time been kept in chains, but when she seemed to grow less discontented, the chains were dropped. There was then another attempt to escape, and it was apparently while she was again in chains that she was allowed to have regular talks with Nachtigal, who brought her daily to and from her master's house. Eventually she quarrelled with her master's free wife; being on this account threatened with transfer to another master, she ran away again, breaking her chains, and leaving her small son behind, this time for good.[24] In Bagirmi, two slave women, assigned by Abu Sekkin to Nachtigal, who was having trouble in getting his domestic work performed, also had their feet fastened together with short, heavy chains. They soon ran away, to Nachtigal's secret satisfaction.[25] The propensity of slaves to run away was apparently sufficiently strong in Bagirmi to make the right of one important official to retain all fugitives who were not reclaimed by their masters a valuable perquisite.[26] 'Some slaves', said Baba of Karo, 'have been with your family so long that they become like your grandmothers,' and when slavery was stopped in Hausaland, nothing much happened, so she reported some sixty years later, in her father's slave compound. The fact, however, that 'some slaves which we had bought in the market ran away' at that time suggests that not all of them had been perfectly contented with their lot.[27]

The legal texts also took account of the fugitive contingency, in a multitude of incidental provisions: in tax assessment, a runaway slave was counted for some taxation purposes (*zakat al-fitr*), but not—even if the owner hoped

[24] ii, 98–9.   [25] ii, 620.   [26] ii, 612.
[27] Mary Smith, 1954, 78, 67.

1. Bagirmi slave-raid against the Pagan Kimre, 1872.
Nachtigal, ii, facing, 628.

2. The attack on Musfeia, 1823. Denham and Clapperton, 3rd edition, 1828. i, facing 315.

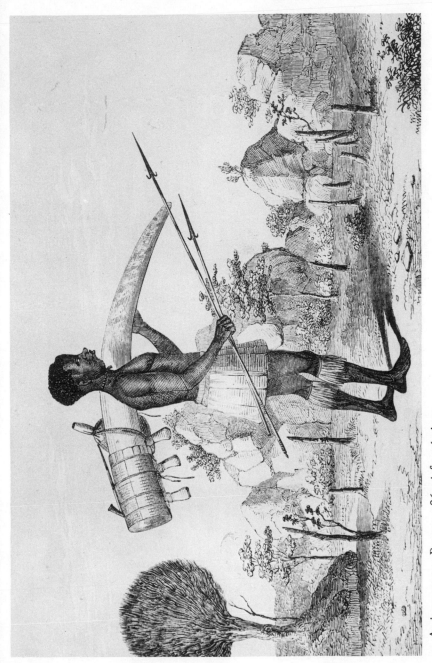

3. An ivory porter. Burton, 1860, i, frontispiece.

4. A slave caravan. Richardson, 1848, i, frontispiece.

5. A Negress in Morocco. O. Lenz, *Timbouctou,*
Paris, 1886, 395.

6. A slave in the block. J. Buttikofer, *Reisebilder aus Liberia*,
Leiden, 1890, ii, 181.

7. Above, foot irons and, below, man-
acles for slaves, from the Fulani of
Ngaundere in Adamawa. S. Passarge,
Adamaua, Berlin, 1895, 261 and 262.

8. A Ghadames bill of sale, including gold, slaves,
slave-girls, hides, pillows (or pillow-cases?), ivory, herbs
(senna?), perfume, camels, sacks (or perhaps sheaths,
scabbards), and household slaves (perhaps eunuchs).
Richardson, 1848, i, 114.

9. Nachtigal's first grave, in Liberia. Buttikofer, 1890, i, 440.

to regain him—for others (ordinary *zakat*);[28] and a marriage involving a runaway slave as dowry was invalid.[29]

Even when the ordinary day-to-day life of a slave was tolerable, insecurity continued to be a normal characteristic of the slave condition, for a variety of different, and unpredictable, circumstances might lead suddenly to his or her sale or transfer. A Kanuri, whom market shortages had cut off from his kola nuts, the favourite luxury of Bornu, might, so Nachtigal said, when kola came back into the market, part with his horse or his concubine in order to buy some.[30] A slave who accompanied his master on a journey might find himself left behind in some strange place as payment of some toll-obligation which his master had to meet, or as a contribution to a present to some magnate along the road.[31] Or a slave-owner who fell on hard times might feel that in order to improve his liquidity position he had no alternative to selling some of his slaves.[32] Slaves might be requisitioned as compensation, or as fines. In Vai country, in the seventeenth century, the compensation for adultery with a wife of the king was gifts or slaves.[33] Among one people in the Nassarawa Province of northern Nigeria, if a murderer was caught he was handed over to the family of the victim to be killed; but if the murderer escaped, a male or female slave, depending on the sex of the murdered person, was presented to the bereaved family.[34] In Mauritania, blood-money might include slaves: the loss of an ear was compensated by the gift of a woman slave, while lesser wounds received varying numbers of camels.[35] Slaves forming part of the marriage gift of a fiancé to his intended bride would normally return to his

[28] Khalil ibn Ishaq, i, 121, 127.   [29] *ibid.*, ii, 47.
[30] i, 669.   [31] iii, 323.   [32] iii, 321.
[33] Ogilby, 1670, 411.
[34] F. F. W. Byng-Hall, 'Notes on the Bassa Komo tribe', *Journal of the African Society*, October 1908, 20.
[35] Norris, 1968, 19.

home; but the law allowed the bride's father to sell such slaves, if more money were needed for the trousseau.[36] Denham said that corporal punishment for slaves was rare in Bornu, but the fact that Bornu slave-owners were more than once seen by him in tears at having had to sell a slave[37] was a poor consolation perhaps for the slave thus uprooted again from his home.

Nor did the emancipation of a slave necessarily assure to his descendants unquestioned social acceptance; the taint of slavery in the family genealogical tree sometimes continued to be a liability. Some illustrations of the disabilities from which a member of a distinguished family might suffer if he happened to have a slave as a mother are noted below (pp. 124–6), and the tension which has continued in Mauritania between the Negroes whose ancestors were once slaves and other sections of the population has also been mentioned (pp. 44–5). In Liberia in 1874 the Negro American traveller, Benjamin Anderson, was told that the Mandingoes of Musadu had such 'a hard-hearted and unalterable opinion respecting the freest man if he has once been a slave' that he thought it prudent to cut out from a Monrovia newspaper which he had been given for distribution in the interior of the country a passage which 'contained an unsavoury revelation about our once being slaves'.[38] In quite recent times a social distinction is said sometimes to remain in marriage alliances,[39] and cases are known of West Africans who had planned a marriage with an American Negro going to the United States for the wedding ceremony to avoid any risk of unpleasantness with their family at home.

The extent to which the slave population reproduced itself is a disputed question on which our authorities have

[36] Khalil ibn Ishaq, ii, 55.

[37] Denham and Clapperton, 1826, A, 334.

[38] Benjamin Anderson, *Narrative of the expedition despatched to Musahdu by the Liberian Government . . . in 1874*, Monrovia 1912, 29.

[39] Trimingham, 1968, 93.

little to say. Lugard once asserted that 'it is a known fact that slaves do not increase naturally to any appreciable extent',[40] but this so-called demographic law has been categorically rejected by other writers as a 'myth'.[41]

Jobson in the seventeenth century spoke of Gambian Mandingo Muslims and their slaves, 'which slaves they suffer to marry and cherish the race that comes of them'.[42] According to Clapperton, male slaves in Sokoto were given wives on reaching the age of eighteen or nineteen, and their children were also slaves.[43] Barth was surprised to see so few home-born slaves in the Sudan, except among the Tuareg who deliberately encouraged this. He concluded that a domestic slave was rarely allowed to marry and that this absence of reproduction was a main factor in maintaining slave-raiding.[44] Referring particularly to Tripoli, Nachtigal noted that Negroes were always eager to marry with as little delay as possible. But the climate of Tripoli did not suit them, and their descendants were neither numerous nor very vigorous.[45]

Slave revolts

The outbreak of revolts such as have been noted in various parts of the world from time to time is one channel through which slave discontent might find expression. Revolt, however, required organization and courage and persistence, so that the absence of slave revolt at any time cannot be regarded as conclusive proof that slaves were not discontented.

Revolts by Negro slaves in Mesopotamia are reported as early as 696,[46] and in the late ninth-century Basra was for

[40] Lugard, 1893, i, 169.
[41] M. I. Finley, *Slavery in classical antiquity*, Cambridge 1960, 60.
[42] Jobson, 1623, 84–5.   [43] Clapperton, 1829, 213–4.
[44] Barth, 1857–8, ii, 151–2.   [45] i, 17–18.
[46] G. Mathew, 'The East African coast until the coming of the Portuguese', in Oliver and Mathew, 1963, 101.

a time held by slaves from East Africa who had been employed in the saltpetre mines of the lower Euphrates.[47] The history of Brazil, another overseas export market, was also for a long time, up to the early nineteenth century, marked by slave insurrections of one kind or another.[48] Within Africa, it has been suggested that slave revolts were a threat to sixteenth-century Songhay.[49]

Nachtigal had nothing to say on this subject, unless his account of the Qairawan merchant who preferred to trade with Wadai in ivory rather than in slaves, whose irritable temperament was likely to make them troublesome,[50] is relevant, and presumably no specific incident of this kind came to his notice. Some European travellers thought that slave-owners in Africa were sometimes inclined to underestimate the risks of slave retaliation. Clapperton, noting the preponderance of slaves in the population of Kano in 1827, warned his Arab friends to 'keep a good lookout', quoting the precedent of slave revolt in St Domingo (now Haiti).[51] Speke found the slaves in Zanzibar 'spellbound', not realizing that 'if they chose to rebel, they might send the Arabs flying out of the land'[52]—the spell was not broken until a little more than a century later.

The apprehensions expressed by these travellers were,

[47] Ibn Khaldoun, *Histoire des Berbères et des dynasties musulmanes de l'Afrique septentrionale*, tr. Baron de Slane, Algiers 1854, ii, 106; Freeman-Grenville, *The mediaeval history of the coast of Tanganyika*, Oxford 1962, 29, 34 (hereafter Freeman-Grenville, 1962 B). Some who escaped when this rebellion was finally crushed are said to be among the ancestors of the Ma'dan, the marshmen of southern Iraq, who have attracted considerable attention in recent years (G. Maxwell, *A reed shaken by the wind*, London 1957, 17–20).

[48] Kent, 1965, 162.

[49] D. A. Olderogge, 'Feudalism in the western Sudan in the sixteenth–nineteenth centuries', *Sovietskaya Etnografia*, 1957, summarized in *African Abstracts*, 1959, 11–12.

[50] iii, 267.   [51] Clapperton, 1829, 171–2.

[52] Speke, 1863, xxvi.

however, perhaps themselves exaggerated. The contrasts between Haiti and Kano may well have been more important
than the similarities. According to a modern historian, although there was sometimes considerable turmoil among
the free population of Hausaland, there were no slave re-
bellions there throughout the last century.[53] This has been
explained in terms of the comparative ease with which
slaves there were able to work and accumulate property for
themselves, and the fact that the claims which masters
could make on them were fairly precisely defined, so that in
some respects they enjoyed more *de facto* freedom than some
of those who were technically free men[54] (compare Thomson's like comment on East African slaves, pp. 99 n, 102
above). A similar psychology may be reflected in the employment of slaves rather than free men as soldiers.

There were evidently some real dangers from slave unrest.
Individual murder was one. A North African merchant told
Clapperton, in Hausaland in 1824, that his slaves never
knew in which room he would sleep, and that he always
kept a dagger and loaded pistols under his pillow. The
merchant said that all the Arabs did the same, fearing to
be murdered by their female slaves, as, he added, often happened.[55] That this was no foolish fear seemed to be established when Clapperton learnt in Kano in 1826 that a
Ghadames merchant had been found strangled in his bed,
one of a succession of such episodes.[56] A cleric from Sennar, teaching in Wadai, was murdered there by his concubines.[57] We have already described the fears in Mauritania,
lest slaves exercise their supernatural powers to the same
end of assassination (see above p. 68). For a much earlier

[53] M. G. Smith, 'The Hausa system of social status', *Africa*, 1959,
242.
[54] Sellnow, 1964, 97.
[55] Denham and Clapperton, 1826, B, 132.
[56] Clapperton, 1829, 171.   [57] Trimingham, 1962, 140.

parallel, Leo Africanus said that the people of Gaoga, the Bulala branch of Bornu, formerly free, came under the domination of a self-established king who got his start in life when, as a slave, he murdered his master and sold his goods for horses. With the mounted force thus acquired, the ex-slave himself captured more slaves, whom he traded to Egypt for more horses, until he was strong enough to rule the whole of Gaoga (see above p. 82).[58]

There were also larger-scale risings. These were frequently associated with runaway slaves, and may have been as often attempts at self-defence against recapture as outright revolt; where the threat of recapture did not exist the escaped slaves sometimes settled down quite peaceably in their own new homes. Such developments seem to have been particularly a feature of East Africa. In 1506 a Portuguese visitor to the north-west coast of Madagascar found there a dense population of refugee slaves from Malindi, Mombasa and even Mogadishu.[59] In the nineteenth century a town, Barder, was reported on the Juba river in present-day Somalia, where an Arab trader had taken advantage of discontent among local slaves to lead them in revolt.[60] In 1867 it was estimated that more than 10,000 slaves had fled to the river Ozi, on the mainland opposite Pate island, whither a chief, Fumo Lotti, proscribed by the sultan of Zanzibar, had earlier withdrawn. The chief established a new state there, with two strong towns, Vittou and Mogogoni. The first rule of the state was to give liberty to all who crossed its borders. New arrivals were encouraged to build homes and clear farms, and were en-

---

[58] Leo Africanus, A, iii, 835; B, ii, 482.

[59] R. K. Kent, 'Madagascar and Africa: II. the Sakalava, Maroserana, Dady and Tromba before 1700', *Journal of African History*, 1968, 526.

[60] Harris, 1844, i, notes by Lieut. Wilmot Christopher attached to frontispiece map.

rolled in armed defence companies.[61] These towns appear
to be in the same area and of the same sort—if they are not
in fact exactly the same towns—which Lugard visited in
1890. He mentions three names, Fuladoyo, Magongeni
(= Mogogoni?) and Mwaiba, putting them on his map in
the immediate hinterland of Malindi. He describes them
as large stockaded villages, colonies of runaway slaves, and
adds that he understood that they had beaten the Arabs in
battle some years before. Now, the Arabs were talking of
carrying war against Fuladoyo. Lugard devised a compro-
mise, according to which the fugitives should be given an
opportunity to earn sufficient money with which to com-
pensate their former owners.[62] He was, however, unable
to see this scheme through.[63] The struggles between the
Arab traders and the local chief Mirambo, in the later
nineteenth century, for control of the Tabora area in Tanganyika were complicated by slaves who, armed by their
Arab masters to fight against Mirambo, ran away and instead fought against the Arabs.[64]

There are West African instances too. About 1756 slaves
in Futa Jallon revolted and built for themselves a fortified
town, Kondeeah, which successfully resisted repeated as-
saults by the disgruntled ex-owners and their allies.[65] In
1838 the Koranko slaves in Kukuna rose against their Susu
masters and established a fortified town in which runaway
slaves were encouraged to settle.[66] Another fugitive slave
fortress, the village of Gamon between the upper Senegal
and upper Gambia rivers, had indirectly considerable impact

[61] E. F. Berlioux, *The slave trade in Africa in 1872*, translated,
London 1872, 47–8; some of the escaped slaves had come overland
several hundred miles, from Somali territory.

[62] Lugard, 1893, i, 224 ff.   [63] *ibid.*, i, 298–9.

[64] V. L. Cameron, *Across Africa*, London 1885, 157.

[65] A. G. Laing, *Travels . . . in West Africa*, London 1825,
126–8, 405.

[66] Fyfe, 1962, 283.

on the course of events in upper Senegambia at the beginning of European colonial control there. As a young man,
the Muslim cleric Momodu Lamine had been mistreated by
the people of Gamon; and in later life his attempts at revenge led to widespread fighting, much of which had nothing to do with Gamon, and to Momodu Lamine's appearance
in 1885-7 as a major political and military leader.[67] One
revolt was recorded near Boporo in Liberia in 1866, when
latent discontent was brought to a head by the decision to
sell some of the slaves of a local magnate who had died leaving an estate encumbered with a heavy load of debt. In this
case the slaves took possession of the town where they lived,
counting on support from a neighbouring free tribe which
was at variance with their masters. Their ostensible allies,
however, betrayed them, and the revolt was eventually
crushed with barbaric severity.[68]

Another category of slave revolt was that undertaken by
Muslim slaves against non-Muslim masters. The risings in
Brazil, early in the nineteenth century (see p. 107), were of
this kind. Muslim slaves and freedmen have been identified
as the main instigators of these; at the time of the main
rebellion, in Bahia in 1835, the police believed that there
was an *imam* exercising some authority, but they never
discovered him;[69] Arabic amulets were much suspected as
tokens of revolt, and to be found carrying such an amulet
might earn a freedman deportation, or a slave several hundred lashes.[70] The revolts have been described as 'religious
wars',[71] a direct repercussion of the Fulani *jihads* of the
early nineteenth century, and of the drive of Islam into the

[67] H. J. Fisher, 'The early life and pilgrimage of al-Hajj Muhammad al-Amin the Soninke (d. 1887)', *Journal of African history*,
1970, 55-6.
[68] Benjamin Anderson, *Narrative of a journey to Musardu*, New
York 1870, 41-4.
[69] Verger, 1968, 341, 349.   [70] *ibid.*, 337-40, 358.
[71] *ibid.*, 361-8.

northern part of the Yoruba country, from which had emerged a considerable number of Hausa and Yoruba prisoners of war. A little ironically, many Yoruba regarded that particular phase of the Fulani *jihad* in Yorubaland which led to the establishment of the Ilorin emirate, as primarily a revolt of Muslim slaves against their Yoruba masters.[72] Samuel Crowther, enslaved as a youth during these wars, and later to become a bishop in the Anglican church, attributed the troubles of the time in Yorubaland to some Yoruba Muslims, some Fulani immigrants, 'and such foreign slaves as had escaped from their owners'.[73] Although the first prominent trouble-maker in Ilorin, Afonja, who sought to break away from his traditional Yoruba loyalties, was later himself overthrown and killed by his erstwhile Muslim colleagues, yet his connections with Islam had strengthened his appeal to Hausa slaves, whose defection in turn further weakened the loyalist Yoruba forces.[74] There were also revolts by Muslim slave officials against Muslim rulers (see below pp. 166–7).

Special provisions had sometimes to be made for the runaway Muslim slaves of non-Muslim masters, and even of Muslim masters living outside *dar al-Islam*, that is, territory under recognizably Islamic authority. Al-Hajj Umar wrestled with this problem, recommending that a slave who fled to *dar al-Islam* from a Pagan master should become a free man—even if the slave were not a Muslim. Opinions differed, continued al-Hajj Umar, concerning slaves who adopted Islam but did not flee to *dar al-Islam*: some said that these, according to Muslim law, became theoretically free immediately upon conversion, and that this freedom would be extended to them in practical reality should a Muslim army ever invade the Pagan territory in which they lived; but others thought that perhaps the army should take possession

---

[72] Clapperton, 1829, 25, 28, 39, 172, 204.
[73] Quoted in Curtin, 1968, 294, 299.   [74] *ibid.*, 295–6.

of such slaves. If a Pagan slave converted to Islam before his Pagan master, he became free, but not if the master converted first—although some lawyers did argue that a Muslim slave, fleeing from a Muslim master who lived outside *dar al-Islam*, became free on entering *dar al-Islam*.[75] These legal details, painstakingly analysed by scholars, might acquire considerable practical importance in the case of a Muslim reformer waging religious war, endeavouring to extend *dar al-Islam* and to attract as many adherents as possible—and such a man, *par excellence*, was al-Hajj Umar himself.

Occasionally, the fugitive Muslim slave found himself as far outside *dar al-Islam* after his flight as before; but in such case, if he held fast to his religious convictions, he might become the pioneer of Islam in a new area. The first Muslims, for example, to establish themselves in the Eastern Cape in South Africa were runaways from Cape Town, who settled at Uitenhage about 1809.[76]

[75] Willis, 1970, 150–1.
[76] S. A. Rochlin, 'Origins of Islam in the Eastern Cape', *Africana Notes and News*, 1956, 22.

CHAPTER V
THE DOMESTIC SCENE II: SLAVES IN THE FAMILY

Domestic demand for slaves

This and the succeeding chapters examine the various kinds of demand which provided an assured foundation for the domestic slave trade in Muslim tropical Africa. The list is probably not exhaustive, and the categories are not mutually exclusive. A slave might be in more than one category at the same time: a Circassian woman, for example, would be at the same time a concubine and a luxury slave, or a senior officer might be at once a eunuch, a soldier, and a royal slave. Equally a slave might pass successively through several categories: a girl might embark as prize money allotted to a fortunate soldier, be passed on as tribute to an overlord, serve him as concubine, and perhaps end her days as an elderly spinner artisan. Nor, of course, are these categories confined to the domestic market; as early as the seventh and eighth centuries, for instance, East African women turned up in China as part of the tribute paid to the Chinese emperor by vassals in Java and Sumatra.[1]

Concubines

The demand for slave girls as concubines was an important continuing element in the African slave trade, domestic and

[1] Mathew, in Oliver and Mathew, 1963, 107–8.

for export, providing at the same time one of the reasons for insisting often that slaves should form a substantial part of any tribute. It was this slave profession in particular which sometimes led, quite naturally, to the fullest incorporation of the slave within the master's family. Female slaves who had crossed the Atlantic might become concubines; visitors to Bahia, early in the eighteenth century, alluded to the ease with which some slave women became the mistresses, even the wives, of the Portuguese.[2] But the domestic trade within Africa, and exports to the Muslim world, were distinct in the degree to which the need to supply concubines was a dominant and conscious motive.[3]

By the introduction of a clear and carefully defined distinction between wives and concubines, Islamic law considerably alters the common African pattern of polygyny. This distinction is expressed in various ways: for example, although a husband must share his nights equally amongst his wives, a concubine of his is not necessarily entitled to this favour, even if she is *umm al-walad*, mother of the child.[4] A few restrictions do hedge the owner's right to his slave women as concubines. For instance, he should not have sexual relations with two slave sisters; if he feels drawn to this, he should sell one of the sisters, or arrange for some

---

[2] Verger, 1968, 70.

[3] The special position of concubines in Muslim African society was again recognized during the progress of the abolition of slavery during European colonialism. In British East Africa, for example, a decree in 1897 allowed slaves to claim freedom if they wished, but this right was denied to concubines except in unusual circumstances, on the ground that family life should not be disturbed; see B. S. Cave, 'The end of slavery in Zanzibar and British East Africa', *Journal of the African Society*, 1909, 26, 29.

[4] Ibn Abi Zayd, 178. The *diya*, or blood-money, for the abortive foetus of a free wife and of a concubine are the same, but only if the concubine was carrying her master's child. If she was pregnant by someone else, then the *diya* of the foetus was one-tenth the estimated value of the mother (Ibn Abi Zayd, 248).

form of liberation to get rid of her.[5] Again, in the case of a female slave who has been made *al-mu'taqah ila ajl*, that is, she has been promised freedom at the expiry of a certain time, although her master may require her to work, and may, provided that the time is not just nearly over, take her property, he may no longer sleep with her.[6] In some parts of Africa, the seclusion of slave women is somewhat less than that of free: in Ghadames, only half-caste and slave women—apart from the splendidly independent Tuareg women, who would even make up their own desert caravans with no men other than their small sons[7]—moved freely about the town.[8]

The distinction between wives and concubines is sometimes rephrased as between free wives and slave wives. This is misleading. The number of wives is legally limited to four, but these may be either free or slave; the number of concubines is unlimited, but these must be slave. Since a free woman may not be taken as a concubine, some jurists have argued that the prohibition of the sale, gift or transfer of any person as a slave must end the Muslim system of concubinage.[9]

The legal marriage of slave women is in some respects identical with that of free women: in the division of the husband's nights, for example, the slave-wife has equal rights with the free.[10] In other respects it is subject to certain limitations: only slave women who are Muslim are eligible to marry a Muslim, though he may marry free women who are Muslim, Christian or Jewish;[11] and, while a free Muslim may marry as many as four slave Muslim women—if he

[5] Ibn Abi Zayd, 186–8.   [6] *ibid.*, 222.
[7] Richardson, 1848, i, 332.   [8] *ibid.*, i, 119, 226.
[9] Lugard, 1933, 10.   [10] Khalil ibn Ishaq, ii, 63.
[11] Theoretically, any sexual relations with women, whether free or slave, who are not of one of these three religions are forbidden, but this is scarcely observed in tropical Africa.

fears temptation and is without the means to marry free women—the slaves in this case would not be his own but the slaves of another, his own being available as his concubines if needed.[12] The divorce formula for a slave wife differed somewhat from that for a free.[13]

For the marriage of slave men, the law again makes some distinctions. In some schools of law, the slave man can marry only two wives; but the Maliki school, which is our chief concern in tropical Africa, allows him four.[14] These wives may be slave or free; but a Muslim woman may not marry her own slave, nor the slave of her son.[15] Lesser points of legal detail might be multiplied: the oath of continence, if taken by a free husband, must bind him for at least four months, but for a slave only half that period is required.[16]

A slave, man or woman, may marry only with the master's consent.[17] But a slave in certain categories—a *mukātib* slave, and a slave authorized to take part in trade—might buy a concubine, even without his master's permission.[18]

The distinction between slave and free appears also in the penalties attached to fornication, adultery and calumny (see also above p. 8). For fornication, a slave, man or woman, receives fifty strokes; a free person, if not *muhsan*, i.e. not fully legally responsible for his or her acts, receives 100 strokes, and may be banished or jailed—but slaves,

[12] Ibn Abi Zayd, 178.   [13] *ibid.*, 182.
[14] *ibid.*, 178; Khalil ibn Ishaq, i, 30. Barth (1857–8, iv, 274) records that the Fulani theocracy of Masina, in the first half of the nineteenth century, challenged that of Sokoto to reduce the number of allowed wives to two. Barth attributed this to the extreme orthodoxy of Masina; but it may perhaps have been a slightly guarded way of saying that the Sokoto Fulani were no better than slaves. Richardson (1848, i, 390) was told by a trader in Ghadames that it was the custom to marry two wives when going to the Negro lands.
[15] Ibn Abi Zayd, 178; Khalil ibn Ishaq, i, 30.
[16] Khalil ibn Ishaq, ii, 98.   [17] Ibn Abi Zayd, 180.
[18] Khalil ibn Ishaq, ii, 27.

and free Muslim women, are not banished; the free and *muhsan* fornicator is stoned to death.[19]

References to concubines are present in African Islamic history from the very beginning. Al-Bakri recorded how one of the conquerors of North Africa, Abd al-Malik bin Marwan, received as his share of the booty from the conquest of Jalula, near Qairawan, 600 dirhems, which he invested in buying a young girl.[20] The slave girls of Awdaghast were renowned in the eleventh century.[21] The pilgrimage of Mansa Musa, ruler of Mali in the early fourteenth century, provided further evidence of this interest. On arrival in Cairo his numerous retinue avidly bought female slaves, singing girls, Ethiopian slaves and cloth from the Turks, spending so much gold as to reduce its exchange value sharply to an extent from which it had not recovered twelve years later.[22] On this occasion the demand for slaves may have been stimulated by Mansa Musa's indoctrination in orthodoxy, for he had previously been in the habit of using the daughters of his free subjects as only slave women should be used. He was reproached in Cairo for his licence. Is it not permitted even for kings? he asked. Not even for kings, was the reply, and he gave it up.[23] Ibn Battuta, visiting Mali in the 1350s, found a Negro town governor, a pilgrim, who surprised him by understanding some Arabic; he discovered that the governor had in his household a young slave girl, a Damascus Arab.[24] A prominent official in Mali at this time, the interpreter, attended the principal Muslim festivals with his four wives and about 100 slave girls, in beautiful robes, with gold and silver ornamented fillets on their heads, playing instruments and singing along with him.[25] Ibn Battuta also described the people of Tak-

19 Ibn Abi Zayd, 252; see also 190.
20 Al-Bakri, 71-2.   21 *ibid.*, 301.
22 Al-Umari, 78-9, 90-2.   23 *ibid.*, 72-3.
24 Ibn Battuta, A, 334; C, iv, 433-4.
25 *ibid.*, A, 328; C, iv, 411-2.

edda, vying with one another in the number of their slaves
and serving-women, living in luxury and ease, just as the
people of Mali and Walata did. They never sold an educated female slave, or only rarely, and then at a high price.
He tried twice to purchase such a slave, but each time the
contract was subsequently cancelled.[26] In such a case, should
the disappointed prospective purchaser be in a position to
express his anger, extensive disruption might follow: one
Mauritanian war arose from the refusal of the owner of a
slave girl to sell her to a chief who desired her.[27] Ibn Battuta, returning from Mali to Takedda, joined a caravan
which included about 600 women slaves.[28] In Timbuktu,
just after the Moroccan conquest, a new official was appointed to replace one who had died in prison, and the
new appointee appropriated a *harim* of 300 young girls.[29]
In East Africa, inland from Mogadishu and Brava on the
Somali coast, a people called the Maracatos were reported
around 1600 to practise the infibulation of women, especially women slaves, who thus fetched better prices. The
Maracatos also made eunuchs.[30] Early in the seventeenth
century the English trader Jobson met Buckor Sano, an
African merchant on the upper Gambia. '. . . Hee shewed
unto mee,' wrote Jobson,

> 'certaine young blacke women, who were standing by
> themselves, and had white strings crosse their bodies,
> which hee told me were slaves, brought for me to buy.
> I made answer, We were a people, who did not deale
> in any such commodities, neither did wee buy or sell

[26] *ibid.*, A, 335–6; C, iv, 439–40.
[27] al-Shinqiti, 1911, 479; 1953, 95. A variant instance of the same
theme occurs in the Hausa tale of a chief who wished the wife of one
of his slaves. He sent the husband on a journey. But the wife shamed
the chief, saying that the master does not sup of the same vessel as
his dog (Tremearne, 1913, 26–7).
[28] Ibn Battuta, A, 337; C, iv, 444–5.   [29] *Tedzkiret*, 278–80.
[30] Freeman-Grenville, 1962 A, 150.

one another, or any that had our owne shapes; he seemed to marvell much at it, and told us, it was the only merchandise, they carried down into the countrey, where they fetcht all their salt, and that they were solde there to white men, who earnestly desired them, especially such young women, as hee had brought for us.'[31]

Later in the seventeenth century, a Moroccan cleric, driven out by the Sultan, fled to Timbuktu. He sought the protection of the king of Segu, Mamari Biton, whose authority then extended over Timbuktu, and supported his case with a gift of two Andalusian slave girls. (Even in the ninth century, Ibn Hawqal had spoken of white slave damsels from Andalus, selling for 1000 dinars or more.)[32] Mamari Biton refused to surrender the cleric to emissaries sent from Morocco, and even allowed him to levy troops in Timbuktu.[33] Bawa, ruler of Gobir in the eighteenth century, received from the ruler of Nupe 500 female slaves, and 500 boys, each boy bearing 20,000 cowries. Bawa responded with a gift of 100 horses, and female slaves whose beauty outshone the sun, 'beautiful in form and character and resplendent with ambergris and silk'.[34]

The emergence of a more militant puritan Islam, in the late eighteenth and nineteenth centuries, did not fundamentally alter the situation, though some of the leaders behaved with restraint. For Shehu Ahmadu, the founder of the Masina theocracy, tradition apparently recalls only one concubine, a devout woman who could recite the Quran by heart and had studied the religious law.[35] Uthman dan

[31] Jobson, 1623, 120–1.

[32] Sir William Ouseley (tr.), *The oriental geography of Ebn Haukal, an Arabian traveller of the tenth century*, London 1800, 16.

[33] C. Monteil, 1924, 325 & n; M. Delafosse, 'Les rélations du Maroc avec le Soudan à travers les âges', *Hespéris*, 1924, 169–70.

[34] H. R. Palmer, 'Western Sudan history', *Journal of the African Society*, 1916, 269.

[35] Ba and Daget, 1962, vol. i, 52.

Fodio was survived by wives and concubines, who continued living quietly together in Sokoto.[36] In the early nineteenth century, the chief of Mandara, threatened by Adama of Adamawa, a principality in the Sokoto empire, returned a soft answer with a concubine and other presents; Adama, undeterred and undistracted, seized the Mandara capital, though he was able to hold it for only one day.[37] In 1827 Richard Lander, sole survivor of Clapperton's second expedition, accepted with gratitude the emir of Zaria's gift of a slave wife.[38] A Tuareg in Ghadames told Richardson, perhaps vaingloriously, that he had taken an unusual lizard to the Sudan, and had given it to a Negro prince in exchange for a young female slave.[39] Al-Hajj Bashir, first minister of Bornu, had a *harim* of three or four hundred, which he appeared to regard as a sort of ethnological museum, doubtless, added Barth, of a peculiarly interesting kind. He made special efforts to acquire a perfect specimen of each tribe, and told Barth with undisguised satisfaction that he possessed also a Circassian woman.[40] He sometimes antagonized the notables of Bornu by compelling them to cede to him a handsome female slave or a fine horse. Seventy-three sons survived him at his execution in 1853.[41] The accumulation of slave girls in Bashir's *harim* is said on one occasion to have enabled Shaykh Umar of Bornu, hard pressed by Sherif, the king of Wadai, to accept Sherif's offer to halt his threatened advance on Kuka if he were paid 1000 dollars. An Arab trader offered the Shaykh 600 dollars in exchange for young girls valued at 7 dollars per head, the current price in Bornu being then 40 dollars.

[36] Clapperton, 1829, 207, 210.   [37] East, 1934, 23–5.
[38] Lander, in Clapperton, 1829, 304–5.
[39] Richardson, 1848, i, 204–5.
[40] Doughty, 1923, i, 603, the English traveller in Arabia in the 1870s, was once taken, on account of his lighter skin, to his chagrin as the son of a Circassian bondwoman.
[41] Barth, 1857–8, ii, 293–4.

The Shaykh commandeered the most attractive members of Bashir's *harim*, and being able to make up the balance of 400 dollars by other means, could thus buy Sherif off.[42]

The mother of Samori was said to have been captured in a slave raid and reserved for the chief because of her especial beauty; Samori then joined the chief and served him for seven years in return for his mother's release. He and his mother were eventually sent home with a present of slaves and gold. Soon after, early in his independent career, Samori besieged the town of Sanankoro; the townspeople were at last forced to capitulate, and sent him twelve lovely slave girls and gold as a token of their submission.[43] Momodu Lamine, returning from pilgrimage about 1880, and visiting Masina and Segu—in his time both parts of the Islamic empire which derived from al-Hajj Umar—received gifts of concubines at both places, though one story says the ruler of Segu forced him to surrender a girl he had received in Masina.[44] The Mahdist conqueror of Darfur occasionally sent gifts of slave girls, horses, or camels to Khartoum, but was nevertheless finally exiled.[45] The cleric-magician employed by Abushiri in his rebellion against the Germans in East Africa in 1890 asked for 1000 rupees, two handsome boy slaves, and two girl slaves 'with necks slim as bamboos'.[46]

Such exchanges took place also between the Muslims and

[42] A. Schultze, tr. P. A. Benton, *The sultanate of Bornu*, London 1913, 266–7. According to the version of this story recorded in *Documents scientifiques de la Mission Tilho*, 1911, ii, 367, 'les bijoux de ses femmes' provided the other means which Shaykh Umar needed.

[43] Kouroubari, 1959, 545–6.   [44] Fisher, 1970, 61–2.

[45] R. C. Slatin, *Fire and sword in the Sudan*, London and New York 1896, 274.

[46] J. W. T. Allen (tr.), *The German conquest of the Swahili coast: Utanzi wa vita vya wadeshi kutamalaki mrima*, Dar-es-Salaam 1960, 59.

their non-Muslim allies, and amongst their opponents.
When the Muslim ruler of Enarea, in Ethiopia, proposed
an alliance to the Christian ruler of Gojam, the Christian
replied: you are a Muslim and sell slaves, it cannot be;
nevertheless he accepted 100 horns of civet and 50 female
slaves, and sent in return 30 matchlocks, with men versed
in the use of firearms.[47] The Pagan king of Segu, fighting
Shehu Ahmadu, sought the help of a noted Bambara warrior, sending him, so the traditions tell, 6000 horns of Arab
powder, 15,000 of local powder, 6000 slaves, 500 cattle, ten
horses, two ostriches with feet encircled with gold, and a
vedette whose gait was more supple than that of the female
ostrich.[48]

A sometimes important complication arising from concubinage was rivalry among children. In strict law the child
of a free wife and the child of a concubine were exactly
equal in status and privileges.[49] But respect for the law
was not always effective in eradicating the feeling that it
was only right and proper to prefer the son of a free woman
to the son of a bondswoman. The Shirazi, or Persian, emi-
gration to East Africa was said to have been led by Ali, son
of the sultan by an Ethiopian slave, held in little esteem
by his half-brothers, offspring of a Persian noblewoman.[50]
When the sultan Yusuf of Wadai died in 1898, his eldest
son was passed over in the succession because his mother
had been a slave.[51] The distinction was sometimes on the
father's side, not the mother's. Fulani origins, traditionally
derived from a single royal mother, distinguish between her
children by her first husband, a free Arab, and those by
her second, a freed slave. The two main Fulani groups,

[47] Harris, 1844, iii, 53–5.   [48] Ba and Daget, 1962, i, 137–8.
[49] M. Gaudefroy-Demombynes, *Muslim institutions*, London 1950,
136–7.
[50] Freeman-Grenville, 1962 A, 89–90.
[51] Theobald, 1965, 60.

settled and nomad, dispute which has the former, more honoured, descent.[52]

Powerful individuals might rise from concubine birth to great eminence, even despite prejudice, and several folk-tales tell of such triumphs by the despised mother or her child.[53] Abu Yazid, who revolted in 928-9 against the Fatimids of North Africa, was the son of a Negro concubine, born on the banks of the Niger.[54] One story traces the origin of the title Galadima, a very senior official in Bornu, to the appointment of a *mai's* son, born to him by a concubine, to some high position.[55] The founder of the first independent dynasty of Nupe, in West Africa, was not born of a concubine, but was none the less partly tainted by slave status. He came of a chiefly mother in Nupe, while his father was a member of the ruling family in Igala, then over-lords to Nupe. But the father returned to Igala, whither the son himself, Tsoede, was later sent as part of the an-nual slave tribute owed by Nupe to Igala. In Igala, his father recognized him, and took him into his family. Later Tsoede escaped the machinations of his half-brothers, re-turned to Nupe, and set up his own kingdom.[56] Muham-mad al-Fadl, a renowned nineteenth-century ruler of Dar-fur, was the son of a Begu concubine, paid in tribute to the Darfur king by immigrants from the Bahr al-Ghazal. On his succession, Muhammad decreed the Begus free for ever, ended the tribute, and made the buying or selling of Begus a crime punishable by death.[57] Mutesa, later *kabaka*

[52] Lacroix, 1952, 5-6; E. A. Brackenbury, 'Notes on the "Bororo Fulbe" or nomad "Cattle Fulani"', *Journal of the African Society*, 1924, 211.

[53] Tremearne, 1913, 283, 317.

[54] Ibn Khaldun, ii, 530, iii, 201.

[55] P. A. Benton, *Kanuri Readings*, London, 1911, 25-6.

[56] H. A. S. Johnston, *The Fulani Empire of Sokoto*, London 1967, 134-5.

[57] Slatin, 1896, 44-5. Muhammad's mother had been later pro-moted to the position of legal wife. Muhammad himself, as a child, had been placed in the care of the chief eunuch, Abu Shaikh Kura.

of Buganda, was said to be the son of a woman sold into slavery soon after his birth, but this was disputed.[58]

In some cases, such an origin might not prove a serious obstacle: Aliyu Babba, the son of Sultan Bello, though his mother was a Hausa concubine, preceded three of his brothers and one uncle as sultan of Sokoto. His easy-going amiability has been attributed to his Hausa inheritance.[59] Once or twice descent, or pretended descent, from a slave was turned to positively good account: Tippu Tib, the most celebrated of all the eastern Arab slavers and colleague of Stanley, was said to have been recognized king of Mbali, near Manyuema, early in his career, having claimed to be the grandson of the old king's sister, who had long before been sold into slavery.[60]

Several of the foregoing examples show that white slaves were sometimes particularly prized. Leo Africanus commented that, while all the maid-servants of the household of the king of Fez were Negro slaves, the king also had certain Christian captives, Portuguese and Spanish, 'most circumspectly kept by certaine Eunuchs, that are Negroslaves'.[61] In nineteenth-century Katanga, the competing Portuguese and Arab parties each supplied the ruler, Msidi, with a wife at least partly white: one, Maria de Fonseca, was a Portuguese mulatto;[62] the other, Matayu, was brought from the east coast by the Arabs to offset Maria.[63] Maria complained that she had been sold as a chattel.[64] Matayu was ultimately strangled, for poisoning. Another variety much in demand, as well as the white woman, was the Ethiopian, prized for her beauty and amiability.[65]

[58] J. M. Gray, 'Mutesa of Buganda', and H. Mukasa, 'Some notes on the reign of Mutesa', both *Uganda Journal*, 1934, 23, 28, 128–9.
[59] H. A. S. Johnston, 1967, 152.
[60] Ward, 1890, 183–4.   [61] Leo Africanus, A, ii, 482; B, i, 238.
[62] Crawford, 1914, 183–5.   [63] *ibid.*, 295–6.
[64] *ibid.*, 191 n.
[65] A. E. Robinson, 'The Takruri sheikhs of Gallabat', *Journal of the African Society*, 1926, 49; Harris, 1844, i, 217–8, 228.

This was the pattern also in Mecca. There, the white Circassian slaves, male and female, coming from Constantinople, were very expensive, and were never sold in the open market.[66] Negresses were primarily house workers, and only secondarily concubines; Abyssinian women were regarded in the reverse order,[67] and may have excited more real enthusiasm than the Meccan women themselves.[68] In Brazil, several instances were reported in which the greater lightness in colour of a child or woman slave helped elicit more effective sympathy for emancipation.[69]

Nachtigal's observations supplement these impressions of the general importance of concubines. He found the demand for attractive young women clearly reflected in their market prices, and noted incidentally that they were everywhere a significant factor in determining the racial complexion of the population.[70] One of his servants once explained to Nachtigal his hopes of saving enough from the expedition to buy a girl slave. 'If I marry,' he said, 'I can be quite sure that my wife will be unfaithful to me; a slave girl too may be flighty, but I can sell her again as soon as I note her unfaithfulness.'[71] One of the first things that Job ben Solomon, the liberated Muslim slave who created a considerable stir in London in 1733-4, did on his return to his home on the Gambia was to buy a female slave and two horses.[72] A cleric, who claimed also to be a *sharif*, a descendant of the Prophet, and earned a precarious livelihood by teaching and secretarial work for the Awlad Sulayman, went back to Kuka each year with some hundredweights of dates and one or two camels to live frugally with a slave woman there until the teaching season came round again.[73] In Nachtigal's view, indeed, the institution of the concubine slave could be a real blessing for poor people

[66] Hurgronje, 1931, 10-1.   [67] Hurgronje, 1931, 13-4.
[68] *ibid.*, 107, 109.   [69] Verger, 1968, 516-17.
[70] ii, 424.   [71] i, 102-3.
[72] Grant, 1968, 114; Curtin, 1968, 57.   [73] ii, 59.

and for men who had to undertake long journeys. Free wives were seldom inclined to leave their homes and relations, and, according to the religious law, could not be compelled to do so. (Nachtigal may perhaps here have been confusing tribal custom with religious law. Ibn Battuta, discussing the unusual privileges accorded to women among the Massufa Berbers in the western Sahara, included, apparently as one such privilege, the fact that women did not travel with their husbands. Even if one wished to do so, her family would forbid it.[74] One reason why al-Kanemi was available to lead Bornu resistance to the Fulani was that his father-in-law had refused his request to be allowed to withdraw with wife and daughter to Fezzan, to escape the Fulani menace.[75]) If a child was born to a slave, continued Nachtigal, her position was likely to be even more secure than that of a legitimate wife, for only the most compelling reasons could induce a Muslim, however lax in his religious observances, to separate himself from the mother of his children by selling her. She had to exert herself more to ensure that by her industry and amiability she retained the goodwill of her master; there was a risk that she might gain excessive influence over him and become arrogant and extravagant, but in general a concubine involved smaller maintenance and housekeeping costs than did a free wife.[76] The hopeful appearance of the more attractive young women in the Kuka slave market contrasted with the misery and depression of their seniors.[77]

The concubine relationship did not indeed always work out happily. One night on the road to Wadai, Nachtigal's rest was disturbed when his guide's slave girl, covered with blood, rushed in to seek his protection; her jealousy of another slave girl had, it appeared, provoked a violent scene.[78]

[74] Ibn Battuta, A, 321; C, iv, 388-9.
[75] Barth, 1957-8, ii, 660-2.   [76] i, 685.   [77] i, 683-4.
[78] iii, 45-6.

Early in the twentieth century the story was current, concerning one of the towns of the North African coast, of an Arab who killed a Negro slave who would not respond to his advances. He buried her in the house, but her spirit returned each night, in the form of a blue light, frightening away lodgers and doing her former master much harm.[79]

[79] Vischer, 1910, 74.

CHAPTER VI

THE DOMESTIC SCENE III:
SLAVES AT WORK

Free and slave labour

It is generally accepted, and on the whole sound, doctrine in the western world that 'from the experience of all ages and nations, the work done by freemen comes cheaper in the end than that performed by slaves'.[1] There were, however, almost infinite variations of status and practice to be found in Africa, and slave-owners there, who had a scale of consumers' preferences quite different from anything that is now taken for granted in the west, were not easily persuaded by the generalizations, echoing Adam Smith, advanced by anti-slavery advocates—for example by Lugard, who quite reasonably maintained that 'from an economic point of view slave labour and forced labour are the least productive of results in proportion to capital expended'.[2]

Nachtigal found that, especially in the larger centres of population, practically all the menial work was done by slaves, and his firm adhesion to the principle of employing only free wage-earners created great difficulties for him. The performance of a free servant was, in his experience, inferior to that of a slave, and at the same time he expected to be better treated.[3] Clapperton, however, had no high regard for slave productivity, at least in Borgu, estimating

[1] Adam Smith, *Wealth of Nations*, 1937 edition, 81.
[2] Lugard, 1933, 14.   [3] i, 630.

that 'a smart English servant would accomplish their hardest day's work in an hour'; it was fair to recall, he continued, that, if the work was light, the food was light too.[4]

In Kuka Nachtigal never succeeded in recruiting any satisfactory free local resident. He first employed men who had entered his service in Tripoli at the outset of his expedition, and these were later gradually replaced in part by members of a troop of young Moroccan pilgrims who were hoping to make their way to Mecca by putting on acrobatic displays in the towns through which they passed, and by chance had joined the caravan with which Nachtigal travelled from Murzuq to Kuka, and some of whom subsequently quarrelled with their leader. Even these men he found it embarrassing to ask to do work for him which, according to the custom of the country, normally fell to slaves, or worse to slave women. The problem was finally solved by the device mentioned earlier (see above p. 40) of transferring to his service two of Shaykh Umar's slaves on the understanding that they would be freed after their arrival in Egypt.[5] A later observer noted deep-rooted convictions about the appropriate functions of free men and slaves producing some inconvenient short-run economic effects when in the twentieth century the French insisted that slaves in Niger should be freed. Men who had formerly been slaves did much less work than before; they decked themselves out as if they were great men, and, far from being grateful for their liberation, some even reproached the French for not permitting them to keep slaves of their own.[6]

Agricultural workers

The majority of the slave, as of the free, population of sub-Saharan Africa was probably employed in agriculture. In

[4] Clapperton, 1829, 94.   [5] ii, 306–9.
[6] Marty, 1931, 214.

the sixteenth century in Songhay it was normal practice for the *askiya* to appoint in each village a *fanfa*, himself a slave, to distribute the necessary seed to the slave farm workers whom he supervised, and in return a certain part of the harvest was delivered to the *askiya*.[7] In the eighteenth century slave villages in Futa Jallon farmed the valleys, while their Fulani overlords lived above on hilltops or the edges of plateaux.[8] In the Sokoto empire slave farming on the fiefs of great men reached massive proportions. In Adamawa province Barth contrasted the restricted position of the emir Lauwal, many of whose slaves were tied to farm villages, with the greater power of some marcher lords, receiving food supplies from tribute and hence having their slave hosts always available for other service.[9] One town near Sokoto, Magaria, with the villages around it, was inhabited mainly by slaves of the rich of Sokoto, raising grain and tending cattle. In one such village, visited by Clapperton in 1827, the slave-owner was the only free man in a population of 70.[10] Nachtigal observed that of the Arabs settled in Wadai, those engaged in agriculture relied almost exclusively on slave labour.[11]

Various systems were employed to regulate the pattern of slave-farming. Clapperton described the general practice in the Sokoto empire in 1826. A male slave of 18 or 19 would be given a wife, and sent to a village or farm in the country. There he and his wife built a hut, and were fed until harvest by their owner. The owner explained his planting requirements; beyond these, the slave might enclose land for himself. He worked for his owner from daylight to midday, and thereafter used his time as he pleased. At harvest each slave received about a bushel of each sort of grain, plus his own produce. During off-seasons, he had to obey if

[7] Kati, 179–80.
[8] Trimingham, 1962, 170.   [9] Barth, 1857–8, ii, 502–3.
[10] Clapperton, 1829, 192.   [11] iii, 206.

his master called on him to travel or to go to war.[12] The organization of agricultural work among the Hausa Muslims in the latter years of the nineteenth century was still much the same:

> Each slave had his own farming land. . . . In the early morning the slaves and their sons would go to their own farms. At this time of day (9.30 a.m.) they came back and went to the master's farm, the *gandu* fields until Azahar (2.30) when they returned. At noon food was taken out to them at the *gandu* farm. At Azahar they came in and rested, then in the afternoon the men went to their own farm-plots, and their wives and children went to their little plots too.[13]

In East Africa, slave cultivators worked under one of two arrangements. Some cultivated their master's land, paying him an *ijara*, that is a rent, each month, or perhaps annually; in this arrangement, the whole of the crop remained to the slaves, and the rent calculations took account of the abundance or paucity of the harvest. Under the other scheme, the master took the whole of the main harvest, sometimes even reaping it at his own expense; but he gave plots of land to his slaves, which they might cultivate for themselves on Thursdays and Fridays. Slaves under this arrangement paid no *ijara*.[14]

Somewhat similar schemes may survive the emancipation of the slave. Among the southern Tuareg today, many former slaves live as independent farmers, or as nomads organized in clans rather like their former masters. Freed slave farmers cultivate land owned by the Tuareg, with

---

[12] Clapperton, 1829, 213–14; Reade, 1864, 582.
[13] Mary Smith, 1954, 41.
[14] Beech, 1916, 147; he adds that slave-owners on the second system appeared more prosperous than those relying on *ijara*.

half shares in the crops; the landowner must pay for the cultivator's food for six months, and must supply half the seed and other necessaries. It is not many years since the cultivator received only one-fifth of his harvest.[15]

Although the free man as well as the slave of necessity often turned his hand to farming, there were many peoples among whom, or localities in which, agriculture was regarded as a sphere specially appropriate for slave labour. Among the Vai, for example, trade was esteemed a more fitting occupation for freemen, while women and slaves farmed;[16] and the same situation is implicit in several of the cases already cited in this section.

Further, within the general agricultural category slaves sometimes became specialized labourers with specific skills. We have already remarked the reluctance of the people of Tidjikdja to eliminate slaves lest there be then no one to care for the palm trees (see p. 68). On the east coast, tappers of coconut palm wine were among the most highly skilled and valuable slaves, comparable with traders, sailors and fishermen.[17] At Teyma oasis, in Arabia, where palm trees grew to a height of 15 fathoms, a few people only, and these all Negroes, dared to climb them for the fruit.[18]

Among the Trarza Moors of the western Sahara, slaves were expert in the collection of gum arabic, principal export of the region. At harvest time, the Trarza went to the gum-bearing districts, and settled there. Daily the slaves were sent out to collect the gum. In the evenings fires were lit, to inspect what had been gathered. Should a slave have brought too little, his masters would reprove and perhaps beat him; but the slave himself would in any case be

[15] Nicolaisen, 1963, 198.
[16] S. W. Koelle, *Narrative of an expedition into the Vy country of West Africa . . .* , London 1849, 29.
[17] Beech, 1916, 148.   [18] Doughty, 1923, i, 286.

ashamed to see one of his colleagues surpass him in the work.[19]

The list of such varieties of slave agricultural work might easily be extended. In Murzuq, Nachtigal found the simple operations required for diverting water into the irrigation channels in the gardens there were sometimes performed by oxen, but more commonly by donkeys or slaves.[20] In the Bornu villages he noted that the care of animals was usually entrusted to male slaves, while female slaves concentrated on domestic work.[21] The tending of livestock is a recurrent slave occupation: a visitor to Abeokuta, in southern Nigeria, in 1850 met a Fulani slave from Sokoto, apparently a Muslim, who had served his new masters for fifteen years, caring for their cattle.[22]

Perhaps the most important function of the slave as an agricultural specialist came in nomad economies. The traditional derivation of the name Timbuktu explains that it means 'the old woman', and refers to an old slave woman with whom the nomads left their goods when the place was just beginning to develop as an entrepôt.[23] This derivation is etymologically unlikely, but it does suggest the sort of settled role, within a primarily nomadic society, which slaves are believed to have fulfilled. Nachtigal thought that the relative scarcity of slaves in such poorer regions might have encouraged the inhabitants in their devotion to the nomadic life: in effect, that they were nomads at least partly because of lack of slaves.[24] Conversely, it has also been suggested that nomads, for instance some of the Tuareg, feeling that the accumulation of slaves was inconsistent with the

[19] al-Shinqiti, 1911, 494; 1953, 116 (the French account is slightly abbreviated here).
[20] i, 91.   [21] ii, 391.
[22] Bowen, 1857, 133. On one of the slave farms of a notable of Abeokuta Bowen met also a Hausa Muslim slave who, he was told, wished to escape from such servitude to a non-Muslim (137).
[23] al-Sadi, 36.   [24] ii, 97.

maintenance of their traditional way of life, kept the number of their slaves to a bare minimum, settling the surplus in villages where they had to pay tax.[25] It seems more likely, however, that the settled work of the slaves and the pastoralism of the nomads complemented one another in an essential fashion. The Tuareg, for example, cannot exist on pastoralism alone: good years are too few, and good times in each year too short—other food, from cultivation and the caravan trade, is necessary. Again, those in the Ahaggar mountains frequently have their camels grazing three hundred miles or more from their sheep and goats, and slaves were needed for these latter stock; indeed slave herdsmen, more knowledgeable perhaps than their Tuareg master about certain varieties of livestock, might have considerable influence.[26]

The transatlantic export trade and that from the interior of East Africa to the clove plantations of Zanzibar,[27] or the French island plantations of the Indian Ocean,[28] were also intended to supply mainly agricultural or plantation workers.

Farming was sometimes combined with trading. At Iendwe, near Lake Tanganyika, in the later nineteenth century, both Arab and Wanyamwezi caravans, trading for slaves and ivory, used to halt and farm, slaves and wives doing the work, while subsidiary expeditions went in search of trade.[29] At nearly the same time Hausa traders in Adamawa sometimes stopped and farmed with their wives and slaves, thus feeding themselves and gaining some surplus for further trade with the local people.[30]

25 Deherme, 1908, 396.   26 Nicolaisen, 1963, 442.
27 Gray, in Oliver and Mathew, 1963, 216–17.
28 Alison Smith, 'The southern section of the interior, 1840–84', in Oliver and Mathew, 1963, 268–9.
29 Thomson, 1881, ii, 16–18.
30 H. Dominik, Kamerun, Berlin 1901, 76; cit. J. Lippert, 'Die Bedeutung der Haussanation . . .', Mitteilungen des Seminars für Orientalische Sprachen in Berlin, 1907, 208–9.

Occasionally the slave trade rendered valuable assistance in introducing new crops. Portuguese slavers brought the peanut from America to West Africa in the sixteenth century,[31] and coffee is said to have been introduced first from Ethiopia into the Yemen—this was perhaps also a result of the slave trade, and Galla slaves might be found in the Arabian peninsula in the nineteenth century who told of the coffee trees at home.[32]

Artisans

Of artisans, many of whom were apparently free men, Nachtigal gave no systematic account, but slaves were mentioned by him as assisting an architect or builder, or participating in domestic cotton handicrafts.[33] Slaves from Massenya, capital of Bagirmi, had a good reputation as weavers.[34] Both building and cloth work have been common tasks for slaves. Judar Pasha, conqueror of Timbuktu for Morocco in 1592, used the services of slaves from various Timbuktu households to build a fortress in the city.[35] In Hausaland in 1826 Clapperton witnessed bands of men and women slaves, accompanied by drums and flutes and singing in chorus, passing to and from the river with water to mix clay for repairing the city walls; each great man had his part of the wall to build, as the Jews built the walls of Jerusalem each man opposite his own house.[36] In Timbuktu in 1828 Caillié saw slaves working as masons and bricklayers,[37] just as slaves in Mecca itself were often employed in building, and in other heavier work such as quarrying. In Mecca, young slaves were sometimes put to such

[31] M. A. Klein, 1968, 37.   [32] Doughty, 1923, i, 247.
[33] i, 622–3.   [34] ii, 669.
[35] J. C. Hunwick, 'Ahmad Baba and the Moroccan invasion of the Sudan', *Journal of the Historical Society of Nigeria*, 1962, 319.
[36] Clapperton, 1829, 98; Nehemiah iii, 28.
[37] Caillié, 1830, ii, 344.

work in the hope that they would thus also acquire a more fluent command of the Arabic language.[38]

Clapperton spoke of Nupe slaves in Sokoto in 1824, the men considered the most expert weavers in the Sudan, the women the best spinners.[39] Spinning was generally assigned to married women, or to some favourite old female slaves.[40] In Borgu also, where slaves were numerous, the men included weaving among their various tasks, while the women spun and prepared the yarn for the loom.[41] Female slaves were not always judged solely on their merits as concubines; south-east of Mandara the Musgo women were particularly disagreeable in appearance, but were very trustworthy and capable of great labour.[42]

Nachtigal also mentioned slaves belonging to the people of Ngigmi, the northernmost Bornuan town on the road from Murzuq to Kuka, who were employed in the salt-works to the south of the town, in a village whose name, which Nachtigal gave as Kindschalia, meant 'the slave place'.[43] Slave salt-mines are of considerable antiquity in the Sahara; Ibn Battuta described those of Taghaza.[44] As late as the 1930s reports of peculiarly horrible conditions in the salt-mines of the western Jouf were still current.[45] Ibn Battuta observed slaves also mining and casting copper, in Tadkeda; both men and women took part.[46]

Nachtigal's friend Lamino (see above p. 13) was particularly proud to include among his several thousand slaves a group of skilled female cooks from all the countries between the Nile and the Niger.[47] Barth had travelled with a slave-

[38] Hurgronje, 1931, 11.
[39] Denham and Clapperton, 1826, B, 113.
[40] Clapperton, 1829, 221.   [41] ibid., 94.
[42] Denham and Clapperton, 1826, A, 69–70.
[43] i, 570.   [44] Ibn Battuta, A, 317–18; C, iv, 377–8.
[45] W. Seabrook, The white monk of Timbuctoo, London 1934, 259; J. Wellard, Lost worlds of Africa, London 1967, 145–6.
[46] Ibn Battuta, A, 336; C, iv, 440–1.   [47] i, 601.

raid against the Musgo, in 1851, on which this same Lamino
was present, and had praised at that time the excellent cook-
ing of one of Lamino's slave women who was accompanying her master.[48] As early as the eleventh century the female slave cooks of Awdaghast, in the western Sahara, were
highly valued, selling for 100 mithqals, gold pieces, or
more.[49] In the nineteenth century in Rio de Janeiro, skilled
cooks, Negro slaves, were in great request.[50] Even where
such *cordon bleu* standards were not maintained, female
slaves might cook and even sell their creations on the
market, as Clapperton noticed in Borgu and Sokoto—the
food included fried fish, the fish caught by young slaves.[51]

Among the Fulani, a people devoted to their cattle, the
work of butchering was always left to slaves. This custom
was used symbolically to stir up in revolt Ali, Sarkim Gobir,
a Hausa chief who had collaborated with the Fulani after
their *jihad*, and had received appointment by Bello, Fulani
sultan of Sokoto. Hausa resisters sent Ali a set of butcher's
knives, thus indicating that he was merely a slave of the
Fulani. This device succeeded in persuading him to throw
off his allegiance.[52]

Slaves took part in many other types of work also; Christian slaves sawed wood in Fez,[53] and there were slave drum-
mers in Sokoto.[54] Tremearne's Hausa stories include a

---

[48] Barth, 1857–8, iii, 129.   [49] al-Bakri, 300–1.

[50] J. Candler and W. Burgess, *Narrative of a recent visit to Brazil*,
London 1853, 38–9.

[51] Clapperton, 1829, 94, 211.

[52] Johnston, 1967, 130 and n. In many parts of tropical Africa,
where the need to guard against eating ritually unclean food is real,
Muslims exercise a virtual monopoly of butchering. But in North
Africa the trade is scorned: in Kabylia, only the Akli, black or mulatto descendants of slaves, are butchers; and it is the Homria, offspring of Mzabite men and Negro women, who form a separate caste
at Ghardaïa and act in Algiers as butchers or scavengers (X. de Plan-
hol, *The world of Islam*, Cornell 1959, 66–7).

[53] Leo Africanus, A, ii, 442; B, i, 203.

[54] Clapperton, 1829, 254.

passing reference to 'the market of the Filani Slaves who bring wood'.[55] Technically skilled people might, on being enslaved, pass at once into special service. In Tripoli, doctors went straight to the Dey, and were the best-treated slaves; one, a French naval surgeon, captured in 1668, has left an account of his experiences.[56]

Caravan workers

The absence of adequate means of transport has often been adduced as one of the most important reasons for the persistence of slavery in Africa before the development of modern means of communication.[57] Leo Africanus twice mentioned slaves as essential for caravans in the Sudan: for caravans going in search of gold, over paths too rough for camels, slaves carried merchandise as well as food for their masters and guards (and presumably for themselves);[58] and large bodies of slaves helped to protect the merchants of Agades on the dangerous route between Kano and Bornu, being speedily set to some useful business at each halting place to avoid idleness.[59] The most important function of the slaves owned by Mandingoes in the Boporo area in Liberia, where slaves in the 1860s were said to outnumber free men by three to one, was to serve as 'carriers for their masters in the trade of salt and country cloths'.[60]

In the employment of porters, as elsewhere, it was not al-

[55] Tremearne, 1913, 340. For non-Muslim examples, Newitt (1969, 76–7) mentions that slaves on the Portuguese *prazos*, or grants of crown land, on the Zambesi included among their jobs those of boatman, fisherman, trader, hunter, carpenter, basket-maker, goldsmith, musician, iron-worker, barber, cook, etc.

[56] De la Roncière, 1919, 73–4.

[57] A. McPhee, *The economic revolution in British West Africa*, London 1926, 126–7, 249–50.

[58] Leo Africanus, A, iii, 832; B, ii, 479.

[59] *ibid.*, A, iii, 820; B, ii, 473–4.   [60] Anderson, 1870, 41.

ways easy to draw a clear line between slave and free. Clapperton twice mentioned Hausa and Bornu caravans whose carriers included both men and women slaves, as well as women working for hire.[61] European explorers might prefer hiring porters for wages, but many of those hired were in fact slaves.[62]

Some slaves possessed skills of advantage to an entire caravan. A German explorer, halted by a flooded river, 70 metres across, in the Cameroon, watched a small Hausa caravan cross. All its goods were packed in small portions, and put one by one into a large gourd, which one slave, a powerful swimmer, ferried back and forth. Then the same slave helped over the men and women who could not themselves swim. All crossed safely, and the face of the slave, commented the explorer, Zintgraff, 'shone with proud satisfaction'.[63] A somewhat similar device was described by Nachtigal in Logon.[64] Some slaves round Lake Tanganyika became seamen on Arab dhows,[65] and on the east coast dhow crewmen were one of the most highly valued categories of slave.[66] At Suez, too, slaves were employed on coastal sailing vessels.[67] Even on trans-Atlantic slavers, sailing to Brazil, slaves purchased in Brazil were sometimes among the crews: nearly half the ships between 1799 and 1810 apparently carried some slave crewmen, averaging as many as 14 per vessel.[68] Some of the settlers in the colonies described above (see pp. 110–11), established in the nineteenth century, were runaway slave seamen. Not all slaves were gifted in this way; a young man whom Lander

[61] Clapperton, 1829, 68, 137.   [62] Thomson, 1881, i, 67–8.
[63] E. Zintgraff, Nord-Kamerun, Berlin 1895, 308.
[64] ii, 753–4.   [65] Speke, 1864, 230; Burton, 1860, ii, 96–7.
[66] Beech, 1916, 148.
[67] G. Baer, 'Slavery in nineteenth-century Egypt', Journal of African History, 1967, 421.
[68] H. S. Klein, 'The trade in African slaves to Rio de Janeiro, 1795–1811', Journal of African History, 1969, 541–3.

bought in Zaria was terrified at the prospect of crossing the Niger even in a boat. He was finally persuaded to do so, but fainted immediately on reaching the other side.[69]

The variety of languages which a miscellaneous group of slaves would speak might greatly help a caravan passing through several countries.[70] Slaves too might help to find the way for a caravan in areas which they knew well. Harris told how, on his way towards Ethiopia from Berbera, his caravan, travelling at night because of the extreme heat in the coastal plain, lost its way, until a female slave redirected it 'when all the lords of creation were at fault'.[71] Slaves might also help market the goods of a caravan; Hausa caravans in Nupe sent slaves peddling small wares round the markets and private houses.[72]

Such assistance was not confined to the secular: we have already mentioned (see pp. 67–8) the very real advantages accruing to a trans-Saharan caravan in this century from the fits of spirit possession of a freed slave woman in the party. Nor was the assistance confined to the practical: Richardson recalled how, on a tedious journey in the central Sahara, a slave of the caravan 'amused us with playing his rude bagpipe through these weary wastes'.[73]

In addition to these and other services, sometimes indispensable, rendered by slaves as simple porters, they also sometimes played an important part in the organisation of caravans. Nachtigal mentioned two instances where a slave was assigned a position of responsibility. On the road from Murzuq to Kuka, his team of servants was supplemented by a Hausa slave of one of the leading men of Murzuq, who took the opportunity to send two camel loads of merchandise to Bornu.[74] Apparently—there is no specific refer-

[69] Lander, in Clapperton, 1829, 312–13.
[70] Thomson, 1881, i, 29–30; Speke, 1863, xxvii.
[71] Harris, 1844, i, 208.   [72] Clapperton, 1829, 138.
[73] Richardson, 1848, i, 408.   [74] i, 490.

ence to this—the man returned to his master in Murzuq when he had disposed of the goods. Later, on the expedition to Bagirmi, the horse sent with Nachtigal by the Sharif el-Medeni to be sold to the king of Bagirmi was placed in the care of one of the Sherif's Hausa slaves.[75] When this man fell ill, he had to be left behind with a village chief with one Maria Theresa dollar to cover expenses,[76] and was sent back to Kuka sometime before Nachtigal's return. In Ghadames in the 1840s, Richardson met a slave who was sent every year by his master to buy and sell, 'as if a regular free merchant'. The slave, a little apologetically, assured Richardson that he brought 'few slaves, and mostly goods'.[77]

The attainment by slaves of command positions in caravans is particularly noted in the nineteenth-century East African trade. Cameron in 1874, west of Lake Tanganyika, met a caravan comprised of a few freedmen each with one or two slaves, two small traders with a dozen men each, and the main body of 250 porters divided between an Arab and the slave of an Arab.[78] Such situations were not rare.[79] A man might at the same time be the chief of a large village and the slave of an Arab.[80]

Caravan workers often combined private trade, and even private trade in slaves, with their group responsibilities. Nachtigal's supply difficulties on the road back to Kuka from Bagirmi were greatly increased by the investments in slaves made in Bagirmi by one of his servants and by the guide assigned to him by Shaykh Umar;[81] the story of the frequent and sometimes successful efforts of these slaves to escape is a constantly recurring theme in his account of this part of his travels (see pp. 92–3). Many early European

[75] ii, 482.
[76] ii, 566.   [77] Richardson, 1848, i, 188; cf., 260.
[78] Cameron, 1885, 253; see also 230.   [79] ibid., 58, 61, 218.
[80] ibid., 49.   [81] ii, 635–6, 650.

travellers experienced similar difficulties. Burton told of porters investing their earnings, on reaching Lake Tanganyika, in slaves and ivory; those who bought slaves deserted as promptly as possible, in order to hurry home before the slaves escaped.[82] Speke, travelling with Burton, described how extra cloth had to be given to some of their caravan officials, who had bought slaves and had to make occasional presents to discourage escape.[83] Arnot in Katanga found his porters spending all their earnings on slaves, so that his camp became 'a regular slave-pen'.[84]

A final specialized duty of caravan slaves was to be useful to their masters when they went on pilgrimage to Mecca. When Mansa Musa, emperor of Mali, went on pilgrimage in the fourteenth century, he was preceded by 500 slaves, each bearing a staff of gold.[85] In the nineteenth century, Momodu Lamine (see p. 123) had several slaves who carried before him the 300 Qurans which he had collected during his own long pilgrimage.[86] Other pilgrimage slaves might supply less spiritual paraphernalia: in 1876, in the pilgrimage caravan from Damascus, the Persian aga and his son were followed by a Galla slave, from East Africa, bearing fire in an iron sling, to kindle the nargilies, or hubble-bubbles.[87] Slaves sometimes became a more permanent element in pilgrimage arrangements. At the end of the sixteenth century Idris Alooma, ruler of Bornu, founded a pilgrim hostel in Arabia, with slaves as part of the endowment.[88] A freedman might achieve a post of real authority in pilgrimage organization: the *amir al-hajj*, conductor of the pilgrim convoy, which Doughty observed passing through Arabia from Persia in 1877, was a 'home-born'

[82] Burton, 1860, ii, 74.   [83] Speke, 1864, 264.
[84] Arnot, 1889, 184–5.   [85] al-Sadi, 12–13.
[86] Fisher, 1970, 59.   [87] Doughty, 1923, i, 66.
[88] Ibn Fartua, 11.

Galla; his father had been a slave from Africa, but the son
was born in the house of his master, Ibn Rashid.[89]

Some of these pilgrimage slaves might be used as a form
of travellers' cheques, to help finance the trip.[90] It is possible that some of the slaves from distant lands, such as
those from British India and from the Dutch East Indies
who were observed in the slave market of Mecca in the
1880s,[91] may have served such a purpose. Colonial governments, even in the twentieth century, found the sale of
slaves accompanying pilgrims, and disguised as servants or
fellow pilgrims, particularly difficult to check. The Dutch
attempted to deal with this, for pilgrims from Java, by a
system of passports, coupled with a representative—Muslim
of course—in Mecca. The British Indian government did the
same.[92] In 1960 some Moor or Tuareg notables were reported to have covered part of their pilgrimage expenses by
selling slaves in Arabia.[93]

On the other hand, the purchase of slaves sometimes involved the imprudent pilgrim in financial difficulties.
Mansa Musa of Mali overspent on slaves and other commodities during his celebrated fourteenth century pilgrimage (see pp. 119, 145) and had to borrow money in Egypt
on his way home. A ruler, or *mai*, of Bornu in the seventeenth or eighteenth century gave so largely in alms that

[89] Doughty, 1923, ii, 50; another son of the same slave father was
a 'principal personage' in Hayil, where Ibn Rashid ruled (i, 603).
[90] Ibn Khaldun, ii, 113; al-Umari, 90; Kati, 25–6; Harris, 1844,
i, 379; Trimingham, 1962, 32.
[91] Hurgronje, 1931, 13.
[92] Lugard, 1933, 13. He thought that investigation of the history
of slaves liberated by Consular agents at Jidda and elsewhere might
throw light on methods of enslavement, and he suggested that the
permanent Slavery Bureau set up by the League of Nations in 1932
might undertake this work among other things (1933, 7).
[93] Froelich, 1962, 155; cf. A. H. M. Kirk-Greene, 'The major
currencies in Nigerian history', *Journal of the Historical Society of
Nigeria*, 1960, 141.

he was unable to pay for certain slaves which were brought to him in the Hijaz, until the prayers of his accompanying clerics miraculously transmuted pebbles into gold: he then completed the purchase of the slaves, and resumed his alms-giving.[94] The pilgrimage caravans returning from Mecca to the Middle East often carried with them newly pur-chased slaves to supply the markets there.[95]

Among these various pilgrimage slaves, some became pil-grims themselves, for the pilgrimage of a slave is valid if per-formed with the consent of his master (see above p. 48). An interesting tale is told of Askiya Daud, a sixteenth-century ruler of Songhay, who inadvertently kissed the hand of one of his own slaves among the returning pilgrims; on dis-covering his mistake, the *askiya* at first wished to have the hand cut off, but finally agreed not to punish its presump-tion for the sake of the sacred rites it had performed in Mecca.[96] In the Hanafi school of law, which, however, is almost unknown in black Africa, a slave is allowed to per-form the pilgrimage as deputy for someone else.[97]

The treatment of slaves who were serving as caravan work-ers sometimes partook of the cruelty accorded to slaves on the march as merchandise (see above pp. 92-5),[98] but there is evidence also to suggest that some degree of com-radeship might be achieved amongst the working party on the road. Clapperton in the 1820s, watching a group of Gonja traders in a Hausa caravan passing through Bariba, observed how slave girls, though compelled to carry heavy

[94] el-Nager, 1969, 398-9.
[95] Doughty, 1923, i, 209. But in 1877, he could not see five such slaves in the whole Damascus caravan. A stout Negro lad might be bought from the returning pilgrims for about 60 reals (then about £11), the price of two camels or a common riding camel (i, 553).
[96] Kati, 204-7.   [97] el-Nager, 1969, 16.
[98] German traders in Cameroon complained that their Hausa rivals loaded and overloaded slaves without government interference, de-spite a decree in 1908 regulating the maximum permitted loads (Rudin, 1936, 334).

loads on their heads, yet were 'as cheerful and good-natured as if they were at home grinding corn in their own native country'.[99] It was reported that in a caravan returning from the coast to Futa Jallon, 'even the slaves were relaxed into familiarity never permitted in the towns, while masters would sometimes be seen relieving the servants by bearing their burdens'.[100]

Luxury slaves

The wealthy might indulge in luxury slaves, whose work was often of a more frivolous nature. The Bornu dignitaries of Nachtigal's time, who attended Shaykh Umar when he was planning a new capital, had long files of slaves to carry their meals on the hour-and-a-half journey to the site, so that they might continue there to enjoy the comfortable living to which they were accustomed.[101] One corpulent dignitary, encumbered by the bulky garments which were fashionable in Kuka, was assisted in mounting his horse by some half-dozen slaves, who then trotted after him, carrying his weapons and other accoutrements,[102] and a similar practice was followed by others.[103] Clapperton in Sokoto in 1824 had interceded on behalf of the slave of an official, whose job it was to run by the side of his master's horse carrying spears; for pretending lameness he had been heavily shackled, a severity however which Clapperton said was rare.[104] In his hours of ease Nachtigal's corpulent friend sat surrounded by his female slaves, some of whom massaged his unwieldy legs, while others kept him cool with fans or amused him with their piquant conversation.[105]

Nachtigal was once confronted with the prospect of be-

[99] Clapperton, 1829, 75–9.   [100] Canot, 1928, 139.
[101] iii, 17.   [102] i, 590.   [103] i, 621.
[104] Denham and Clapperton, 1826, B, 100–1.
[105] i, 604; ii, 290–1.

coming a luxury slave himself. While he was virtually a prisoner in Tibesti, a visitor from Borku thought it might be a good idea to purchase both him and his Piedmontese servant, who later turned Muslim and left Nachtigal's service. They would have some interest as curiosities, but as they would be worthless as working slaves, no more could be offered for them than one good strong camel.[106]

Nachtigal's story confirms the view that in many parts of Africa the possession of a large number of slaves had become a status symbol.[107] In a country such as Bornu, rich in slaves, there was, as he observed, an endless number of luxury servants[108] who, serving only the changing whims of their masters, had lost almost completely any capacity they may have had for regular useful work.[109] In Kano in 1851 Barth contrasted the host of idle, insolent slaves following a rich governor on horseback with the half-naked, half-starved slaves on sale, in rows like cattle, in a market shed.[110] The influential slaves of distinguished masters, Nachtigal noted, imitated their masters' habit of ostentatiously wearing more clothes than was at all suitable for the normally high temperatures of Kuka.[111]

The urge to accumulate slaves remained strong even when there seemed to be no obvious immediate use to which they could be put. This was especially noticeable in Ba-

[106] i, 337–8.
[107] 'Slaves were valuable property, but they also had prestige value'; F. Mahoney and H. C. Idowu, 'Peoples of the Senegambia', in Ajayi and Espie, 1965, 136. Visitors to Bahia, early in the eighteenth century, were struck by the numbers of domestic slaves, and by the way in which slave-owners loved to make a parade of these to show off their wealth (Verger, 1968, 70).
[108] i, 631.
[109] Though such a factor is scarcely susceptible of precise analysis, it is perhaps worth recalling the possible, or even probable, ill-effects on the masters, of having such slaves. Doughty in Arabia commented on a young prince: 'For his age he was corrupt of heart and covetous; but they are all brought up by slaves!' (1923, vol. i, 614).
[110] Barth, 1857–8, ii, 108.   [111] i, 620–1.

girmi. At the time of Nachtigal's visit there, the king, Abu
Sekkin, and his followers were living in conditions of such
stress that it was quite impossible to offer Nachtigal hospitality befitting the royal dignity. Food supplies were desperately short, but nevertheless Abu Sekkin continued to
press his tributaries to discharge their obligations to deliver
slaves to him, and with his own people made numerous
slave-raids on the Pagans in the surrounding country, although the hostility thus provoked added greatly to his supply difficulties. It was more than three months before any
of the slaves captured on these raids could be channelled
into the export market, and in the meantime the domestic
market was so glutted that, even with the supply being
diminished by the ravages of disease, they could be purchased for next to nothing.[112] Adult men could be obtained
for less than a quarter of the normal Kuka market price,
and small children, unlikely to be able to stand the rigours
of a difficult journey, were almost given away.[113] Nachtigal explained that Abu Sekkin had been driven into the
Pagan regions by hunger and lack of money; without an
adequate supply of slaves he would have had nothing with
which to reward his faithful followers or to pay his debts.[114]
The urge to push on with the accumulation of slaves, even
in such highly unfavourable conditions, may however also
be plausibly interpreted as indicating that the principle
enunciated by Adam Smith in his analysis of the economics
of slavery, 'the pride of man makes him love to domi-
neer',[115] was also a powerful element in the economic structure of Bagirmi.

[112] ii, 652.
[113] ii, 634, 652.   [114] ii, 610.
[115] Wealth of nations, book iii, chap. 2.

CHAPTER VII

THE DOMESTIC SCENE IV: SLAVES AND THE STATE

Slaves, in addition to performing various duties such as those described in the previous chapter, on behalf of the ordinary slave-owning citizen, might also discharge important responsibilities on behalf of the state. This chapter discusses such state functions under four headings: slaves as colonists, slaves as soldiers, royal slaves, and the special category of eunuchs.

Colonists

Colonization has a long and varied history in Africa, as parties of immigrants enter new territories, and there endeavour to maintain their own distinct way of life in their own separate societies. Some of these attempts at colonization have led to the subjugation of the original inhabitants; sometimes, in revenge as it were, the original inhabitants have absorbed the newcomers; or it may be that the two groups settle into some sort of partnership. The period of European imperialism, in the colonies of settlement in Africa, is a recent and powerful illustration of this; the same basic pattern was also discernible in some of the Muslim movements of expansion in the nineteenth century, particularly for example in the policy of al-Hajj Umar, exhorting his Tokolor countrymen from the Senegal regions to

settle among the Bambara on the upper Niger; and it has
been going on, quite independently of European or Muslim
influence, in countless instances throughout the continent,
sometimes, as in the Bantu expansion, on a most grand
scale.

Occasionally slaves have played an important part in such
colonization, serving various purposes: the role of slaves as
colonists, however, is in one respect peculiar, for it may be
that the slaves themselves, if they are for instance newly
captured prisoners of war, are not representative of the culture of the colonizing authority, but are, at least at the beginning, only handy instruments of that authority.

One aspect of the expansion of Kano in the fifteenth century was the establishment of imported prisoners in special
towns: one official is said to have founded twenty-one such
towns, of 1000 slaves each, and from these settlements first-
born virgins later supplied the royal *harim*.[1] In the nineteenth century Adamawa was a country of slave colonies,[2]
and slave agriculturalists helped more quickly to settle and
absorb the territory surrounding towns newly conquered by
the expanding Fulani emirate there.[3] King Ali of Wadai's
policy of settling the Bagirmians whom he had captured in
1872 with a view to accelerating the economic development
of his country has already been mentioned (see pp. 39-40).

Slave colonies also helped in providing bases for distant
travel in commercial and religious pursuits alike. We mentioned that as early as the ninth century Asian slave merchants were established in Fezzan (see p. 72); one of the
rulers of Bornu, whose probable date is about 1000, set up

[1] *Kano Chronicle*, in Palmer, 1928, iii, 109-12; M. G. Smith,
'The beginnings of Hausa society', in J. Vansina and others, *The
historian in tropical Africa*, London 1964 (hereafter M. G. Smith,
1964 B), 351.
[2] Barth, 1857-8, ii, 478, 509-10.
[3] C. V. Boyle, 'Historical notes on the Yola Fulani', *Journal of the
African Society*, 1910-1, 85.

three slave settlements in Fezzan,[4] and it seems a reasonable guess that these had some commercial significance. Turning again to the theme of slaves and pilgrimage, on various occasions we are told of substantial numbers of slaves settled *en route* by intending pilgrims. Dunama, ruler of Bornu early in the twelfth century, went on pilgrimage three times, and each time established 300 slaves in Cairo; finally the Cairenes, so the story runs, fearing some ulterior motive on his part, caused him to be drowned.[5] Among the earliest Muslim visitors to Hausaland was a party of learned men and others who passed through, going towards Bornu and coming from the west; a number of these people, including some slaves, stopped and settled among the Hausa.[6] The seventeenth- or eighteenth-century Bornu *mai* mentioned above (p. 146) whose name is given, perhaps erroneously, as Ali bin Umar, is remembered as having settled 5000 slaves in Bagirmi, and 4000 in each of two places in Wadai, leaving them there on his journey to Mecca and confirming them on his way home.[7] What lay behind such settlements is not clearly known; perhaps the slaves were, through farming and other activities, to amass supplies for the use of the returning pilgrims.

Slave colonists in the desert, attending to oases, also helped mobility, in addition to supplying an essential economic counterpart to the nomadic activities of the original Saharans (see p. 138). Without the oases the desert would have been an impenetrable barrier between the Mediterranean world and tropical Africa.[8] And without slaves many oases would have gone untended. Many, but not all, for, in

[4] Ibn Fartua, 67.   [5] Ibn Fartua, 11; Barth, 1857–8, ii, 275, 635.
[6] *Kano Chronicle*, 111.
[7] el-Nager, 1969, 134–5, 395 ff., reproducing an unpublished manuscript.
[8] Barbour, *A survey of northwest Africa*, London 1959, 342–3.

Richardson's words, 'many a happy oasis is without a slave'.[9]
He visited one, Sidi Mabed, near Ghadames. He had been
told that the people of Sidi Mabed disapproved of slave-
holding, and he went there in hopes of finding sympathizers
with his own strenuous abhorrence of slavery and the slave
trade; but the explanation of one of the villagers was, alas,
disappointing: 'If we had money we would have slaves; we
have no slaves, because we have no money.'[10]

Soldiers

Slave participation in military activities has a long history.
The following are a few examples from within the Sudan.
In the fourteenth century, when Yaji, the first Muslim ruler
of Kano, failed to take an enemy town by means of the
prayers of his newly arrived Muslim subjects, he then followed the advice of a shrewd slave and the expedition was
crowned with success.[11] In the sixteenth century, Askiya
Daud of Songhay reduced the whole army of the empire to
slavery. Previously, the askiya had inherited only the horse,
the shield and the javelins of each soldier; now he would
inherit everything. As for the askiyas' continued habit of
taking the daughters of their soldiers as concubines, the
chroniclers resignedly commented, 'We are the Lord's, and
to Him we must return'.[12] The Funj, in the eastern Sudan,
employed an extensive slave army. The growth of that empire led to the settlement of a standing army of slaves, mainly
from the Nuba mountains of Kordofan, in villages around
Sennar, where Bruce found them in 1772. These may
have played some small part in spreading Islam among their
own people, though Bruce thought that they were them-

[9] Richardson, 1848, i, xxviii.   [10] ibid., i, 285-6.
[11] Kano Chronicle, 105-6.
[12] Kati, 211; Rouch, 1953, 206; Quran, Surah ii, 157.

selves hardly Muslim, and we do not know how many of them ever saw their homes again.[13]

Slave soldiers formed a special category in foreign trade both as imports and as exports. In North Africa bands of European slaves sometimes formed an élite army corps; the same was true of Negro groups exported from the Sudan.[14] Slaves from East Africa were important in India, especially as soldiers, as early as the fourteenth or fifteenth centuries.[15] Ahmad Graan, Muslim scourge of Ethiopia in the six-teenth century, sent Ethiopian slaves to the Turks in Arabia and received a large body of Janissaries in return.[16] Alooma of Bornu, at the end of the same century, also had Turkish help.

> Among the benefits which God (Most High) of His bounty and beneficence, generosity and constancy con-ferred upon the Sultan was the acquisition of Turk-ish musketeers and numerous household slaves who be-came skilled in firing muskets.[17]

In the seventeenth century the pasha of Tripoli sent fifty young Europeans to Bornu in an exchange which included, among other things, 200 horses and some muskets from Tripoli, and 100 young men and 100 girls from Bornu. The succeeding *mai* of Bornu, in view of the satisfactory performance of these Europeans, sent to ask for some more, accompanying his request with 200 young slaves and several eunuchs. He received the solicited Christians, and 50 horses too.[18]

Special regulations sometimes applied to the weapons

[13] Stevenson, in Lewis, 1966, 210–11.
[14] al-Umari, 114, 146–7.
[15] Mathew, in Oliver and Mathew, 1963, 121 and n.
[16] Harris, 1844, ii, 234; Pory, introduction to Leo Africanus, A, i, 52.
[17] Ibn Fartua, 11.   [18] De la Roncière, 1919, 79, 83–4.

which slave soldiers might use. These regulations might
be restrictive: among the Tuareg, the servile classes were
not allowed to wear a sword, nor to carry an iron spear,
these being distinctions of a free man;[19] but slaves did
carry some sort of weapon, and in the old days, when cattle-
raiding and warfare formed part of the Tuareg way of life,
they often accompanied their masters on raids.[20] In other
cases, however, slaves were encouraged in the exclusive use
of certain weapons. We do not know if Alooma's Turks,
mentioned on the previous page, were slaves, but clearly
some, if not all, of the soldiers who carried the newly acquired firearms were. Clapperton, observing Sultan Bello's
unsuccessful attack on the Hausa capital of Gobir in 1826,
noticed that all the forty-one muskets marshalled by the
Kano contingent among the attackers were handled by
slaves, not one by a Fulani.[21] Such arrangements may re-
flect the desire of the ruler to keep these weapons strictly
under his own control; the king of Ethiopia did not like to
let the guns of his matchlockmen out of his sight.[22] Perhaps
also the old aristocracy found the new weapons undignified
and unworthy. A parallel instance, though not involving
firearms, appears among a branch of the Danakil, in the
area of modern French Somaliland. They deemed unlawful
in their own persons the use of the bow, and maintained
some 100 Somali archers; these were originally prisoners of
war, who, though naturalized among their captors, retained
their own language and never intermarried with the Danakil.[23] Slaves themselves were not always exempt from a
similar conservatism, as the inability of the Egyptian Mam-

[19] Barth, 1857–8, i, 237.   [20] Nicolaisen, 1967, 442.
[21] Clapperton, 1829, 186.
[22] Harris, 1844, i, 371; ii, 57, describes the general of the gun-
men, riding a gaily caparisoned mule, richly attired, followed by
fifty attendants—'but he too is a slave, as was his father before him
and as his son will be after him'.
[23] Harris, 1844, i, 225.

luk dynasty to adjust to firearms, in attempting to resist the rise of the Ottomans, indicates.[24] Distinct foreign groups, serving specialized military functions and sometimes carrying particular weapons, were of course not necessarily slaves. In Ashanti, for example, a royal bodyguard of Hausa, hired by the king, used the Snider rifles in the royal armoury.[25]

In the nineteenth century the employment of slave troops continued, though some of the more thoroughgoing Islamic theocracies appear not to have relied on this device extensively. In East Africa, Arab and Swahili traders deployed slave soldiers. About 1840 a regular Arab colony was established in the Tabora area, in modern Tanzania, under Abdullah bin Salim, a recognized leader, with 200 armed slaves.[26] The armed slaves of the Arabs played a prominent part in the Muslim *coup d'état* which, temporarily, placed power in Buganda in Muslim hands in 1888.[27] Ngongo Lutete, a former slave of Tippu Tib, became himself a powerful chief in the Congo. At first allied with the Arabs against the Congo Free State of King Leopold, he changed sides in 1892. He and his 1500 men, armed with guns, were a help to the Belgians, despite the embarrassment caused by their rushing on to the field after each battle to eat their slain enemies.[28] Rabih, another noted slaver, may himself have once been a slave, but this is disputed.[29]

In the eastern Sudan, after the Egyptian conquest of the area by Muhammad Ali in 1821, Nubians were recruited into the administration's slave army, the *jihadiyya*, just as in Funj times; and this army was subsequently taken over

[24] D. Ayalon, *Gunpowder and Firearms in the Mamluk Kingdom*, London 1956, 47.
[25] A. B. Ellis, *The land of fetish*, London 1883, 215.
[26] Smith, in Oliver and Mathew, 1963, 270.
[27] Oliver, 1965, 106–7.   [28] Slade, 1962, 108 ff.
[29] Trimingham, 1962, 218; Schultze, 1913, 282, 300–1; Lippert, 1899, 243–4; Macleod, 1912, 143–4.

by the Mahdists. Ex-soldiers, or runaways, returning home in this later period might thus have spent considerable time in a strongly Muslim environment.[30] Salih Shanqa, a Takruri notable at al-Qallabat, on the Sudan-Ethiopia border, had a personal retinue of 4000 slaves, who carried firearms for him in war, and cultivated his villages in peace; with these, together with tribesmen and Egyptian government troops, he held the Mahdists at bay for some time.[31]

In Bornu, in the central Sudan, there are repeated references to slave troops and officers. Al-Kanemi was always attended on his expeditions by about 100 chiefs and favourite slaves.[32] The commander-in-chief of the army at that time, Barca Gana, a dedicated Muslim, had fallen to al-Kanemi as a slave when only 9 years old.[33] Slaves were among the losses which al-Kanemi suffered when his attack on the Fulani empire in 1827 failed.[34] Barth in 1851 found Uba, the northernmost Fulani town in Adamawa, restricted in size after being plundered by Ramadan, a slave and officer of al-Kanemi.[35] Barth himself urged the transfer of a few hundred lazy slaves from the Bornu capital to some fortified place in the potentially rich, but then desolated by Fulani and Tuareg raiders, province of Ghambaru, so that people there might resume farming under armed protection.[36]

Nachtigal found the same situation. In Bornu, he reported, there was little effort to maintain a centralized armed force, and for his military expeditions the Shaykh for the most part depended on the contingents, mounted or on foot, which his leading dignitaries were prepared to equip. The position of those who were formally designated as mili-

[30] Stevenson, in Lewis, 1966, 211–12.
[31] P. M. Holt, The Mahdist state in the Sudan, 1881–1898, 1958, 148 ff.
[32] Denham and Clapperton, 1826, A, 162–3.   [33] ibid., A, 104.
[34] Clapperton, 1829, 252.   [35] Barth, 1857–8, ii, 417.
[36] ibid., ii, 225.

tary commanders will be examined below (see pp. 168–9). But in addition, every courtier and official, even if his post was non-military, maintained a considerable number of armed men, if he wished to establish any claim to the esteem of the Shaykh and of the people. The chief *qadi*, for example, kept 100 horsemen. Most of these soldiers (and of the soldiers in Bagirmi too)[37] were slaves, and the commanders of these contingents were also themselves often of slave origin. Lamino employed fifteen captains, described by Nachtigal as 'higher ranking slaves',[38] to command his force of 1000 horsemen, 300 of whom were equipped with the quilted armour of the country. The structure of the military forces of Bornu therefore ensured a considerable permanent demand for slaves, though it need not of course be assumed that all these men spent their working hours exclusively in martial manoeuvres. The guardian of Shaykh Umar's rickety cannon (who was not, however, described as a slave) could not live on his artillery commission, and combined with it a merchant's business.[39]

Turning to the western Sudan, in Masina, which perhaps of all the theocracies kept closest to an orthodox model, Shehu Ahmadu, the head of state, kept few captives. Those that came to him, for instance as booty, he freed, often giving them posts which bound them to the community and made them sure auxiliaries. Captives who took part in the first battle, in 1818, which led ultimately to the establishment of the theocracy, were freed; Shehu Ahmadu bought and emancipated any whose masters would not release them in charity.[40] Celebrating the deeds of a slave warrior in the forces of Hadeija, a Fulani emirate in rebellion against Sokoto in the mid-nineteenth century, tradition states that the blood of his foes cemented his hand to his spear, so that after the battle it could only be freed with oil and hot wa-

[37] ii, 605. [38] i, 599, 727.
[39] i, 747. [40] Ba and Daget, 1962, i, 40.

ter.[41] Some of the earliest followers of al-Hajj Umar, who launched a *jihad* against the Bambara in 1850, were slaves, whom he instructed in Islam and to whom he entrusted some of his most important military commands; it is likely that these men were freed.[42]

An example from the Sokoto empire indicates that not all the slaves engaged in military activities were men. Clapperton said of Bello's attack on the Gobir capital in 1826 (see p. 156), that the most useful person there, as well as being as brave as any, was an old female slave who had nursed five former governors of Zamfara, and who rode astride a scruffy horse giving water to the wounded and thirsty.[43] The sultan of Bagirmi possessed a large number of female slaves who accompanied him everywhere, even into battle, it being their duty there 'to taunt cowards to an assumption of courage'.[44]

The military tradition continued into European colonial times; the native battalions of the Italians in Eritrea contained many Galla, mostly freed slaves. Freed Galla slaves fought too in the Italian forces in Libya against the Arabo-Turks.[45] And, in muted form, the same tradition crossed the Atlantic; in Brazil in the 1860s, for example, some citizens, confronted with the possibility of being drafted for military service, the country then being at war with its southern neighbours, sent instead slaves who had been specially liberated for this purpose.[46]

One specialized military use of slaves was as slavers. In Bagirmi Nachtigal noted with some disgust that slaves themselves joined in the slave-raids, and with no less zest than their masters helped to tear to pieces the bodies of the vic-

[41] East, 1934, 79.
[42] M. Delafosse, *Haut-Sénégal-Niger*, Paris 1912, ii, 306.
[43] Clapperton, 1829, 188.   [44] Macleod, 1912, 169.
[45] Cerulli, 1922, 14.   [46] Verger, 1968, 518.

tims who were killed.[47] Such employment was of considerable antiquity in the area; Alooma used slaves in slave-raiding, and sometimes to massacre prisoners, in the late sixteenth century.[48] In East Africa slaves, or ex-slaves, were often their masters' most effective agents in slaving.[49] The few cases of deliberate cruelty to slaves which Cameron observed were perpetrated not by Arabs but by owners who were themselves slaves or had recently been freed.[50] On the other hand, there are occasional instances of ex-slaves being used in anti-slavery operations. In 1832 the Liberian authorities in Monrovia mounted a column against a Muslim potentate, called the Sultan of Brumley, on the St Paul's river. He had started raiding when the Monrovians refused to send back some of his slaves who had escaped to Monrovia (compare p. 189 below). The Liberian force was accompanied by 120 freed slaves, serving as scouts.[51]

The prospect of acquiring slaves was also sometimes a sort of pay supplement scheme for soldiers on active service, an African army equivalent to the prize money of western navies. Al-Kanemi rewarded his followers with the slave produce of Bornu's wars.[52] The Arabs fighting Mirambo, in East Africa, gave a slave and a concubine to anyone bringing in the trophy of a fallen foe.[53] Bello, sultan of Sokoto, once attempted to apply the proper legal division of booty, but after three expeditions his troops went on strike, refusing to fight for another man's booty, and Bello reverted to the old practice whereby each man took what he could lay his hands on. Even at the height of his reforms, Bello had not gone so far as actually to stockpile women and children captured by individual soldiers for

[47] ii, 627, 631.   [48] Ibn Fartua, 22–3, 28.
[49] Speke, 1864, 211–12.   [50] Cameron, 1885, 256.
[51] Johnston, 1906, i, 151–2.
[52] Denham and Clapperton, 1826, A, 326.
[53] Cameron, 1885, 111–12.

later redistribution, but merely included them in his calculations of the total value of the booty.[54] On the contrary,
a poem of Futa Jallon describing a raid by the *almami* about
1863, in conjunction with the clerics of Touba, one of the
main Islamic religious centres of that area, mentions 12,000
captives who were assembled and then distributed, each
participant in the campaign receiving his share.[55] Each of
the Shuwa Arabs who had an obligation for military service
in Bornu had the right to half his booty if it consisted of
slaves, horses or cattle, and the whole if it consisted of inanimate objects such as clothing, ornaments, etc. Captured
weapons were however reserved for the government.[56]
Those who participated in Abu Sekkin's slave-raids had to
hand over to the king half of any slaves whom they captured, but retained for themselves the other half, and any
animals that they might pick up.[57] Nachtigal did not explain how this rule was interpreted when, as presumably
often happened, a warrior captured an odd number of the
enemy, three, or perhaps only one. Among the Hausa,
whose raid into Gwari country initiated the adventurous
story of the hero of Sir Abubakar Tafawa Balewa's novel,
Shaihu Umar, the rule was that 'if a man were to capture
three slaves, the Chief would take two of them, and he
would be allowed to keep one'.[58] In the 1860s al-Hajj
Umar's men marched to the attack, confident of either conquering slave women here (men prisoners were regularly
killed) or winning the large-eyed girls of paradise.[59] But
in al-Hajj Umar's army itself there was discontent with the

[54] Haj Said, *Histoire de Sokoto*, attached to *Tedzkiret en-Nisian*,
306–7.
[55] Sow, Alfâ Ibrâhîm, *La femme, la vache, la foi: écrivains et
poètes du Foûta-Djalon*, Paris 1966, 231–3.
[56] ii, 440.   [57] ii, 642.
[58] M. Hiskett's translation, 1967, 22.
[59] Mohammadou Aliou Tyam, *La vie d'El Hadj Omar*, tr. H.
Gaden, Paris 1935, 95–6, 98–9, 122, 132–3, 137.

rules for booty distribution: free Muslim soldiers were required to surrender the canonical one-fifth of their captured slaves and goods; slave warriors, or *sofas*, had to give up one half; while the *tuburu*, those who had been forced to convert and follow al-Hajj Umar, received nothing by right, but only by somewhat arbitrary grant.[60]

It is sometimes a delicate task to distinguish adequately between such practice and that followed by some European colonialists. For example, after a battle in 1887, when the French defeated the army of Momodu Lamine, the Soninke leader on the upper Senegal, seventeen women of Momodu Lamine fell into French hands. The French commander, Galliéni, asked them, through his interpreter, if they would like to marry instead some of his African *tirailleurs*. Their answer is not recorded. Galliéni, assuming that they would not mind—*que leur importait de changer d'esclavage?*—distributed them to the seventeen men who had most distinguished themselves in the battle just finished, giving each his choice in descending order of valour.[61]

Royal slaves

Slave soldiers were often an important element lending strength to the state, and reliance on such soldiers, and on slave officials of all kinds, was a recurrent feature of African governments aiming at centralization and, often, at despotism. An early example is perhaps ancient Mali, where slaves may have played an important part.[62] During Ibn Battuta's

[60] Willis, 1970, 152.

[61] Lieut.-Col. Galliéni, *Deux campagnes au Soudan français: 1886–1888*, Paris 1891, 120–2. M. A. Klein, 1968, 238, mentions another case, which became notorious when one soldier so rewarded later offered his bride for sale.

[62] C. Monteil, *Les empires du Mali*, 1930, 141; N. Levtzion, 'The thirteenth- and fourteenth-century kings of Mali', *Journal of African History*, 1963, 351; Mauny, 1961, 341, 374.

visit to Mali the king's wife fell into disfavour for her excessive pretensions; one sign of her ostentation was to ride
each day with men and women slaves in attendance. Finally one of her women slaves informed against her.[63] For
Hausaland from about 1350 onwards, M. G. Smith has
argued persuasively the importance of the interrelationship
of many factors—among them Islam, slave raiding, slave
tribute, slave export, slave settlements, slave officials, eunuchs and concubines—in the development of centralized
and sometimes dictatorial governments.[64] The sultan of
Kano, about 1500, was threatened by a revolt by one of his
chief officials, the *dagachi*; the sultan survived this and
subsequently dismissed the *dagachi* and replaced him with
a slave.[65] Under Pasha Mansur of Timbuktu, in the early
eighteenth century, the pasha's slaves, or *lagha*, became
excessively insolent, and so abused the people that it became
unsafe even to venture to the mosque for prayers. Runaway
slaves took refuge with the *lagha* and were never returned.
Kabara, the Niger port of Timbuktu, was entirely in the
hands of the *lagha*; the traditional governorship stood va-
cant. Trouble came to a head when the *lagha* murdered a
prominent *sharif*. The pasha was then deposed, and all
lagha who could be caught—one was dragged from sanc-
tuary in the *imam*'s house—were executed.[66] Between 1870
and 1880 the Fulani rulers of Zaria, within the Sokoto
empire, appointed slave generals to command their standing
armies, as much in this instance through fear of internal
revolt as a means of defence against invaders.[67] In Katsina
city, also within the Sokoto empire, towards the end of the
nineteenth century royal slaves 'so troubled the market that

[63] Ibn Battuta, c, iv, 417–19.
[64] M. G. Smith, 1964 A, 164–94; 1964 B, 351–3.
[65] *Kano Chronicle*, 112.   [66] *Tedzkiret*, 27 ff.
[67] M. G. Smith, 1959, 242.

its members rebelled and thrice drove back the royal slave cavalry'.[68] In a situation not exactly parallel, since the slaves were not his own, Kalema, the late nineteenth-century Muslim *kabaka* of Buganda, losing popular support, relied increasingly on the Arabs and their bands of armed slaves.[69] The first emir of Adamawa appointed by the British, though he was the correct legal successor, was unpopular because he preferred court favourites and slaves to the old Fulani aristocracy, and he was deported in 1901.[70] In some cases, however, where the Fulani leaders clung closer to the nomadic tradition, and preferred to tend their farms and cattle rather than to dance attendance at court, the advancement of slaves to high political office was not so much resented; Sambo, founder of the Fulani emirate of Hadeija, obtained from his colleagues express consent for such aggrandisement.[71]

These examples make it clear that as a weapon of strong government slaves were a delicate instrument. There were many episodes in addition to those listed above where the excesses of slaves provoked a popular reaction. The iniquity of slaves, arousing divine vengeance, was one of the causes assigned for the defeat of Songhay by the Moroccans in 1591, but we are not told exactly in what this iniquity consisted.[72] In Kayor, in modern Senegal, the exactions of the *tyeddo*, or royal slave soldiery, finally drove the Muslims of Kayor to revolt, instigated by their *qadi*, at the end of the seventeenth century. On this occasion the rising was successful, and a prince who had converted to Islam took the

[68] M. G. Smith, 1964 A, 178.
[69] J. M. Gray, 'The year of the three kings of Buganda', *Uganda Journal*, 1950, 37–8.
[70] Boyle, 1910–11, 88–9.
[71] J. M. Fremantle, 'A History of the region comprising the Katagum division of Kano province', *Journal of the African Society*, 1911, 314.
[72] Kati, 272.

throne.[73] The Kayor Muslims again revolted a century
later; this time the *damel*, or ruler, put them down, and sold
them into slavery.[74] In the mid-eighteenth century the ruler
of Darfur was said to have completely alienated free men by
the preference which he showed for slaves, showering upon
them riches and positions of honour. He was eventually defeated in an expedition against Wadai, when his free subjects, already exasperated by the burdens imposed upon
them to facilitate his military preparations, and also resent-
ful of the slight inflicted on them when slaves were placed
in the front line of the battle, free men being relegated to
the second place, refused to rally to his support when his
slave guards began to waver in the final decisive conflict.[75]
In 1760 the Funj dynasty in the eastern Sudan lost the last
remnants of its power, having during the period of its decline relied more and more upon a slave army.[76]

Where it was a Muslim government that evoked such resentment, we may guess that the cause of the faith sometimes suffered. But in other cases, when it was the hand of
non-Muslim, slave-supported, rule that lay heavy upon the
people, popular resistance sometimes found succour in Islam: this was true in the Woloff states of West Africa,
where tension between royal slaves on the one hand and
peasantry and free chiefs on the other was a factor speeding
up the Islamization of the peasants.[77]

There was, moreover, also a danger that the royal slaves
might come themselves to dominate, or to undermine, their
master. At the end of the thirteenth century the imperial

---

[73] Cheikh Tidiane Sy, *La confrérie sénégalaise des Mourides*, Paris
1969, 39.

[74] V. Monteil, 'Lat Dyor . . . et l'Islamisation des Wolofs du
Sénégal', in Lewis, 1966, 343-4.

[75] iii, 373-4; A. J. Arkell, *A history of the Sudan up to A.D. 1821*,
London 1961, 221.

[76] Trimingham, 1968, 25.   [77] M. A. Klein, 1968, 19 n.

throne of Mali was seized by a freed slave, Sakura.[78] An exiled royal slave played some part in encouraging, presumably for revenge, the Moroccan conquest of Songhay.[79] One of Muhammad Bello's sons apparently died of disgruntlement after quarrelling with the slaves whom his father had settled on him.[80] While several subordinate rulers in the Sokoto empire of the nineteenth century tried to govern their respective emirates independently of the Fulani aristocracy, relying largely on eunuchs and slaves, the abler despots, in order to encourage rivalries, frequently redistributed offices among their slaves, gave critical functions to freemen or kin when advisable, and sometimes summarily executed senior royal slaves. Nevertheless, as a member of the dispossessed Hausa dynasty of Katsina observed of the throne slaves: 'These were the rulers; the Fulani had power in name only. The king was in the hands of his slaves.'[81] In the time of Abdulahi, 1855–83, there was a revolt of the palace slaves of Kano, which was however quelled.[82] The potential unreliability of slave support is further illustrated in the case of Tukur, who succeeded his father as chief of Tibati, one of the major principalities within the Adamawa emirate. Tukur drove out his rival brother, Ardo Hammadu. But Hammadu later sent secret messages to the chief slaves in Tibati; some deserted to him, while others, remaining at their posts, became his clandestine supporters. Finally Hammadu attacked Tibati, and Tukur, abandoned by his slaves, was defeated and killed.[83] And to turn again to Kayor, which we have already cited for other slave difficulties, in the later nineteenth century the royal slaves wished

[78] Levtzion, 1963, 345 and n.
[79] H. de Castries, 'La conquête du Soudan par el Mansour', Hespéris, 1923, 445–6, 452; al-Sadi, 215–16.
[80] C. E. J. Whitting (tr.), History of Sokoto, Kano [1948 ?], 25; Said, 341.
[81] M. G. Smith, 1964 A, 179.   [82] Kano Chronicle, 131.
[83] East, 1934, 47–9.

to depose the *damel*, Lat Dyor. Lat Dyor frustrated this conspiracy, and dismissed the chief of the slaves; but this man did in the end contribute to Lat Dyor's overthrow.[84]

At least in the larger political units visited by Nachtigal —Bornu, Logon, Bagirmi and Wadai—the heads of state deployed huge slave establishments, both household and military. No clear distinction was made between slaves who were the ruler's personal property and 'slaves of the state'. Shaykh Umar of Bornu needed slaves, for example, to look after the collection of wild animals kept in some huts near the west gate of his palace.[85] Long trains of his slaves carried the guest meals which he gave to distinguished visitors to his capital, or the gifts which he made on festive occasions.[86] Over 100 of his slaves carried the evening meals distributed during Ramadan in 1870.[87] Ibn Battuta, in fourteenth-century Mali, regarded the similar slave service accorded to the commanders there at the end of each day during Ramadan, when the fast was broken at the sultan's palace, as rather disreputable, for each commander was then attended by twenty or more female slaves all completely naked.[88] On these occasions in Bornu slaves received customary gratuities, for which more or less regular rates had become conventional.[89] There was a well-defined hierarchy in Shaykh Umar's household, and the head slave who controlled the distribution of gifts did much better out of the gratuities than his menial subordinates. The king of Wadai gave meals to distinguished people in the same way,[90] but the use of such duties by his servants as an opportunity to supplement their incomes was sternly forbidden by him.[91]

Many of the tasks of the royal household slaves were simi-

[84] V. Monteil, in Lewis, 1966, 345.
[85] i, 635.   [86] i, 579; iii, 10.   [87] i, 743.
[88] Ibn Battuta, A, 330–1; C, iv, 423–4.
[89] i, 605–6.   [90] iii, 230.   [91] iii, 67.

lar to those undertaken by the slaves of other important men, though sometimes on a larger scale. But there were also slaves who occupied positions of great political and military importance. Nearly all the military commanders of Bornu, the *kashellawa*, were 'slaves of the head of the state',[92] and the most important of them sat in the *nokena*, or State Council, alongside some of the Shaykh's sons and brothers and freeborn representatives of the four main sections of the population. Nachtigal listed the names of 30 *kashellawa*.[93] Though called slaves, at least two were described as chiefs of Kanuri tribes,[94] two others had succeeded to their fathers' positions, and they were allowed a great deal of latitude in determining the size of the military contingents which they would recruit. Nachtigal believed that on the whole the strength of the forces under their control had diminished; by 1870 the detachments commanded by one or two had fallen to an almost derisory figure, and the total number of soldiers under the *kashellawa* was less than the total maintained by non-military dignitaries (see p. 159). The military commanders in Logon similarly had been originally slaves.[95]

Most Bornu court officials, said Nachtigal, were slaves or of slave origin.[96] Some offices were always held by free men, but why different offices were treated in different ways was not explained. At least some slave officials owned their own slaves. Nachtigal mentioned one slave, the Fulani Ibrahim, who had twenty years before held the important post of *digma*. By 1870, Nachtigal discovered with some embarrassment, Ibrahim had been deprived of all effective power; had he known beforehand of Ibrahim's fall, he would have been less eager to look him up.[97]

Nachtigal's account of the origins of the Dalatoa tribe in western Kanem illustrates the possible preference for slave

---

[92] i, 583, 723–4.   [93] i, 725–6.   [94] i, 724.
[95] ii, 538.   [96] i, 715–21.   [97] i, 714.

officers. After the seat of government moved from Kanem to Bornu, about 1400, the Tunjur Arabs were made guardians of Bornu's eastern flank. Later, when they adopted 'a disagreeably independent position', a Hausa slave, Dala, was appointed instead, and from him descend the Dalatoa.[98]

With succession often ill-defined, and suspicion and jealousy within the royal family commonplace, the ruler might naturally prefer his principal servants to be entirely dependent upon him. In Bornu especially, a centuries-old dynasty which free men might still cherish and respect had been displaced comparatively recently by the family of al-Kanemi, an outsider, though friendly, twice called to rescue a weak and despairing monarch from Fulani attack.

Slaves also played an important role in the court of Wadai. The king had a corps of 500 pages, including a special detachment, 'those who are used for important messages', some twenty slave boys from 12 to 16 years old, who distributed the king's instructions. A man summoned to a royal audience could tell from the slave's demeanour whether a favour was to be expected, or whether there was reason to fear for his life.[99] Service in this group frequently led later to promotion to a high political post. Employment as messengers was a common duty for slaves; in the Sokoto empire, the ruler sent his orders to fiefholders through eunuchs or throne slaves.[100] One of Sultan Bello's messengers was an old female slave, herself owning nearly forty men and women slaves; she was, Clapperton observed, 'a shrewd old woman, of strong natural sense'.[101] In Darfur in the early twentieth century, sultan Ali Dinar's last *wazir*, the foremost official in the kingdom, had begun his career long before as Ali Dinar's slave boy.[102]

[98] ii, 252–3.   [99] iii, 232–3.
[100] M. G. Smith, 1964 A, 177.
[101] Clapperton, 1829, 249.   [102] Theobald, 1965, 212.

Eunuchs

Though the making of eunuchs was said to have been strictly forbidden to his followers by the Prophet Muhammad, African rulers, in their search for reliable civil servants, sometimes found eunuchs attractive, in the lower ranks for looking after the *harim*,[103] but in higher political offices also, since there could be no temptation to found a rival dynasty. Around 1800, for example, the prince of Muscat, fearing lest his African dependency of Zanzibar become too independent, appointed eunuchs as his representatives there, dividing civil and military power between them.[104]

The best-known early source of eunuchs in Africa was in Ethiopia. Here, despite the efforts of the king of Amhara to forbid the practice, castration continued to be performed in the fourteenth century in the town of Washlu, the care of the survivors being the speciality of the Muslim principality of Hadya.[105] The Ethiopian slaves whom Mansa Musa and his suite bought in Cairo (see above p. 119) were presumably eunuchs. Ethiopian eunuchs were already known in Arabia, for the servitors and doorkeepers of the mosque in Medina, all eunuchs, included Ethiopians. The head of these, not himself an Ethiopian, in Ibn Battuta's time, confronted with the temptations of Joseph in Potiphar's house, had followed the example of Origen.[106] An Ethiopian eunuch was in charge of the Zanzibar customs at the beginning of the nineteenth century, and later be-

103 The status of *harim* keeper was sometimes a degraded one, and might be alleged in insult: Amda Seyon, conquering ruler of Ethiopia in the fourteenth century, had been incensed by his lowland Danakil enemies taunting him as a eunuch, fit only to care for women (Harris, 1844, ii, 230).
104 Freeman-Grenville, 1962 A, 198.
105 al-Umari, 16–17, 32.
106 Ibn Battuta, B, i, 175; C, i, 279–80.

came *hakim* or magistrate as well.[107] In Ethiopia itself, the market was dependent on domestic demand as well as on exports. Harris, visiting in the nineteenth century, found many eunuchs among the king's servants.[108] Many supervised women slaves, but one assumed command of a garrison town during the king's absence, and the whole court went into deep mourning for the death of the chief eunuch.

Another important early source was Nupe. The exchange of ten horses for twelve eunuchs between the rulers of Nupe and of Kano in the mid-fifteenth century has been mentioned above (see p. 81). Queen Amina of Zaria, variously dated as early fifteenth or mid-sixteenth century, also received eunuchs from Nupe.[109] The institutions of mass-slavery and of eunuchs both flourished in Kano. The first to appoint eunuchs as important state officials there was Muhammad Rimfa, in the later fifteenth century.[110] In the time of Abubakr Kado, who in the later sixteenth century concentrated exclusively on religious duties, both eunuchs and clerics became very numerous in Kano.[111] Early in the seventeenth century, Wombai Giwa, presumably a eunuch, became so powerful and likely to revolt that he had to be dismissed from his office.[112] Kutumbi, ruler of Kano in the second quarter of the seventeenth century, was always attended by 100 eunuchs, handsomely dressed and with gold and silver ornaments.[113]

In Songhay, too, eunuchs had an important place in the civil service. Leo Africanus spoke of a private palace of the *askiya*, containing a great number of concubines and slaves, kept by eunuchs.[114] He also said that Askiya Muhammad

---

[107] J. Gray, in Oliver and Mathew, 1963, 212 n.
[108] Harris, 1844, ii, 26, 56, 57, 75, 167, 369; iii, 301.
[109] Alhaji Hassan and Shuaibu Na'ibi, *A chronicle of Abuja*, Lagos 1962, 3; *Kano Chronicle*, 109.
[110] *Kano Chronicle*, 111–12.   [111] *ibid.*, 114.
[112] *ibid.*, 117.   [113] *ibid.*, 119.
[114] Leo Africanus, A, iii, 827; B, ii, 471.

I attacked and killed the Hausa king of Gobir, and made eunuchs of his grandsons.[115] A eunuch was in charge of the *askiya*'s extensive wardrobe.[116] The chief of the palace eunuchs, Ali Folon, played almost the part of regent towards the end of Askiya Muhammad I's reign.[117] Askiya Ishaq II, defeated by the Moroccans, attempted to slip away with gold and silver, royal emblems, thirty of the best horses in the royal stables, and forty eunuchs.[118] A little ironically, many of the early leaders of the Moroccan expeditionary and occupation forces were themselves Andalusian eunuchs.

The tradition continued. Sultan Bello's house in Sokoto in 1826 had two entrances, one of which was guarded by a great number of eunuchs, presumably because his *harim* was there.[119] Eunuchs attended Bello's army in the attack on Gobir in that year (see above p. 156).[120] Atiqu, Bello's successor, sent a eunuch to enlist al-Hajj Umar's prayers on behalf of a besieged Fulani town.[121] The chief eunuch of the sultan of Agades called on Barth when he arrived in town.[122] In 1910 a eunuch was monitor at the French government-controlled madrasa in Timbuktu.[123] Eunuchs were not peculiar to Islam in West Africa; in Yoruba traditional government, for example, they also played an important part.[124]

Eunuch officials in Bornu were also mentioned by

[115] *ibid.*, A, iii, 828; B, ii, 473; Rouch, 1953, 204.
[116] Kati, 260–1.
[117] Rouch, 1953, 192 and n; al-Sadi mentions Ali Folon several times, but not as a eunuch.
[118] Kati, 273.   [119] Clapperton, 1829, 208.
[120] *ibid.*, 185.   [121] Said, 328–9.
[122] Barth, 1857–8, i, 398.   [123] Seabrook, 1934, 189–90.
[124] R. Smith, 'The Alafin in exile', *Journal of African History*, 1965, 69; S. Johnson, *The history of the Yorubas*, London 1921, 59–60; P. Morton-Williams, 'An outline of the genealogy and cult organization of the Oyo Yoruba', *Africa*, 1964, 253–8; Clapperton, 1829, 38.

Barth.[125] Denham had earlier seen the sultan of Mandara accompanied by thirty of his sons and six favourite eunuchs.[126] Nachtigal found eunuchs playing an important part in the administrative structure of Bornu, Bagirmi, Wadai and Darfur, but noted that there were no eunuch officials in Logon, despite its proximity to Bagirmi, one of the chief sources of eunuchs in central Africa.[127] Their role was especially significant in Bagirmi; Nachtigal listed the names of at least twelve eunuchs who had responsible administrative posts in the Pagan regions which were subject to Bagirmi, and noted that in that country military commands were also often in the hands of eunuchs.[128]

The origin of the traffic in Bagirmi was fairly precisely dated by Nachtigal as during the reign of the *mbang*, or king, Haji Muhammad el-Amin, 1751–85. Eunuchs had always been employed in Bagirmi, Nachtigal said, to look after the royal *harim*, but up to that time they had been imported from Bornu, and their high price severely limited the number that could be purchased. On one occasion the king bought several at fifty slaves apiece; the *fatscha*, the chief minister and military commander, protested against this extravagance, and proposed that in future home production should be substituted for imports. The death rate was very high. Nachtigal was told that of the first 100 boys subjected to castration in Bagirmi only thirty survived, and other estimates have put the mortality rate at 80 per cent.[129] The previous course of Bagirmi trade was however reversed, Bagirmi becoming an important exporter of eunuchs to other countries, with corresponding benefits for the royal exchequer.[130]

A later account, published in 1907, also gave King Haji the credit for inaugurating the making of eunuchs in

[125] Barth, 1957–8, ii, 290, 648.
[126] Denham and Clapperton, 1826, A, 130.   [127] ii, 538.
[128] ii, 615.   [129] Deherme, 1908, 373.   [130] ii, 710–11.

Bagirmi; this account, though recognizably based upon the same popular traditions as those upon which Nachtigal had drawn, differed in some of its details from his story. Haji, it was said, learnt the value of eunuchs either while he was in Mecca or from some of the potentates whose courts he visited while on pilgrimage. Returning from Mecca, he purchased a eunuch in exchange for fifty slaves from the sultan of Mandara, and then when it was pointed out to him that this was a rather expensive procedure, he took instruction in the techniques of castration, and subsequently made his own eunuchs. His successor, Burkomanda, who died around 1844, was said to have had 1003 of them, but never allowed any of his subjects to maintain them. Some fifty eunuchs still survived in the early years of the twentieth century, relics of the days of Bagirmi's independence, but by that time no further additions were being made to their number.[131]

Most of the forty or fifty eunuchs whom Nachtigal found at the court of Wadai came from Bagirmi; castration was also sometimes inflicted in Wadai as a judicial punishment on local wrongdoers, and the royal corps of eunuchs was also reinforced by young Tubu and Bedeyat captured when making raids into Wadai territory. Some eunuchs were employed exclusively in the management of the king's very large *harim*, but, as in both Bornu and Bagirmi, others held high and responsible positions, including military commands. The *harim* duties of one eunuch were combined with responsibility for the relations of the government with

[131] H. Gaden, 1907, 441–2. All the other references to eunuchs below, except those otherwise identified are from this article by Commandant Gaden, who had lived in Bagirmi; he wrote after Bagirmi had come under French control, his information being derived from conversations with political refugees who had come from the neighbouring countries into Bagirmi during the troubled years of the early twentieth century as well as with Bagirmians.

the Arab population;[132] another, who, while Nachtigal was
in Abeshr, died as the result of a drunken quarrel between
two eunuchs near the royal palace in which their retainers
had joined, was a *kamkolak*, the title held by the highest
ranking administrative officials of the country.[133] In Darfur, too, the head eunuch was one of the most important
officials in the country, acting as tutor to Muhammad al-
Fadl before his accession to the throne,[134] and as regent
when Muhammad became king at the age of 11 or 12 (see
above p. 125 n. 57).[135]

It was rare for eunuchs to be made in Bornu in the nineteenth century. Shaykh Umar did so only on one occasion
when a score of captives from a raid on the Pagans in the
south were castrated. The Shaykh preferred to get them
from Bagirmi, and in Nachtigal's time the top officials in
his domestic household, as well as some of the provincial
officials, e.g. the governor of Ngornu, the second town of
Bornu, were eunuchs.[136] These, according to Nachtigal,
were more important and more respected than most of the
other court officials whom he listed,[137] and the standing
and revenues associated with their positions in earlier times
had been maintained practically without change. One of
these eunuchs was often sent abroad on confidential missions; another was keeper of the royal privy purse, responsible for giving, on the instructions of the Shaykh, appropriate gifts to foreign guests and the chief recipient of the
gratuities which these favoured persons were expected to
offer in return (see above, p. 168). This man has been described as 'the real master of Bornu for half a century'.[138]
Nachtigal would apparently not have rated his importance
quite so high; most of his references are to occasions when

[132] iii, 231.   [133] iii, 55.   [134] Slatin, 1896, 44–5.
[135] iii, 385, 386, 430.   [136] ii, 484.   [137] i, 722.
[138] *Encyclopedia of Islam*, i, 751, 753, 1911–3; cf. C. C. Ifemesia,
'Bornu under the Shehus' in Ajayi and Espie, 1965, 291.

the eunuch brought to him tokens of Shaykh Umar's good-will, but he did comment in general terms on the influence which the slaves at court could exert in the distribution of the sources of income which in theory were at the exclusive disposal of the Shaykh.[139] Lamino had a few eunuchs, and indeed, according to Nachtigal, sometimes had extensive castration operations carried out under his own direction,[140] and in Wadai the king had given eunuchs to several of his dignitaries. In general, however, the maintenance of eunuchs was, in Bagirmi, Bornu and Wadai, a privilege jealously preserved for the ruler of the country.

[139] i, 715.   [140] i, 599, 685.

CHAPTER VIII

THE DOMESTIC SCENE V: SLAVES AS CURRENCY

With so many different uses for slaves, it is not surprising that they circulated sometimes as a means of exchange, even almost as a form of currency. In any predominantly barter economy it is often difficult to differentiate clearly between transfers of goods in discharge of legal obligations to pay tribute or taxes, conventional or courtesy presents, and exchanges of goods which are definitely barter. Slaves have been widely used for all these purposes, and provided it is remembered that in practice one category shades almost imperceptibly into another, it will be helpful to comment on this use under each head separately.

Tribute

From the earliest period of the history of Islam in Africa, slaves were frequently mentioned as tribute or taxes paid to political superiors. Uqbah bin Nafi, who conquered several places in North Africa and Fezzan in the 660s, imposed on various rulers an annual tribute of 360 slaves, cutting off an ear or a finger of some of the rulers as a perpetual reminder of their obligations.[1] Even earlier, the Muslim conquerors of Egypt had begun levying slave tribute from Christian Nubia. This continued, with some interruptions,

[1] al-Bakri, 33–5.

into the fourteenth century, and was discontinued only when a Muslim became king of Nubia. In this case, as in some others, the payment of tribute was not easily distinguishable from exchange, for Nubia at the same time received annually from Egypt grain, cloth and horses.[2]

Here are some later examples. About 1400 Kanajeji, a son of the first ruler of Kano to adopt Islam, received slave tribute from the Kwararafa in exchange for horses; he oppressed some of his enemies to the extent of obliging them to surrender many of their own children as slave tribute.[3] From about 1450 each ruler of Katsina on his accession sent 100 slaves as tribute to Bornu, though his sovereign rights do not seem otherwise to have been affected.[4] Leo Africanus described the presentation around 1500 to the king of Fez by a neighbouring prince of 100 Negro slaves, men and women in equal numbers, 10 eunuchs, 12 camels, a giraffe, 10 ostriches, 16 civet cats, a pound of civet, a pound of ambergris, and almost 600 oryx skins.[5] In 1584 the ruler of Songhay, receiving an embassy bearing gifts from Morocco, responded with still more costly gifts, chiefly slaves and eunuchs.[6] Ngolo, the powerful eighteenth-century king of Segu—Segu and its rulers, however, were but slightly tinged with Islam—began his career when his village used him to pay the government in lieu of tax.[7] On the east coast, the sultan of Pate used to receive from each of the heads of some subordinate tribes tribute of one slave and 20 dollars.[8]

In the nineteenth century, slave tribute was very common. A Bornuan, kidnapped and sold into slavery at the

[2] Arkell, 1961, 186–9, 199–200; Y. F. Hasan, *The Arabs and the Sudan*, Edinburgh 1967, 21–8, 91, 107.

[3] *Kano Chronicle*, 107.

[4] Barth, 1857–8, ii, 78–9; M. G. Smith, 1964 B, 348 n.; Palmer, 1928, iii, 83.

[5] Leo Africanus, A, ii, 308–9; B, i, 139.   [6] al-Sadi, 193.

[7] C. Monteil, 1924, 44–6.   [8] Freeman-Grenville, 1962 A, 248

opening of the century, said that his country had received an annual tribute of 1000 slaves from the Kwararafa kingdom to the south-west.[9] The Kwararafa in turn may have received some slaves in the tribute which their own vassals paid to them.[10] The newcome ruler of Dar Fertit, a vassal state neighbouring Darfur, kept in his overlord's good graces by an annual gift of 200 slaves, together with a little myrrh and ivory.[11] Much of our information for this period concerns the Fulani empire of Sokoto. From eight of the ten Fulani emirates listed by Clapperton as paying tribute to Sokoto in 1826, the offerings included slaves.[12] A visitor to Ilorin in 1855 reported the presence there of a messenger from Sokoto, with a demand for 200 slaves.[13] Such emirates themselves received slave tribute; at least one freed slave in Sierra Leone had been paid to Bauchi in this way.[14] Pagan enclaves or neighbours acknowledged the paramountcy of the Fulani by paying a capitation tax, supplying armed levies, or giving slaves.[15]

In 1851 Barth was told that the emir of Adamawa, the main slave centre for the Fulani, received in annual tribute about 5000 slaves as well as horses and cattle, a figure which Barth thought rather high.[16] From this tribute, and the produce of its own raids, Adamawa passed a part to

[9] Koelle, *Polyglotta Africana* 1854, 21, 10.

[10] Ruxton, 1908, 380.

[11] G. Douin, *Histoire du règne du Khédive Ismaïl*, Cairo 1936, vol. iii, part i, 451; the newcomer was Muhammad al-Hilali, who had set out from Morocco intending pilgrimage, but was distracted by the needs and opportunities in Dar Fertit, and settled there. Rabih killed him in 1872.

[12] Clapperton, 1829, 215–16.

[13] C. S. Groves, *The planting of Christianity in Africa*, London 1954, reprinted 1964, ii, 62.

[14] Hair, 1965, 197.

[15] M. G. Smith, 1964 A, 185; Lacroix, 1952, 29; Hogben and Kirk-Greene, 1966, 450.

[16] Barth, 1957–8, ii, 503; Lacroix, 1952, 34.

Sokoto. As many as 2000 slaves might be sent from Adamawa, perhaps half of them reaching Sokoto.[17] Zubayr,
emir of Adamawa 1890–1901, having received permission
from Sokoto to war against Hayatu, a dissident member of
the Sokoto ruling family, set out in company with a Sokoto
agent, and on the way stopped to capture some slaves, sixty
of whom were handed over to the agent for the sultan of
Sokoto.[18]

All kinds of business might be facilitated by supereroga-
tory slave tribute. In the time of Zubayr the chief of Gabow
died and left four sons, who, seeking the succession, re-
paired to the emir. One, Atiku, had nothing to offer; but he
promised the *wazir* fifty slaves, and thus gained admission
to the emir; he promised the emir 300 slaves, and gained
the inheritance. Then, to meet his commitments, he enslaved some even of his fellow Fulani, even clerics. Zubayr,
angry, summoned his chiefs, Atiku among them. No chief
came with a gift of more than thirty slaves, except Atiku
who brought 100, in fine gowns, trousers and fezes, each
on a horse. Zubayr was thus mollified, and Atiku lived out
his days in peace.[19] Earlier, when Adama, first Fulani emir
of Adamawa, died, one of his chiefs, in semi-rebellion, refused to come to the capital to acknowledge Lauwal, Adama's successor. Lauwal sent a messenger to summon the
recalcitrant chief, Buba Njidda. After a somewhat unsatis-
factory parley, Buba Njidda's head slave offered the messenger 500 slaves as something with which to buy kola nuts, an
offer which the messenger treated with scorn.[20] Again,
when Buba Njidda retook possession of a certain territory
he gave 1000 slaves to Sokoto, 1000 to Yola, the capital of
Adamawa, and 100 to a one-man boundary commission.[21]
Examples outside the Sokoto sphere include a present of

[17] Boyle, 1910–11, 82, 86–7; Zintgraff, 1895, 291; East, 1934, 21.
[18] East, 1934, 113–15.   [19] *ibid.*, 107 ff.
[20] East, 1934, 35–7.   [21] Lacroix, 1952, 34.

500 slaves to the pasha of Tripoli in 1822 from an Arab who hoped thus to persuade the pasha to remove the sultan of Fezzan,[22] and tribute in slaves and ivory paid to Darfur by the Bahr al-Ghazal tribes.[23] In this last instance, and probably in many others, an offending tributary could be raided, with equally gratifying results, if tribute were not forthcoming.

Nachtigal recorded several similar transactions. The ruler of Fezzan, he said, had been compelled during the seventeenth century to accept an obligation to pay an annual tribute to Tripoli of 4000 mithqals in gold, half of which was payable in slaves.[24] Bagirmi had the duty, dating from the early years of the nineteenth century, to send to Wadai every year 500 slaves, 30 young girl slaves, 30 horses and 1000 tobes.[25] An attack by Wadai on Darfur in the late eighteenth century was said to have been heralded by refusal to pay the customary annual tribute of a girl of royal blood for the *harim* of the king of Darfur.[26] The king of Bagirmi sent an annual gift of slaves to the ruler of Bornu, though there was no tributary obligation to do so.[27] There was some question about the adequacy of the gifts exchanged between the kings of Wadai and of Darfur in 1873–4, but even the least pretentious of them included at least one slave-girl.[28] On his accession to the throne of Wadai, the king of that country sometimes showed his respect for the sultan of Turkey by sending a number of eunuchs to Constantinople.[29] Presents of slaves were one of the means used by the king of Wadai in his unsuccessful efforts to seduce the turbulent Awlad Sulayman from their somewhat uneasy allegiance to Bornu.[30] One Bagirmi chief

---

22 Denham and Clapperton, 1826, xxii–xxiii.
23 Slatin, 1896, 47.   24 i, 168.   25 iii, 281 n.
26 iii, 367.   27 ii, 481.   28 iii, 482.
29 iii, 228.   30 ii, 47–8.

who had to deliver 100 slaves annually to the king sought
his master's aid for their collection,[31] and one official in
the capital of Wadai received from a village in his administrative district an annual tax of ten slaves, 300 strips of cotton cloth, and 150 pitchers of honey.[32]

Not surprisingly there was sometimes trouble over the
quality of the slaves offered as tribute; the custom of the
king of Bagirmi of sending his oldest, ugliest and most use-
less slaves to Wadai was one of the provocations which
moved the king of Wadai to attack him in 1870.[33]

The hazards of slaves on the march, already described
(pp. 91–3), sometimes interfered with the proper flow of
tribute. Barth, in 1851, witnessed one instance of this. He
had accompanied a slave-raid into Kanem, carried out by
the Awlad Sulayman Arabs on behalf of the Bornu authorities. An officer of al-Hajj Bashir, the leading Bornu
dignitary, also accompanied the expedition, in order to take
back the Bornu share of the spoil. The most handsome of
the women slaves was particularly destined for al-Hajj
Bashir himself, in view of his special interests (p. 122). But
this woman, even before she had been handed over to the
Bornu officer, escaped, and was eaten by wild beasts, only
her clothes, ornaments, and some bones being found. The
affair occasioned, said Barth, a great deal of unpleasant
conversation.[34]

Nachtigal's comments throw no light on the reasons for
using slaves for these purposes in some cases but not in
others. In any event, slave tribute was not exacted merely,
or perhaps even mainly, because the slaves might later be
advantageously exported to Tripoli, Cairo or Constantinople. It was also believed that the recipients of such tribute
would find the slaves really useful at home.

---

[31] ii, 655.
[32] iii, 142; cf. i, 701; ii, 537; iii, 125, 182, 238, 463.
[33] ii, 724.   [34] Barth, 1857–8, iii, 71–2.

Alms and presents

The general acceptability of slaves under this heading was another element which helped keep up the demand for them. We have already described the use of slaves as presents to clerics, and to teachers and students of religion (see above pp. 41–4). Similar generosity might be exercised on behalf of lay recipients, whether prompted by religious or other motives. Of the sultan of Kilwa, who was surnamed Abu'l-Mawahib, the giver of gifts, Ibn Battuta reported in 1331 that he once gave away his own clothes to a beggar, perhaps a religious mendicant; the sultan's son took back his father's clothes, and gave the beggar instead ten slaves, and the sultan was so impressed by the popular acclaim evoked by this generosity that he himself added ten more slaves and two loads of ivory.[35] Leo Africanus, then aged 16, once deputized for his uncle, visiting a prince in North Africa, and reciting poems, some by his uncle and some by himself, in honour of the prince. Leo received 100 ducats and two slaves for his uncle, 50 ducats and a good horse for himself, and 10 ducats for each of his two servants.[36] Later, at the court of Gaoga in the central Sudan, Leo saw a merchant of Damietta give the king a gallant horse, a Turkish sword, a royal robe and several other articles, receiving in return five slaves, five camels, 500 ducats and 100 ivory tusks.[37] Uthman dan Fodio too, founder of the Sokoto empire in the nineteenth century, was renowned for his generosity in slaves, camels and provisions, especially to *sharifs*, descendants of the Prophet.[38] A *sharif* named al-Habib once came to Ali, a later sultan of Sokoto, and explained that he would

[35] Ibn Battuta, B, ii, 381; C, ii, 194–5; Freeman-Grenville, 1962, B, 108.
[36] Leo Africanus, A, ii, 305–7; B, i, 136–8.
[37] *ibid.*, A, iii, 835; B, ii, 483.   [38] Clapperton, 1829, 205.

not pretend to have come on pilgrimage to the tomb of
Uthman or for any other pious purpose, but honestly admitted that he had come for money. Commending his frank-
ness, Ali gave him drafts for five horses on Zaria, and for
200 slaves on Adamawa; honouring the draft, the emir of
Adamawa added 50 slaves as a personal token.[39] When
Canot, the nineteenth-century slave-trader, left Futa Jallon
after his visit there, he was given various presents by the
ruling family, including five slaves. The son of the *almami*
of Futa Jallon, 'like a gentleman of taste, despatched for my
consolation the two prettiest handmaidens he could buy or
steal in Timbo', capital of the state.[40]

Not only Muslims gave slaves as alms or presents. King
Jesus I of Ethiopia, 1680–1704, sent back a few slaves and
a young elephant with emissaries who had visited him from
France, though by various misadventures all the gifts were
lost.[41] Amai, Christian ruler of Nubia, who visited Cairo
early in the fourteenth century, included slaves among the
gifts which he took with him on that occasion.[42]

Nachtigal was once pressed by the king of Wadai to accept a slave who had become particularly attached to him
on account of his treatment of leprous ulcers.[43] He noted
two instances where slaves figured as part of a marriage
dowry, evidently a widely accepted convention. It was, he
said, standard practice among the well-to-do of Bornu for
the bride's father to include a slave among the presents
given to a prospective son-in-law,[44] and in Wadai slaves
were included among the presents which a bridegroom
gave to his bride.[45] In Sokoto in 1826 the dowry given by
a family of good condition consisted of young female slaves,
and many household and personal goods which were carried in procession on the heads of the wife's female slaves

[39] Said, 351–3.   [40] Canot, 1928, 173.
[41] Arkell, 1961, 217–20.   [42] *ibid.*, 197–8.   [43] iii, 99.
[44] i, 739.   [45] iii, 253.

when she first went to her husband's house. If the husband slept with one of his wife's dowry slaves, he had next day to supply a new virgin slave of equal value; this, it was said, never occasioned any dispute.[46] Leo Africanus reported that in Fez 'the meaner sort' usually gave for a daughter's dowry 30 ducats and a female slave worth 15 ducats.[47] Among the Vai, the bride was purchased with presents and slaves, and the dowry included a slave.[48] Until a few years ago, it was customary for the Tuareg brideprice to include a slave girl.[49]

The difficulty of defining the exact difference between one transaction and another (see above, p. 179) arises with gifts, just as at other points in this chapter. Tributary obligations for which there was no ready means of enforcement tended to become a little hazy, and it might be difficult to determine whether there was any element of tribute in the transmission of such things as the eunuchs sometimes sent by the kings of Wadai to Constantinople as a mark of respect (see p. 183). Similarly, the slaves presented to the official in charge of the Darfur frontier post by the caravan with which Nachtigal travelled from Wadai to Darfur in 1874 might be variously classified as a gift or a transit-toll.[50]

The eunuchs despatched to Mecca and Medina for the service of the holy places there constituted a rather special category. As marks of respect comparable with the eunuchs sent to Constantinople, Nachtigal mentioned only pious gifts of money as being despatched to Mecca and Medina.[51]

[46] Clapperton, 1829, 213.
[47] Leo Africanus, A, ii, 448; B, i, 209.
[48] Ogilby, 1670, 392-3. When Sau, the father of Doalu Bukara who in the nineteenth century invented the Vai script, died, Sau's son-in-law received among other presents a slave (Koelle, 1849, appendix, 5). The grammatical examples cited by Koelle (1854, Outlines, 95, cf. 108) for the Vai language include such sentences as, 'We will give you eight slaves, four for the diviners and four for the Muslims'.
[49] Nicolaisen, 1963, 440.   [50] iii, 323.   [51] iii, 228.

Eunuchs were, however, also sent there, as they were to Constantinople, only rarely from Bornu, but more frequently, though irregularly, from Bagirmi and Wadai. In 1852 Barth met an envoy from Medina in Massenya, who had come to ask for eunuchs to guard the Prophet's tomb.[52] The last such despatch was about 1895. The satisfaction which one of the eunuchs who went to Mecca at that time found in his work there has already been noted (see p. 5). Another old Bagirmian eunuch, after many years of service in charge, he said, of the Zam-Zam well, returned from Mecca in the later years of the nineteenth century to end his days peacefully in Abeshr.[53]

Slaves as currency

The leader of a trading caravan from Futa Jallon to the West African coast in the nineteenth century, too sensible to fall captive under the romantic spell of the mere name of Timbuktu, did nevertheless prefer the market of that city.

> 'Ah!' said the astute trafficker, 'no market is a good one for the African, in which he cannot openly exchange his slaves for whatever the original owner or importer can sell without fear! Slaves . . . are our money.'[54]

Nachtigal also noted how slaves came to be regarded as one of the more useful substitutes for money. They became, in effect, a store of value, albeit one which medical hazards made extremely risky.[55] The reasons for the failure of Nach-

[52] Barth, 1857–8, iii, 372.
[53] Gaden, 1907, 439–40, 442–3, 445.
[54] Canot, 1928, 135–6.
[55] cf. J. F. Ade Ajayi, 'West African states at the beginning of the nineteenth century', in Ajayi and Espie, 1965, 254: 'Slaves were used in large transactions as a form of currency.' Also, Report on Lagos for 1891, 58, cit. McPhee, 1926, 234: 'The slave has become the cheque book of the country, and has been necessary for all large

tigal's friend, the Sharif al-Medeni, to return home from
Kuka included the epidemics which thinned the ranks of
the slaves whom he had accumulated, along with ivory
and ostrich feathers, to finance the journey.[56] Human as
well as medical factors might complicate the utility of slaves
as a form of money. In the mid-nineteenth century, in
Boporo, a Muslim centre in Liberia, one man lent another a
slave to take on a journey in the direction of Monrovia.
Near Monrovia, once within which slaves were by law free
(see above, p. 161), this slave ran away, and the lender had
later to bring an action against the borrower, to recover the
lost value.[57]

It was perhaps not surprising that, in the unusually
straitened circumstances of Abu Sekkin, fugitive king of
Bagirmi, he should try determinedly to satisfy his obligations
of hospitality and to pay for the horses which had been
brought to him from Bornu by pressing Nachtigal to accept
some slaves.[58] The proprieties, in fact, were eventually observed by a gift of ivory.[59] But in quite different circumstances, on his way to Abu Sekkin's camp, Nachtigal was
offered a dozen slaves by a village chief who wished Nachtigal's party to reinforce his own men on a raid.[60] Even in
Kuka, where a more or less satisfactory currency system
existed, based on the Maria Theresa dollar and the cowrie,
barter transactions were still common and slaves were often
offered in payment of debts, the offer of old slaves who had
outlived their usefulness being indeed one of the devices
used to evade the payment of debts to foreign merchants.[61]
On several occasions Nachtigal himself had trouble because
a debtor wanted him to accept slaves at least in part settle-

payments. Unfortunately he has a trick of dying while passing from
hand to hand, and it is possible that the less perishable currency
[silver coin] will oust him from the commercial field.'

[56] i, 639–40.   [57] Bowen, 1857, 81–2.   [58] ii, 654.
[59] ii, 655.   [60] ii, 592.   [61] i, 704.

ment of an obligation,[62] or he found it impossible to raise a
loan from his friends because they had nothing to offer him
but slaves or camels.[63] Payment in slaves was in itself quite
a respectable financial operation, sometimes used by Lamino
who enjoyed a high reputation as an honest and trustworthy
debtor.[64] The possession of a good supply of slaves not only
strengthened the social standing of men of rank, but also
made them better credit risks.

In the use of slaves as currency, or in any other commercial transaction in which they served a role somewhat akin
to currency, it is difficult, just as it is at many points in this
survey, to distinguish how much arises from the original
Islamic heritage, and how much from the local African custom. The legal texts repeatedly make special mention of
commercial regulations applying to slaves. The law of sale
includes frequent references to slaves;[65] purchase *en bloc* is
forbidden for slaves, clothing, or anything else that can be
counted easily;[66] a guarantee for a slave is valid, if explicitly
stipulated or part of local procedure, for three days at the
total responsibility of the seller—such a guarantee, extended
to a year, insures only against madness, elephantiasis and
leprosy;[67] it is illegal to sell certain things, such as a runaway slave or camel;[68] anything may be made the object
of a loan, save slave girls and silver dust;[69] if a female
slave is given as security, a child born to her after the contract is agreed becomes part of the security, but her goods
do not unless special provision is made for this.[70]

In these and other like provisions, it is clear that the religious law provides considerable precedent for regarding
slaves in an economic, almost a fiscal way. Yet at the same
time there are similar precedents to be found in parts of

[62] iii, 6, 19.
[63] ii, 306.   [64] i, 602.   [65] Ibn Abi Zayd, 200 ff.
[66] *ibid.*, 212.   [67] *ibid.*, 210.   [68] *ibid.*, 208, 214.
[69] *ibid.*, 206.   [70] *ibid.*, 236.

Africa where there has been little Muslim influence. For example, an American traveller near Badagry, in Yorubaland, in 1850 saw the corpse of a slave bound in mats and suspended, several feet above the ground, between two stakes. This, he was told, was the customary mode of burial for a slave who died while in pawn for debt, so that his original owner, the debtor, on returning from the interior, should know that the creditor had not sold him.[71] In Katanga and the surrounding area, a system called *nkole* was in force, whereby the aggrieved party might seize someone, someone perhaps only very remotely connected with the offender, in any dispute. If the offender still declined to offer adequate compensation, the innocent third person who had been seized might be enslaved, and thus himself provide the compensation.[72] An introductory survey—which does not, however, mention Islam—has been made of pawnship in a wide region of Central Africa.[73] Observers sometimes called it debt slavery, or even domestic slavery; the pawn owner in many instances acquired hereditary rights, and the status of pawn was itself heritable. Pawns, in this area, seem to have been more important as compensation for an injury, leading to a strengthening of the pawn owner's lineage, than in any narrower economic sense. A somewhat parallel system, called panyarring, obtained in West Africa, where it was apparently much abused in order to provide recruits for the Atlantic trade.

A slave who might be used as a medium of exchange, in any of the forms just described, was peculiarly liable to that

[71] Bowen, 1857, 101.

[72] Crawford, 1914, 9 ff. He tells of a family of four taken as *nkole*; the father was killed, and the two daughters made concubines of the aggrieved chief. Just after, the chief died, and one of the girls was buried alive with him. Crawford (195-6) also mentioned two boys bartered for one man.

[73] Mary Douglas, 'Matriliny and pawnship in Central Africa', *Africa*, 1964, 301-13.

insecurity which has been noted earlier as inherent in slave status (see pp. 103–5). One of the favourite slaves of King Muhammad of Darfur, Adam, who attained a position of great importance shortly before Nachtigal's visit to that country, acquired the nickname of Tarbush from an episode which vividly illustrated this hazard. Having been presented with a tarbush by a passing merchant, the king gave instructions to express his thanks by the counter-present of a slave. An official, who had a grudge against Adam, handed him over to the merchant, and it was with some difficulty that he was retrieved to resume his career in the king's service.[74]

[74] iii, 397–8.

CHAPTER IX

THE SLAVE MARKET IN KUKA

The slave section, an important part of the great market held every Monday in Kuka, was supplied from three main sources. Some were captured in government raids in the surrounding Pagan territories south, west and south-west of Bornu; others came from tribute paid by vassal princes, who carried on continuous warfare against their Pagan neighbours to discharge this obligation; and some came through trade with nearby Hausa countries, Adamawa, and especially Bagirmi.[1] Slave dealers set up their booths, protected from the sun and rain, on the south side of the eastern market, and there were displayed slaves of both sexes and all ages, with or without chains, from all the Pagan countries south of the Sudan states.[2] Slatin gave a comparable picture of the slave market in Omdurman during the Mahdiya.[3] Hurgronje described the slave market in Mecca in most amiable terms.[4] Comparing Mecca and Cairo, in the 1880s, he said:

> No unbeliever comes to Mekka, while the Azhar Mosque [in Cairo] has been defiled by the feet of English men and women. In Mekka there is a slave market. In Egypt slaves can only be bought in secret, as if it were a sin.[5]

[1] i, 701. [2] i, 683-6.
[3] Slatin, 1896, 557. [4] Hurgronje, 1931, 14-15.
[5] ibid., 185.

An African Muslim cleric, visiting Freetown in 1792, told the governor that Freetown 'ranks next in holiness to Mecca and Medina, for no slave lives or is sold here'.[6] The visitor, it seems likely, had studied a little what it might please the Governor to hear.

The price structure in the Kuka market clearly indicated the general supply and demand situation. It seems probable, though Nachtigal did not specifically say so, that most slaves were females. Of those who eventually got through to the caravans for the Mediterranean, it has been estimated that some 60 per cent were young women, and another 10 per cent children under the age of ten.[7] In one caravan of 400–500 which passed through Qatrun from Bornu to the coast when Eduard Vogel was there towards the end of 1853, most of the slaves were girls or children under 12. Vogel saw at most fifteen men, and was told that they would not be relieved of their chains until they reached Murzuq.[8] As men were more likely than women to be killed during a slave-raid, women and children would usually be in a majority when the booty was rounded up at the end of the day. At the same time the demand for women, both as concubines and for domestic service, was much livelier than the demand for men, so much so that at all ages, despite the disparity in supply, the price of women was usually higher than that for men. In East Africa, too, Burton in 1860 reported the price of females as everywhere about one-third higher than that of males.[9] This was in contrast with the conditions in the United States, where female slaves usually brought about three-quarters of the price of male slaves of

[6] Diary entry of 3 November 1792 of Lt J. Clarkson, in *Sierra Leone Studies*, March 1927, 95–6.
[7] Boahen, 1964, 128.
[8] 'Eduard Vogels Reise nach Central-Afrika', *Petermanns Mitteilungen* 1855, 251.
[9] Burton, 1860, ii, 376.

similar age.[10] On the West African coast, where the pattern
of American demand had some effect, Canot reported that
women slaves who were over 25 years were subject to a 20
per cent. price reduction, though if such 'were staunchly-
built, and gave promising tokens for the future', their price
was the same as that of able-bodied men. Children, he
added, were rarely purchased at the coastal factories, but
might be traded advantageously in the local towns.[11]
Somewhat surprisingly, Leo Africanus, costing presents
given to the ruler of Fez in the early sixteenth century,
valued men above women: good men slaves he put at 20
ducats, women slaves at 15, eunuchs at 40, and civet cats at
200.[12]

Much of the demand for women depended a good deal
on the individual tastes of the buyer; in the Kuka market
young women commanded prices ranging from 40 to 100
Maria Theresa dollars. Consumers' freedom of choice in
this connection might lead to unexpected consequences; in
accordance with the principle that only the testimony of
people of the highest moral probity was admissible in a
court of law, an otherwise respectable citizen of Cordova
was once rejected as a witness on the ground that on one
occasion he had been so smitten with desire for a slave girl
as to pay for her a sum far in excess of her real value.[13]

The *sedasi*, the boy who measured six spans from the
ankle to the tip of the ears—the word comes from the Arabic
sudasi, applied also to a six-letter word, a hexagon, and so
forth—aged usually from 12 to 15, was a more standardized
item of commerce in Bornu, and movements in his cost indicated the general situation in slave prices. A foreign mer-

[10] *Encyclopedia of the Social Sciences*, New York 1934, vol. 14,
85.
[11] Canot, 1928, 90 n.
[12] Leo Africanus, A, ii, 308–9; B, i, 139.
[13] N. J. Coulson, 'Doctrine and practice in Islamic law', *Bulletin
of the School of Oriental and African Studies*, 1956, 220.

chant, enquiring about the state of the market, would ask, How much are *sedasi*? *Sedasi* figure in the popular songs and poetry of the central Sudan: a Shuwa Arabic poem, recounting the deeds of the folk hero Abu Zayd, tells how he offered, for a splendid white mare which he eventually acquired by the cheaper method of murdering its owner, 99 old women, 99 slaves of five spans, and 99 *sedasi*.[14] A praise singer at the court of Bornu claimed that the *galadima* had rewarded his poetry with a present of twelve slave girls and twelve *sedasi*.[15]

There was, in addition, a brisk demand in Bornu for both boys and girls in the five-span group, from 10 to 13, the girls again generally more expensive than the boys; seven-span boys, 15 to 20, brought good prices, though they were more difficult to train, and more likely to run away. Older men suffered even more from these defects, and were not much in demand. They were, moreover, likely to keep up a spirit of discontent among their womenfolk, and one case was actually recorded in Bagirmi where, partly for these reasons, some captured men were resettled, with an appropriate number of women, on the site of a devastated village.[16] For older women who could be used in household work somewhat higher prices were paid than for men of the same age.

Eunuchs, mainly from Bagirmi, seldom came into the open market, as they were usually sold privately to dealers who were confident that they could dispose of them among the magnates of the Muslim world in Europe, Asia and Africa.[17] Nachtigal also saw offered for sale in the Kuka market, for export to the north, deaf and dumb slave girls,

---

[14] J. R. Patterson, *Stories of Abu Zeid the Hilali in Shuwa Arabic*, London 1930, 24 and 3.

[15] J. R. Patterson, *Kanuri songs*, Lagos 1926, 22.   [16] ii, 651.

[17] According to Gaden (1907, 436), the sultans never sold eunuchs, but sometimes presented them to other sultans or sent them to Mecca and Medina for the service of the holy places.

much sought after as servants for the wives of these magnates, and dwarfs, a favourite plaything for Muslim princes;
no prices were recorded for them, though they were said to
be less costly than eunuchs. The Dinka deaf-mute whom
al-Hajj Ahmed Tangatanga, Nachtigal's patron on the road
from Wadai to Darfur, purchased from a young Arab in
1874 has already been mentioned (see above p. 13). Bornu
dwarfs evidently enjoyed widespread popularity. In 1653
the *mai* of Bornu sent some 125 slaves to the pasha of Tripoli, including twenty eunuchs and five dwarfs.[18] Clapperton's party found a Bornu dwarf near Badagry in 1825,
and tried to buy him his freedom; but the slave did not wish
to be sold, and his master refused to part with him.[19]

Nachtigal's price list for slaves in the Kuka market in
1870[20] is summarized below. The Maria Theresa dollar, in
which all prices were quoted, was at that time worth about
4 marks.[21]

An old man	4 to 5 MT dollars
An old woman	6 to 10
A strong adult man	12 to 14
A middle-aged woman	10 to 15
A young adult man	15 to 18
A 7-span youth, aged 15 to 20	16 to 22
A 6-span boy, 12 to 15, or a 5-span girl, 10 to 13	20 to 25
A 5-span boy, 10 to 13	16 to 20
A young girl or woman	40 to 100
A boy eunuch	50 to 80

It is interesting, for purposes of comparison, to note that
at the same time the price of a fine riding horse, bred by
the Shuwa or Tubu, was 20 to 40 dollars, and of a good
strong riding horse of the usual local breed, 15 to 25 dol-

[18] de la Roncière, 1919, 82–3.   [19] Clapperton, 1829, 16.
[20] i, 692.   [21] i, 702.

lars. A northern camel which had come through the desert
sold for up to 15 dollars, a camel from the Tuareg, or from
Kanem or Wadai, for 15 to 40 dollars. In 1871 Nachtigal
paid 30 dollars for the maintenance for more than nine
months of two servants and a horse left behind by him in
Kuka while on his expedition to the Awlad Sulayman; this
included paying a woman to carry water and cook two meals
daily for his men. Among the Teda of Tibesti, a good camel
was worth about as much as a *sedasi*; its price in Kawar,
about half-way between Murzuq and Kuka, was said to be
from 25 to 35 dollars in 1869, which was a good deal more
than the price of a camel in Fezzan at that time.[22] In Darfur in 1874 a *sedasi* cost 30 dollars.[23]

Clapperton quoted prices in cowries in Sokoto which
showed very much the same ratio between men and women
as in Nachtigal's Kuka; a youth aged 13 to 20 cost from
10,000 to 20,000 cowries; a virgin girl of 14 or 15 commonly
cost about 30,000; an exceptionally handsome woman might
fetch 40,000 or 50,000.[24] At the Yoruba capital in the same
year, he found horses selling for from 80,000 to 100,000
cowries, while prime slaves were 40,000 to 60,000.[25] By
1852, prices in the Sokoto market had apparently risen: a
lad 'of very indifferent appearance' was sold for 33,000
shells, while a pony fetched 30,000.[26]

Somewhat more elaborate comparisons of relative slave
prices are available for the Cairo market in the nineteenth
century. The price of black girls was usually, though not
always, a little higher than that of boys. The price of black
adults was higher than that of boys by 50 to 100 per cent.,
and eunuchs fetched double or three times the price of
black male adults. Abyssinian boys were a little more expensive than Negroes, the difference rising to 100 per cent. in
the higher age brackets. Abyssinian girls cost from 25 to 600

[22] i, 460.   [23] iii, 484.   [24] Clapperton, 1829, 222, 232.
[25] *ibid.*, 59.   [26] Barth, 1857–8, iv, 180.

per cent. more than Negro girls, and white Circassian girls were sometimes ten times as expensive as Abyssinian girls.[27]

Oversupply cut prices. In the glutted market of Bagirmi in 1872, old men could be purchased for 2 to 3 dollars; women, old or young, for 5; children of 6 or 8 could be exchanged for an ordinary Bagirmi or Bornu shirt, which in Kuka cost three-quarters of a dollar.[28] A comparable glut was recorded after a successful campaign by Samori's troopers in the west, at about the same time: 6 chickens were sold for one slave, a sheep for three slaves, a cow for ten[29]—but these prices may have been the consequence also of a shortage of food on that occasion.[30] In Katanga in 1887 Arnot saw Arab slavers buy a man for 10 yards of calico; he was told that women and children would fetch 12 to 16 yards.[31] Children too small to walk were usually thrown away; Arnot soon acquired a small family of them.[32]

[27] Baer, 1967, 427.   [28] ii, 652.
[29] Kouroubari, 1959, 563.
[30] V. Monteil, *L'Islam noir*, 1964, 101.
[31] Arnot, 1889, 205.   [32] *ibid.*, 183–4, 213–15, 243.

CHAPTER X

CONCLUSION
ANTI-SLAVERY MEASURES

In countries actually or nominally under the control of the Sultan of Turkey, more or less vigorous efforts were being made at the time of Nachtigal's travels to enforce anti-slave-trade edicts. It was, however, nowhere easy to ensure the effective administration of these, partly because many people benefited materially from the trade, which to them appeared perfectly legitimate and natural. Early in 1826 the British Consul in Tripoli estimated that the Pasha there had lost about £10,000 during the lull in the slave trade resulting from nothing more serious than the presence of British missions in the interior.[1] For governors and other officials in distant provinces, both the temptations to evasion and the difficulties of supervision were increased. Some provincial officials, very poorly paid, indifferent to the broader political considerations which weighed with their distant masters in Cairo or Constantinople, and perhaps with a direct monetary concern in the trade, accordingly made only perfunctory efforts to enforce the law.

Richardson's experience in Ghadames, in the 1840s, although no anti-slave-trade laws applied there at the time, shows the financial importance of the trade. The market in Tunis had already been shut, and slave-dealers were seeking

[1] F.O. 76/20, Warrington to Hay, 29 January, 1826, Public Record Office, London.

outlets in Algeria.[2] The governor of Ghadames levied a duty of 10 dollars per head on slaves; this was a very heavy tax, apparently 25 per cent or even more of the sale value of the slaves.[3] At one time, the governor had to borrow money from Richardson, and was able to repay it only when a caravan of forty slaves arrived and the tax on them had been paid.[4]

According to Eduard Vogel, the transit toll on slaves levied at Murzuq in the latter part of 1853 was three *mahabub* per head, a *mahabub* being worth, in Nachtigal's time, a little less than a Maria Theresa dollar. Just as Vogel was leaving Murzuq, the Pasha added another *mahabub* to the toll. Vogel estimated that the three *mahabub* toll was equivalent to an *ad valorem* tax of about 5 per cent. The general transit toll levied on other goods on their way to the Mediterranean coast was 12 per cent, except on ivory, on which 3 per cent was paid.[5]

By the time of Nachtigal's visit sixteen years later, the transit toll on slaves had been reduced to two Maria Theresa dollars; according to Nachtigal, this might bring to the Governor an annual income of 40,000 marks, a figure which suggests annual imports of some 5000 slaves, substantially more than his regular salary, and in this the official responsible for administering the control in the most southerly oasis of Fezzan, Kawar, also had his share.[6] Officials were reluctant to abandon such a lucrative source of revenue; while Nachtigal was in Fezzan instructions against the slave trade were frequently issued, but if the arrival of a slave caravan were expected, the instructions were held back

[2] Richardson, 1848, i, 269, 355.
[3] *ibid.*, i, 253–4, 355. The price of slaves in Ghadames which Richardson mentioned ranged from twenty to fifty dollars (i, 253–4, 258–9, 263, 293).
[4] Richardson, 1848, i, 269, 293.
[5] *Petermanns Mitteilungen*, 1855, 251–3.
[6] i, 132–3, 701.

until the slave tax had been paid.[7] Towards the end of 1869 one such caravan from Bornu was admitted into Murzuq secretly by night, though the Governor took care to collect his tax.[8] It was suggested that, in view of the current risks, he had demanded and received double the usual amount, though apparently Nachtigal did not vouch for the accuracy of this report. Early in 1869 small slave caravans were met daily on the road between Tripoli and Murzuq, and enquiries about slave prices were taken quite as a matter of course, like enquiries about the prices of corn, oil or butter.[9] Prohibition measures could be evaded by concealing the slaves, formerly brought openly into the town markets of Murzuq and Tripoli, in suburban gardens or in nearby villages, where they could be disposed of one by one.

There was still in 1874 considerable uncertainty about the rigour with which the ban upon the slave trade would be applied in practice in the outlying provinces of Egypt under the regime of Khedive Ismail. The caravan with which Nachtigal travelled on the last recorded stage of his journey, from Darfur to el-Obeid, the capital of Kordofan, included many slaves. Some were part of the ordinary households of masters travelling in the caravan, but others, including a considerable number of 'hot' slaves (see above pp. 40–1), were intended for sale.[10] The news received as the caravan approached el-Obeid, that it had become impossible to sell slaves in Egypt, caused great concern.[11] It was rumoured that the *mudir* in el-Obeid had confiscated all the slaves in the town, not only recent purchases, but also those that had been bought a long time before, though the latter had subsequently been returned to their owners on the instructions of the Governor-General of the Egyptian Sudan. The members of the caravan engaged in long debates about the course to be followed in face of this depress-

[7] i, 133.   [8] i, 480–1.   [9] i, 64.
[10] iii, 489.   [11] iii, 495.   [12] iii, 502–3.

ing prospect; it was eventually agreed that as many slaves as possible should be sold before leaving Kordofan, and that the others should be sent back to Darfur.[12] Some of the slaves intended for sale still, however, remained, and a Nile merchant who came out to meet the caravan took possession of all of them, confident that his skill in concealing slaves unnoticed in the villages of the district, combined with the venality of the Egyptian officials, would make it easy to hold them until the government once more relaxed the strict application of the edict prohibiting imports of slaves.[13]

Similar smuggling was described on the road from Gondar to the Egyptian Sudan in 1855. Doka, a Sudanese village, had formerly been an important slave-trade centre between Ethiopia and Sennar. By 1855, the trade was illegal. (It was also illegal in Ethiopia under Theodore, but smuggling went on there too.)[14] In Doka there were no European consuls to receive information and make the necessary representations to the authorities. The Coptic civil servant and the Muslim kashif or judge were not so remorseless. The Muslims of Gondar were said to keep their slaves concealed in cellars under their houses. (Slave pits were not uncommon, witness the caves under Cape Coast Castle on the coast of modern Ghana, and the remains in Darfur.[15]) The slaves were moved only at night, and then with their mouths stuffed with rags lest they should cry out.[16] Cameron, west of Lake Tanganyika in 1874, observed the use of a wooden snaffle to gag slaves, in an area where there was considerable local kidnapping and slaves might be offered for sale to a passing caravan when still quite close to their own homes.[17]

Even among the high authorities responsible for issuing edicts against the slave trade, there was in Nachtigal's time

[13] iii, 505.   [14] Krapf, 1860, 466–7.
[15] Arkell, 1961, 213–14.   [16] Krapf, 1860, 470.
[17] Cameron, 1885, 256.

a certain ambivalence of attitude. There was said to be still some effective demand for slaves in Constantinople, and the Governor-General of Tripoli apparently felt no embarrassment in including among the commissions assigned to Bu Aischa the collection for the Sultan of Turkey not only of some lions and tigers, but also of a few eunuchs, 'for which there was a considerable demand in the palaces of the great men of Constantinople, and which form the most acceptable present to the powerful men responsible for the dealings of dignitaries who live far from the capital with the Commander of the Faithful'.[18] In Kuka, Bu Aischa collected both for himself and for the Governor-General of Tripoli a considerable number of slaves, and some which were presented to him he exchanged for ivory and ostrich feathers.[19] When he finally departed more than two years after he had set out from Tripoli, he took with him a large company of slaves, including eunuchs, deafmutes and dwarfs.[20] On the other hand, there was also perhaps a desire to avoid awkward publicity; Nachtigal thought, for example, that the initial reluctance to allow him to join Bu Aischa's caravan might have been based on a wish to restrict his opportunities of seeing how even the highest authorities still connived at the slave trade.[21]

In the slave markets in the Sudan countries themselves, there was no objection in principle to the slave trade, nor any effort, however half-hearted, to abolish it. The difficult adjustments created in these countries by an enforced steadily diminishing export demand for slaves have already been noted (see above pp. 76–7), and Nachtigal drew attention to this as an important contributory cause of the decline of Murzuq. In earlier years no Murzuq merchant could engage in trade with the Sudan without buying and selling slaves, so that, as part of their business contracted, the in-

[18] i, 481.   [19] ii, 15.   [20] iii, 3–4.   [21] i, 482.

centive to maintain their trading connections correspondingly weakened.[22]

However much officials might drag their feet in carrying out the perhaps reluctant instructions of their masters, the trade was none the less clearly on the way out. The number of slaves which earlier had passed annually through Fezzan Nachtigal believed to have been between 5000 and 8000. By 1869 this had been reduced by at least two-thirds.[23] A caravan which went north with two of Nachtigal's servants after his first arrival in Kuka carried with it 1400 slaves, but by that time such caravans were rare.[24] Slave parties were encountered much later, but they were very small. Even in 1906, a little south of Qatrun, a British traveller met a trader from Tibesti who had with him half a dozen slave children whom he had bought in Wadai in the hope of selling them in North Africa.[25]

The trans-Saharan slave trade is now virtually a matter of ancient history. The subsequent course of domestic slavery in the Sudan countries, as they collapsed under the pressure of superior European power, is another story. Many of Nachtigal's African friends were more or less aware that among the numerous unaccountable eccentricities which they attributed to Europeans an antipathy to slavery was often to be found; nevertheless, just as the ancient Greeks had done, and whatever their social status, they 'always took slavery for granted as one of the facts of human existence', and none of them a century ago was able 'to imagine that there could be a civilized society without slaves'.[26]

[22] i, 24.   [23] i, 133.   [24] i, 701.
[25] Vischer, 1910, 195.
[26] M. I. Finley, 1960, 53, 61.

ADDENDA

After the proofs of this book had reached their final form, we found, a little to our chagrin, two further substantive references in Nachtigal to the subject of slavery. In order to fulfil our undertaking to give Nachtigal's slavery material in its entirety, these two passages are added here. The first might be read in conjunction with the other references to slaves being prepared for their arrival at market, on page 97; the second in conjunction with the discussion of tribute, as on page 184.

Al-Hajj Ahmed Tangatanga, the Dongolan with whom Nachtigal travelled to Darfur, did his best to make his slaves attractive for the Darfur market. He gave them new clothes before they entered the capital, el-Fasher, two slaves riding on a camel, their hair arranged in the favourite Darfur style, and with appropriate applications of the local beauty treatment which involved the use of such things as red clay, butter and cloves.[1]

A vassal tribe might accept the tributary obligation to supply slaves as part of the natural order of things, but nevertheless object strongly when the slaves thus supplied were used for commercial purposes. The Birgid, for example, in eighteenth-century Darfur, were said to have rebelled when some of the female slaves whom they supplied each year as concubines for the king, or as servants in his household, were channelled into the domestic market and sold to the Nile merchants.[2]

[1] iii, 336.   [2] iii, 375.

Bibliography

This bibliography is for the most part limited to items which bear directly and principally on the theme of slavery in Muslim Africa. Of such items, there are very few. Readers interested in exploring the Atlantic slave trade will find in the note on page 1 a sufficient introduction to the very voluminous literature. In the footnotes, all books are cited in full on the first occasion, and thereafter are identified by author and, in most cases, date.

G. Baer, 'Slavery in nineteenth-century Egypt', *Journal of African History*, 1967.

Abubakar Tafawa Balewa, *Shaihu Umar*, tr. M. Hiskett, London 1967. A novel by the late Prime Minister of Nigeria, telling the story of a man who was enslaved.

N. R. Bennett, 'Christian and Negro slavery in eighteenth-century North Africa', *Journal of African History*, 1960.

R. Cohen (ed.), 'Slavery in Africa', Special Supplement, *Transaction*, Jan.-Feb. 1967.

J. D. Fage, 'Slavery and the slave trade in the context of West African history', *Journal of African History*, 1969. A recent and radical reassessment of the African slave trade, primarily about the Atlantic but with some interesting suggestions for Saharan parallels.

H. H. Johnston, *The history of a slave*, London 1889. An imaginary autobiography, based in part on real incidents.

F. D. Lugard, 'Slavery in all its forms', *Africa*, 1933.

Michael Mason, 'Population density and "slave raiding"—the case of the Middle Belt of Nigeria', *Journal of African History*, 1969.

J. N. Nicolaisen, 'Slavery among the Tuareg in the Sahara: a preliminary analysis of its structure', *Kuml* (Aarhus, Denmark), 1957.

Irmgard Sellnow, 'Die Stellung der Sklaven in der Hausa-Gesellschaft', *Mitteilungen des Instituts für Orientforschung*, 1964.

M. G. Smith, 'Slavery and emancipation in two societies', *Social and Economic Studies* (Kingston, Jamaica), 1954.

Index

Abd al-Malik bin Marwan, 119
Abd al-Rahman, sultan of Darfur, 183
Abd al-Rahman, freed slave, 66
Abd al-Salam, 28, 29
Abd Masuma, 49
Abdulahi, Sarkin Kano, 167
Abdullah bin Salim, 157
Abdullahi dan Fodio, 32
Abeokuta, 66, 136
Abeshr, capital of Wadai, 13, 40, 188
abolition of slavery, effects of, 15–16, 21, 44–5, 59, 61, 64, 76, 104, 116 n. 131, 132, 146, 161, 189; European pressure for, 25, 74, 201, 203, 206; influence of Islam on, 27, 28–37, 50. See emancipation
Abubakr Kado, Sarkin Kano, 172
Abul-Mawahib, 185
Abu Sekkin, 25, 91, 104, 150, 162, 189
Abushiri, 123
Abu Yazid, 125
Abu Zayd, 196
Adam Tarbush, 192
Adama, 52, 122, 182
Adamawa, 27, 32, 33, 47, 51, 54, 76, 96, 122, 133, 137, 152, 158, 165, 167, 181, 182, 186, 193
Afonja, 113
afterlife, 19, 162

Agades, 141, 173
agriculture, 13, 39, 41, 42, 44, 51, 56, 68, 132–8, 153, 157, 158
Ahaggar, 14, 137
Ahmad al-Bakkai, 40
Ahmad Baba, 35
Ahmad Graan, 155
Ahmadu, Shehu, 43, 121, 124, 159
Air, 72
Ali, king of Wadai, 38, 39, 152
Ali of Mandara, 61
Ali of Shiraz, 124
Ali, Sarkin Gobir, 140
Ali, sultan of Sokoto, 185
Ali bin Umar, 147, 153
Ali Dinar, 33, 170
Ali Folon, 173
Aliyu Babba, 126
alms, 52, 57, 146, 168, 176; slaves as, 31, 42–4, 76, 184–9, 191
Alooma, Idris, 24, 28, 29, 145, 155, 156, 161
Amina, 172
Anderson, Benjamin, 106, 112
apostasy, 35
Arabia, 9, 45, 46, 54, 101, 102, 122, 135, 145, 149, 155, 171; Arabian nights, 48
Arabic, 36, 49, 112, 139, 195, 196
Ardo Hammadu, 167

Arnot, F. S., 79, 145, 199
Ashanti, 157
'atāqa itq, 52, 59
Atiku, chief of Gabow, 182
Atiqu, sultan of Sokoto, 173
Atlantic slave trade, 1–2, 24,
  46, 72, 78, 85–90, 96, 137,
  142, 191. See Brazil
Awdaghast, 12, 119, 140
Awlad Sulayman, 20, 29, 39,
  100, 103, 127, 183, 184, 198

Baba of Karo, 33, 53, 104
Badagry, 67, 191, 197
Bagdad, 62
Bagirmi, 5, 17, 18, 25, 27, 39,
  54, 63, 64, 67, 72, 77, 82,
  91, 93, 104, 138, 144, 149–
  50, 152, 153, 160, 168,
  174–5, 176, 177, 183, 184,
  188, 189, 193, 196, 199
Bahia, see Brazil
al-Bakri, 71, 85, 119
Balewa, Sir Abubakar Tafawa,
  83, 162, 209
Bambara, 68, 101, 124, 152,
  160
Bantu, 152
Baraghwata, 58
Barca Gana, 158
Barder, 110
Bariba, 147
Barth, H., 11, 20, 28, 32, 61,
  63, 72, 76, 82, 96, 107, 133,
  139, 149, 158, 174, 181, 184,
  188
Basra, 62, 107
Bauchi, 6, 33, 65, 95, 181
Bawa, 121
Beeljie, 87
Begu, 125
Bello, Muhammad, 28, 35, 52,
  95, 126, 140, 156, 160, 161,
  167, 170, 173
Benghazi, 72, 96
Bible, 34, 59 n., 138
Bida, chief town of Nupe, 83

Bilma, 96
Birgid, 207
Blyden, E. W., 46, 47, 50, 89
Boahen, A. A., 64 n., 73, 73 n.,
  194 n.
Bokari, 32
Bombay, Speke's guide, 54
booty, distribution of, 23, 84,
  92 n., 114, 115, 159, 161–2,
  194
Boporo, 112, 141, 189
Borgu, 12, 36, 85, 131, 139,
  140
bori, 6, 67, 143
Borku, 5, 29, 39, 41, 149
Bornu, 5 and passim
Bowen, T. J., 64, 191
Brass, 89
Brava, 120
Brazil, 5, 36, 45, 49, 54, 56,
  66, 108, 112, 115, 116, 127,
  140, 142, 149, 160
bride-price and dowry, 17, 76,
  81 n., 105, 106, 187
Bruce, James, 154
Brumley, 161
Bu Aischa, 38, 96, 205
Buba Njidda, 182
Buckor Sano, 120
Budduma, 14, 17 n., 20, 21, 30
Buganda, 76, 125–6, 157, 165
building, slaves employed in, 39,
  43, 138
Burkomanda, 175
Burton, Richard, 17, 61, 74, 85,
  93, 142, 145, 194
Buxton, T. F., 73

Caillié, R., 138
Cairo, 31, 61, 119, 153, 171,
  184, 193, 198, 201
camels, 14, 43, 58–9, 95, 96,
  97, 102 n., 123, 137, 149,
  180, 190, 198, 207
Cameron, V. L., 144, 161, 204
Cameroon, 18, 27, 142, 147
cannibalism, 18, 19, 26, 86, 157

Canot, T., 86, 87, 88, 89, 95, 186, 195
Cape Coast, 60, 204
Cape Mount, 17
caravans of slaves, 63, 64, 72, 86, 87, 89, 91–8, 144, 148, 182, 202, 203, 206. See porters
cattle, 13, 42, 43, 81, 133, 136, 137, 140, 156, 162, 181
Caucasus, 2
Chad, Lake, 14, 30, 33, 72, 77
children as slaves, 75, 76, 86, 94, 97, 100, 150, 158, 170, 174, 180, 194, 195, 197, 198, 206
China, 115
Christians, and anti-slavery, 24–6, 124, 194; and slaving, 18, 37–8, 46, 54–5, 57, 87, 124, 186; as slaves, 21, 34, 67, 113, 126, 140, 155; in Muslim law, 22, 35, 60, 117–18, 180; missionaries, 26, 76, 79
Circassians, 115, 122 n., 127, 199
circumcision, 46
Clapperton, H., 11–12, 36, 54, 63, 88, 96, 107, 108, 109, 131, 133, 138, 140, 142, 147, 148, 156, 160, 170, 186, 197, 198
cloth and cloth-working, 6, 18, 71, 74, 79, 115, 137, 142, 145, 180, 184, 199. See dress
colonies of slaves, 39–40, 151–4, 155, 159
concubines, 55, 100, 109, 116–29, 161, 162–3, 172, 184, 185, 198, 207. See harim
Congo Free State, 157
Constantinople, 54, 64, 127, 183, 184, 187, 201, 205
conversion, religious, 23, 26–7, 28, 31, 34, 36, 44, 45–52, 62, 63, 67 n., 113–14, 166

cooks, 139, 198
Cooley, W. D., 15
Crowther, Samuel, 113

Dahomey, 16 n., 36, 66
Dalatoa, 170
Dallons, 25
Damietta, 185
Danakil, 74, 156, 171 n.
Dar Fertit, 181
Darfur, 5, 13, 19, 33, 41, 50, 83, 123, 125, 166, 170, 174, 176, 181, 183, 187, 192, 197, 204, 207
Daud of Songhay, 42, 147, 154
Daura, 6
deaf-mutes, 13, 196, 205
Deba, 22, 31
Denham, D., 32, 36, 60, 63, 72, 94, 97, 106, 174
Dimar, 58
Dinka, 13
disease, 13, 53, 67–8, 92, 93, 95–6, 141, 144, 150, 186, 189, 191
diya, 105, 116 n.
Doka, 204
D'Ollone, 18
Dongola, 13, 207
Doughty, C. M., 18, 46, 145, 149 n.
dress, 32, 48, 59, 100, 103, 121, 149, 162, 168, 173, 182, 183, 185, 207. See cloth
Dunama, 153
Duncan, J., 65
dwarfs, 197, 205

ear-cutting, 58
East Africa, 57, 94, 95, 102; Arabs in, 26, 85–6, 99, 110–11; slave exports from, 2, 25, 45, 54, 61–2, 73, 78–80, 115, 138, 155
economic aspects of slavery, 3, 14, 44, 76–7, 131–2; profitability of slave-trade, 74–5, 97;

economic aspects . . . (cont'd)
slaves as medium of exchange,
188–92. See agriculture, mining, pledge or security for
debt, porters, prices and price
relationships
education, 14, 33, 36–7, 42–5,
49, 120, 121, 173
emancipation, 8 n., 20, 26–7, 28,
35, 41, 43, 44, 47, 50–60, 65,
78, 102 & n., 106, 110–11,
113–14, 117, 132, 159, 161,
197
Enarea, 124
Ennedi, 29, 104
enslavement of Muslims, 20, 21,
28–38, 39–40, 166
Eritrea, 160
Ethiopia, 25, 60, 124, 126, 138,
143, 155, 156, 172, 186
eunuchs, 53, 61, 81, 115, 120,
125 n., 126, 164, 170, 171–7,
183, 187, 195, 197, 205
European, colonial policies and
attitudes, 2, 5, 33, 64, 77,
147 n., 151, 157, 160, 163,
165, 175 n.; slaves, 121, 127,
140, 155–6, 174; slaving, 78,
80–1, 85–90, 137

Falaba, 65
Fali, 32
famine, 75–6, 93, 95
Fansiggah, 46
Fatimids, 63, 125
Fez, 42, 126, 140, 180, 187,
195, 202, 206
Fezzan, 5, 38, 42, 61, 64, 71,
72, 95, 98, 100, 152, 179,
183, 198
flags, 26, 32, 33
Freetown, 65, 67, 194
Freretown, 26
Fuladoyo, 111
Fulani, 29, 30, 32, 37, 43, 47,
54, 65, 95, 96, 112, 124, 128,
133, 136, 140, 141, 152, 156,

158, 164, 167, 173, 181, 182
Fumo Lotti, 110
Funj, 154, 166
Futa Jallon, 30, 46, 66, 86, 87,
89, 111, 133, 148, 162, 186,
188
Fyfe, C., 86

Gabow, 182
Gaden, H., 5, 175 n., 188 n.,
196
Galla, 45, 85, 138, 146, 160
Galliéni, 163
Gambia, 30, 85, 120, 127
Gamon, 111
Ganta, 82
Gao, 82
Gaoga, 82, 110, 185
Georgia, 2
Ghadames, 14, 61, 67, 72, 88,
97, 101, 103, 109, 117, 118,
122, 144, 154, 202
Ghambaru, 158
Ghat, 97
Gizima, 19
Gobir, 96, 121, 140, 156, 160,
173
Gojam, 124
gold, silver, 71, 83, 123, 141,
145, 173, 183, 189 n., 190
Gonja, 147
Gordon, General, 64
Goree, 36
Greek, attitude to slavery, 206
guns, 26, 79, 81–4, 124, 155–8,
159
Gwari, 162
Gworam, 33

al-Habib, 185
Hadeija, 32, 159, 165
Hadya, 171
Haiti, 108
al-Hajj Ahmad Tangatanga, 13,
197, 207
al-Hajj Bashir, 96, 122, 184
al-Hajj Jibril, 32

al-Hajj Muhammad el-Amin of
  Bagirmi, 174, 175
al-Hajj Umar, 40, 48, 113, 114,
  123, 151, 160, 162, 173
hakim, 50, 172
Ham, curse of, 34
harim, 87, 120, 122, 152, 171,
  173, 175, 183
Harris, W. Cornwallis, 78, 143,
  172
Hausa, 6, 18, 32, 33, 36, 53,
  67, 83, 100, 104, 109, 113,
  126, 134, 137, 138, 140, 142,
  143, 147, 153, 156, 157, 162,
  164, 167, 173, 193
Hawa, 68
Hayatu, 182
Hijaz, 73, 147
horses, 13, 23, 32, 41, 58, 71,
  81-2, 83, 93, 110, 122, 123,
  144, 148-9, 154, 155, 159,
  160, 162, 173, 180, 181, 182,
  183, 185, 189, 196, 197
'hot' slaves, 39-40, 203
Hurgronje, C. S., 193

Ibadan, 33
Ibn Abi Zayd, 6-7
Ibn Battuta, 4, 71, 119, 128,
  139, 163, 168, 171, 185
Ibn Hawqal, 121
Ibrahim of Bornu, 169
Iendwe, 137
Igala, 125
Ilorin, 113, 181
imam, 43, 47, 50, 92 n., 112,
  164
inheritance, by slaves, 7, 8, 20,
  41, 51, 154; of slaves, 13,
  54-5, 112, 167
Ishaq II, 173
Ismail Pasha, 83, 203
ivory and ivory trade, 79-80, 93,
  108, 137, 145, 181, 183, 185,
  189, 202, 205

Jahanka, 44

Jalula, 119
Jamaica, 49
Java, 115, 146
Jerbah, 59
Jesus I of Ethiopia, 186
Jews, 23, 34, 35, 117, 138
jihad, 21-7, 28, 31, 35, 48, 76,
  92 n., 113, 140, 160
Job ben Solomon, 1, 127
Jobson, R., 54, 107, 120
Judar Pasha, 138

Kababish, 33
Kabara, 164
kaffara, 8 n., 56
Kalema, 165
Kanajeji, 180
Kanem, 5, 14, 28, 29, 63, 64,
  72, 184
al-Kanemi, 29, 30, 128, 158,
  161, 170
Kano, 6, 11, 29, 32, 72, 76, 81,
  88, 90, 108, 109, 141, 149,
  152, 154, 156, 164, 167, 172,
  180
kashellawa, 169
Katanga, 126, 191, 199
Kati, 31
Katsina, 6, 20, 164, 167, 180
Kawar oasis, 38, 198, 202
Kayor, 165, 167
Khalil ibn Ishaq, 6
Khorasan, 62
Kilwa, 185
Kimre, 25
Kindschalia, 'the slave place',
  139
Kirk, Sir John, 21
Koelle, S. W., 37 n., 64, 65,
  78 n., 187 n.
kola, 105, 182
Kondeeah, 111
Kong, 83
Kontagora, 33
Koranko, 111
Kordofan, 5, 50, 154, 203
Krapf, J. L., 45, 46, 75

Kru, 20
Kuka, capital of Bornu, 13, 38,
    41, 43, 60, 61, 82, 91, 92,
    93, 97, 122, 127, 128, 132,
    144, 148, 149, 189, 193-9,
    205, 206
Kukuna, 111
Kutumbi, 172
Kwararafa, 180

Lamino, 13, 139, 159, 177, 190
Lander, Richard, 60, 95, 122,
    142
language, 4, 61-2, 65, 67, 69 n.,
    139, 143, 156. See Arabic
Lari, 63
Lat Dyor, 168
Lauwal, 133, 182
law, Muslim, 7-9, 21-4, 34-6,
    54, 190; Hanafi school, 61 n.,
    147; Maliki school, 6-10, 41,
    52, 57 n., 87 n., 118; status of
    slaves in, 7-10, 21, 48, 92,
    104, 113-14; confusion be-
    tween slave and free status,
    11, 15, 37-42, 59. See eman-
    cipation, inheritance, kaffara,
    mudabbar, mukatib
Leo Africanus, 4, 42, 71, 81,
    110, 126, 141, 172, 180, 185,
    187, 195
Liberia, 17, 18, 19, 37, 66, 81,
    82, 106, 112, 141, 161, 189
Logon, 142, 168, 169, 174
Loma, 19
Lugard, F. D., 60, 85 n., 107,
    111, 131, 146 n.

Mackay, A. M., 76
Madagascar, 110
Magaria, 133
Magongeni, 111
Mali, ancient, 119, 120, 163,
    166-7, 168
Malindi, 111
Malta, 37
Mamari Biton, 121

Mamluks, 156-7
Mandara, 29, 59, 61, 122, 139,
    174, 175
Mandingoes, 37, 44, 54, 86, 106,
    141
Mansa Musa, 52, 119, 145, 146,
    171
Mansur, 31, 164
Manyuema, 95, 126
Maracatos, 120
Maria de Fonseca, 126
markets, 25, 33, 77, 127, 164,
    193-9, 207
marriage, 7, 12, 20, 21, 23, 106,
    116, 117-18, 156
Masina, 43, 51, 118 n., 121,
    123, 159
Massenya, capital of Bagirmi,
    39, 40, 138, 188
Massufa Berbers, 128
Matacan river, 88
Matayu, 126
Mauny, R., 73
Mauritania, 45, 49, 68, 80, 103,
    105, 106, 120
Mbali, 126
Mecca, 5, 21 n., 24, 33, 62, 101,
    127, 132, 138, 145, 146, 147,
    153, 175, 187, 193
Medina, 171, 187
Mesopotamia, 107
mining, 108, 139
Mirambo, 111, 161
Mogadishu, 110, 120
Mogogoni, 110
Mombasa, 21 n., 26, 75, 110
Momodu Lamine, 112, 123, 145,
    163
Morocco, 72, 138, 165, 173, 180
mosques, 43, 46, 164, 171
Mossi, 44
Msidi, 126
mudabbar, 48, 54-5, 56
Muhammad I, of Songhay, 28,
    29, 31, 42, 81, 172-3
Muhammad al-Fadl, 125, 176
Muhammad Ali, 157

Muhammad D'Ghies, 63
Muhammad Rimfa, 170
mukātib, 47, 55, 56, 118
Murabid, 29
Murzuq, capital of Fezzan, 38, 64, 97, 136, 143, 202, 205
Musadu, 106
Musfeia, 32
Musgo, 139, 140
Mutesa, 125–6
Mwaibu, 111

Nachtigal, Gustav, 4 and passim
Nassarawa, 105
Ngigmi, 139
Ngolo, 52, 180
Ngongo Lutete, 157
Ngornu, 176
nkole, 191
nokena, 169
nomads and slaves, 15, 38, 39, 95, 125, 136–7, 140–1, 154, 165
North Africa, 24, 73
North America, 24
Nubia, 63, 157, 180
numbers of slaves, 11–16, 17, 39, 72–3, 76, 77, 95, 97, 101, 120, 145, 181, 182, 193, 206
Nupe, 76, 81, 82–3, 121, 125, 139, 143, 172

oaths, 7, 41, 55 & n., 57–8, 94, 118
el-Obeid, 203
Okrika, 99
Oman, 62
Omdurman, 193
Oubangi, 79
Ozi, 110

Pagan slaving, 8–10, 17–21, 25 n., 53, 136 & n., 174, 187 n., 190–1
Pate, 45, 180
pilgrimage, pilgrims, 5, 33, 46, 48, 53, 62, 64, 94, 96, 101 n.,

119, 123, 132, 145–7, 153, 175, 181 n.
pledge or security for debt, 38, 90, 190–1
Pope-Hennessy, J., 1, 94
porters, 79, 102, 141–8
prayer, 13, 28, 37, 45, 47, 48, 51, 56, 58, 62, 154, 164
prazo, 12, 75, 141
prices and price relationships, 56, 62, 73 n., 81–2, 83, 121, 122, 127, 140, 147 n., 174, 187, 194–9, 201–2
prisoners of war, 22, 34, 38–9, 51, 85, 100, 152
punishment, 8 & n., 36, 38, 49, 68, 86, 87–9, 103, 106, 113, 118–19, 125, 136, 147, 148, 167, 175; enslavement as, 35, 84–91

qadi, 42, 59, 159, 165
Qairawan, 108, 119
al-Qallabat, 158
Qatrun, 194, 206
Quran, 22, 28, 31, 43, 44, 46, 52, 62, 87, 94, 121, 145, 154 n.

Rabih, 92, 157, 181 n.
race, 18, 24, 44–5, 63 n., 106–7, 126–7, 198–9. See Ham, curse of
Ramadan, 24 & n., 26, 47, 53, 56, 57, 61, 67, 168
Ramadan, slave of al-Kanemi, 158
Rano, 6
ransom, 22, 29, 38, 80, 100
Reade, W., 86
religious obligations of Muslim slaves, 47–9, 55–6, 147
revolt, 25, 38, 49, 107–13, 165–6, 167, 172
Richardson, James, 14, 59, 67, 72, 97, 101, 122, 143, 144, 154, 201, 202

Rio Pongo, 87
runaway slaves, 59, 62, 92, 93, 103–4, 111, 114, 136 n., 142, 145, 158, 164, 189, 190

Sa'ad, Nachtigal's servant, 14, 38
Sahara, 1, 5, 14, 143; slave trade across, 1–2, 24, 71–8, 81, 94–5, 120, 152, 194, 201–2, 205–6
Said, Richardson's servant, 59
Sakura, 167
Salih Shanqa, 158
salt, 75–6, 78, 80, 84 n., 87, 121, 141; salt mines, 139
Sambo of Hadeija, 165
Samori, 18, 44, 83, 123, 199
Sanankoro, 123
San Tome, 99
Sanusiya, 64
Saudi Arabia, 73 n.
secret societies, 19, 25 & n., 86
sedasi, 195–6, 198
Segu, 33, 53, 121, 123, 180
Senegal, 15 n., 24, 151
Senegambia, 86, 88, 112
Sennar, 109, 154, 204
sharif, 40, 43, 127, 164, 185
Sharif al-Din, 5
Sharif el-Medeni, 82, 93, 144, 189
Sherif, king of Wadai, 122
Shuwa, 94, 196, 197
Sidi Mabed, 154
Sidi Mustafa, 59
Sierra Leone, 25 n., 36, 47, 65, 66, 72, 85, 86, 88, 181
Slatin, R. C., 193
slaughtering and food, 36, 45, 46, 53, 87, 100, 103, 140
slave-owning slaves, 41, 49
Smith, Adam, 131, 150
Smith, Mary, 33
Smith, M. G., 164
Sokoto, 5, 28, 32, 33, 35, 41, 53, 59, 76, 82, 88, 90, 95,

96, 107, 118, 122, 133, 136, 139, 140, 148, 159, 164, 167, 170, 173, 181, 182, 185, 186, 198
soldiers, slaves as, 62, 64, 134, 154–63
Soliman, Nachtigal's servant, 14
Somalis, 26, 111 n., 156
Songhay, 26, 28, 31, 42, 108, 133, 165, 167, 172, 180
Sonni Ali, 31
South Africa, 114
Speke, J. H., 26, 45, 46, 54, 108, 145
Stanley, H., 126
Suez, 142
suicide, 36, 49, 99, 103
Susu, 111
Swahili, 26, 62, 157

Tabora, 99 n., 111, 157
Taghaza, 139
Tajura, 78
Takedda, 120, 139
Tanganyika, Lake, 142, 144
taxation, 23, 27, 31, 104, 179, 202
Teyma, 135
theocracies, 4. See Uthman dan Fodio, Bello, Sokoto, Shehu Ahmadu, Masina, al-Hajj Umar, etc.
Theodore of Ethiopia, 25, 204
Thomson, J., 95, 109
Tibati, 167
Tibesti, 5, 14, 38, 94, 99, 103, 104, 149, 198, 206
Tidjkidja, 68, 135
Timbo, 66, 186
Timbuktu, 12, 28, 29, 31, 34, 43, 52, 72, 101, 120, 121, 136, 138, 164, 173, 188
Tippu Tib, 126, 157
Tirab, 50
Tokolor, 24, 151
Touba, 44, 162
Trarza Moors, 135

Tremearne, A. J. N., 6 n., 140
tribute, slaves as, 32, 85, 115,
    125, 150, 179–84, 193, 207
Trinidad, 67
Tripoli, 5, 14, 37, 60, 61, 63,
    64, 73, 88, 97, 100, 107, 132,
    141, 155, 183, 197, 200, 203,
    205
Tsoede, 125
Tuareg, 7 n., 8, 15, 20, 58–9,
    95, 97, 100, 102, 107, 117,
    122, 134, 136, 146, 156, 158,
    187, 198
Tuat, 34
Tubu, 77, 197
Tukur, 167
Tunis, 37, 59, 73, 201
Turkey, 73; Turks, 26, 34, 38,
    155, 156, 201

Uba, 158
Ujiji, 93
Ulungu, 99
Umar, shaikh of Bornu, 40, 43,
    49, 54, 60, 97, 122, 132, 148,
    159, 168, 169, 176
Umaru of Bauchi, 33
umm al-walad, 54, 104, 116
Uthman dan Fodio, 28, 29, 32,
    35, 51, 53, 121–2, 186

Vai, 78, 84, 105, 135, 187
Vischer, H., 64, 67, 94, 96

Vittou, 110
Vogel, E., 194, 202

Wadai, 5, 13, 19, 25, 29, 33,
    38, 39, 40, 64, 72, 77, 109,
    128, 133, 139, 152, 166, 168,
    170, 174, 175, 177, 183, 184,
    186, 187, 206
Wanika, 75
Wanyamwezi, 17 n., 85, 137
Washlu, 145
Whydah, 65
wilaa, 61
witchcraft, 18, 68, 85, 89, 109
Woloff, 86, 166
Wombai Giwa, 172
Wurubo, 65

Yao, 79
Yemen, 138
Yola, capital of Adamawa, 182
Yoruba, 36, 64, 65, 113, 173
Yusuf of Wadai, 124

Zambesi, 12, 75
Zanj, 46, 62
Zanzibar, 5, 21, 25, 46, 54, 74,
    102, 108, 110, 137, 171
Zaria, 6, 33, 95, 143, 164, 172,
    186
Zintgraff, E., 142
Zubayr of Adamawa, 32, 182
Zubayr, of the eastern Sudan, 83